SUFFER LESS IN DEATH

SUFFER LESS IN DEATH

Vincent Dodd, R.N.

gatekeeper press™

Columbus, Ohio

Suffer Less in Death
Published by Gatekeeper Press
2167 Stringtown Rd, Suite 109
Columbus, OH 43123-2989
www.GatekeeperPress.com

Library of Congress Control Number: 2021931024

ISBN (hardcover): 9781662909634
ISBN (paperback): 9781662909641
eISBN: 9781662909658

Vincent Dodd, R.N.
Decreasing the mystery, fear, pain, and communication issues
surrounding dying then death.

Dedicated to my father, whose end-stage of the eight-year dying process of his mind and body helped inspire me to finish this book and include a chapter on the mind dying before the body. 1927-2006

Dedicated to my mother, who would enjoy knowing she continues to bring laughter, share of herself, and continue to be a teacher, even after her death. 1925-2015

But most of all, this book is dedicated to you, both the caregiver and the dying.

Twenty percent of all gross proceeds from the sale of this book will be donated to

The Yandle, John D., Sheehan, and Daigle Foundation

Also known as

The Human Bonding Foundation

humanbonding.org

A special thank you to the Editor. To whom I gave 500 run-on sentences, some of them lasting two to three paragraphs, all with way too many commas, too crazy wordy, horribly repetitious, I mean really repetitive, but took those run-on sentence paragraphs and turned them into this halfway respectable book, and now you know why the Editor deserves a special mention. As you can tell this paragraph did not get edited, because I wanted it to be a surprise thank you, it also allows you to see the magnitude of the issues my limited human brain has with the written word.

TABLE OF CONTENTS

<u>Warning:</u>

The title is accurate; this information explores the causes and solutions to our suffering, concerning dying and death of ourselves, others, and even our pets, which will stir your memory and emotions. You are about to begin an unfiltered journey through one of our most actively and even aggressively avoided subjects. Phrases like "I don't want to talk about that" and reading this book are not compatible. We are about to talk about dying then death. As well, "Suffer less" is not "sufferless," we can never dissolve the balances of life or death's ups and downs, the balanced emotions of happy and sad, acceptance and fear, confusion over choices and knowing you did the right thing, or even relief and grief. Yet this book is filled with gems to help you suffer less concerning this dark and unknown subject. Over the past 14 years, since it was first published, people have told me that getting through Suffer Less in Death was hard, but they also expressed there was no doubt it greatly helped them suffer less concerning the dying then death of loved ones, pets, and the fear and planning of their own death. If you find some deeper feelings or past memories coming to the surface that are troublesome and don't go away, seek help, talk it out, or find a qualified counselor. Please remember, the human mind is an amazing and powerful, but limited organ in every last one of us. Seeking help is not a sign of weakness, but rather a sign of courage and strength. It is saying I have the courage to be honest with myself on a deeper level. Be proud to work with your mind and your emotions; in the long run, it only makes life easier and filled with more peace, joy, laughter, and exploration of self and life.

CHAPTER 1

WHY?

"Effective people are not problem minded; They're opportunity minded, they feed opportunities and starve problems."
—Steven Covey, 1932-2012

Pain refused and welcomed

Periodically we must be uncomfortable
Peace and pain
Strife and happiness
All solvent, volatile, and fleeting

When all aligns but not for long
At times we must hurt
At times we will laugh
Balance is hard to welcome

Unfair to expect of others
For they have their own
Together we save self then other
Collectively all less empty

Receiving pain by any means
No, we try to block
Attempting to avoid all is futility
Yet that which arrives can be a gift

I have felt compelled to write this book ever since I took care of a ninety-four-year-old man in the mid-1980s. I was a very new registered nurse in a large inner-city emergency department. This ninety-four-year-old was sent to the hospital from a nursing home because he was bleeding from his rectum. He was also near unconsciousness, had numerous strokes in his life, and his very thin arms and legs were fully contracted. Fully contracted means his limbs were unmovable, all the joints stuck into a permanently bent angle from wasting away in bed, without exercise or physical therapy. His only responses were wincing facial expressions and groans at any movement we did to his emaciated body, meaning very little muscle left.

Had he lived, he soon would have been referred to as cachectic, meaning almost skin on bones.

The type of bleeding he had is known as a gastrointestinal (GI) bleed and is indeed a life-threatening condition. The young intern present at the time wrote an order for me to place a nasal-gastric tube (a tube passed down the nose into the stomach) into this man, to see if he was also bleeding into this stomach. I asked the doctor, "Why? He is ninety-four years old, and this bleeding is a painless and natural way to die." The young doctor said, "We have to. That is not our decision to make, and maybe we can save him." The answer was textbook and legally correct, but I was in shock. I thought to myself that a lower GI bleed was a nice way to die. It is painless; he would first become tired and, as he continued to lose blood volume, he would become unconscious and then die. But, instead, I pushed a firm plastic tube about half the size of a pinkie finger down his nose into his stomach. I placed two large intravenous catheters (IVs) into his arms, and we rolled him onto his side and inserted a large tube, about the size of your index finger, with a camera in the end, into his rectum and up into his colon to see if we could find the bleeding. We found the bleeding. His colon was overrun with cancer; it couldn't be stopped, and he died the next day. Due to these actions, he did not experience a peaceful death—no dignity, no privacy, and, at the time, no rights. I have seen this lack of acceptance of human mortality repeatedly over the past thirty-five years, with the primary ramifications mainly falling on the dying, then the family, and onto all of us. This man's last twenty-four hours were a perfect, sad example.

However, the secondary consequences from our lack of acceptance of imminent and inevitable death reach much further than the suffering of the dying. Numerous studies estimate that 60 to 70 percent of all health care dollars are spent on the last six months of life. Stop and think about that for a minute: Do we have a health care crisis, or an acceptance of our mortality crisis?

The contributing factors to this lack of acceptance of mortality are many. First and foremost is one of the ten characteristics with which all living organisms are initially endowed: "The Will to Live," which deserves great respect for its force. This lack of acceptance is also influenced by the medical staff, families, our legal system, the healthcare system, societal religious views, and at times, thank goodness, by patients themselves. Even an unrealistic expectation of modern medicine could be a contributing factor, because at some point medications and procedures have no ability to be a positive contribution. No matter the cause, it all equals an increase in unnecessary human suffering before unavoidable death. Other effects of our choices may be a little harder to see. When I first published this book in 2007, I started giving talks to empower people to take a more active role in managing both their death and their health care choices in general. I spoke about how our lack of open dialogue and two-way communication with our health care provider leads to unnecessary pain and suffering. This lack of communication can bear negative results in imminent and inevitable death cases but can also potentially increase the death rate by getting in the way or early detection and treatment of cancer.

I was sharing with one particular group the statistics of the percentage of chemotherapy patients that are still receiving chemo within two weeks of, or at the time of, their death. I also shared the concept that not accepting imminent and inevitable death could be adding to the problem of early detection of cancer in some situations. I also explained how when someone arrives at an emergency room triage complaining of chest pain, nausea, shortness of breath, and looks pale and sweaty, we know right away they are having a heart attack. We immediately place them in a wheelchair and we roll them right into the back, tell the attending and a nurse as we roll into a room, and start the treatment that second. Oxygen goes on before the triage nurse leaves the room; when they look this bad, it is an "every minute counts" situation. This immediate action is because, if bad enough, a heart attack can kill someone at any moment. I shared this to say that even though a lump in the breast does not have that fatal instability, it is growing and reproducing quickly, and will have the same effect as the heart attack, if untreated or delayed for too long. My point is this: Rapid reproduction of cells is a characteristic of most cancers. So why do we treat the heart in trouble immediately, but find it acceptable for a woman who discovers a lump in her breast to have to potentially wait days for an appointment to see a doctor, days for radiology studies, days for readings, days to line up follow up for biopsies and or surgery, and/or days to start chemotherapy? That entire time, that cancer is dividing over and over, and possibly spreading further into other organs. I continued that one of the contributing factors to this issue was lack of time and scheduling availability. How many appointments for cancer are used by older patients who are not responding to chemotherapy, instead of for early detection and treatment appointments of cancer in a woman in her forties? I had just finished this speech when a woman raised her hand and asked, "So what you are saying is by me not accepting my death, once I know it is imminent and inevitable, I could be contributing to my granddaughter's need for a total mastectomy or her death?"

I let her know it is not quite that direct, but in the bigger picture it does contribute. I also reminded the group that one of the ten characteristics of all living organisms is The Will to Live. I am not calloused to the will to live, to beat cancer, to live another day no matter what your age; I too have that same drive in me. I have never had a terminal cancer diagnosis, but if I did, I would at least want my oncologist to be painfully honest with me, so I could make highly informed choices about continuing or letting go. I hope my oncologist would have the moral and ethical courage to say to me, "Vincent, your cancer is not responding to the chemotherapy and/or radiation therapy. Would you like to continue with the chemo, or would you like to stop, so maybe you can enjoy your last weeks without nausea and vomiting, or feeling like the chemo truck from hell just hit you and left you in the street? Would you like to enjoy the taste of meals or chocolate, and maybe have a little more strength than the chemo allows ...?" I use that analogy because so many chemo patients have told me that "hit by a truck, or bulldozer" is what the first few days after chemo feel like. If I did have cancer, and my oncologist knew the statistics that I had a 0, or even a poor 10, 20, 30 percent rate of success, I would want and deserve that information. I would like to be able to say, "Let's stop, doctor. I want to enjoy my last laughs and chocolate to the fullest." I would also want the forty- five-year old woman with a lump in her breast, scared to death, to have my next appointment available to her, if my choice could potentially help save her life.

In essence, I am writing this book so you can attempt to keep unnecessary pain and suffering from happening to you, or to someone you love. I am writing this book because, for the most part, the health care field cannot stop this unnecessary pain and suffering because of many influences beyond its control. The medical field has some control, but ultimately it is up to the patient or patient's medical guardian to prevent this unnecessary suffering. Death itself is a very clear-cut objective state. But the process of dying, and the choices we make about our own dying and death, are often subjective and always (hopefully) personal. I am writing this book openly with respect, because you have a right to know more, you have a right to be informed, and you have a right to say "No."

CHAPTER 2

THE RESPECTFUL AND HONEST COURAGE TO WRITE THIS BOOK

"Death is a very narrow theme, but it reaches a wide audience."
—Socrates, 470 BCE – 399 BCE

I Admit Fear

Fear
The prerequisite of all courage

I admit the first
I muster the next

Stalled at times
Accomplished at others

Hum
I must be human

My career in the healthcare system started in the early 1980s when I was accepted into nursing school. My academic training began two years prior, when I was majoring in sociology, with a strong emphasis on death and dying and the institution of family. After beginning nursing school, I started a job with a home care health agency. My title was "home health aide." Mostly I gave bed baths, changed dressings, and, by choice, I gave frequent back and foot massages to the terminal patients. Within a few days of starting, I asked to be assigned to the terminal patients so I could practice what I had learned the previous two years in my academic studies of death and dying. I began to work with the patients and families in what I call "pre-grief" or "cushioning" the imminent death. I would talk with the patients and families frequently and for long periods of time about the more painful subjects of their terminal illness. I found the courage and direction to do so from my amazing sociology teacher, who was the instructor for my Death and Dying course. She also instructed my course on Relationships and Communication, and she turned Sociology 101 into an interesting, diverse, and eye-opening class. She taught us to leave our personal views and opinions out of these conversations, but to still learn to have the conversations. She taught us that at rare times the conversation will be met with resistance and not to force the subjects.

But she also taught us that the person with the terminal illness will often be relieved that someone does want to talk about their terminal situation and their nearing death. As she stated, I found that willingness to talk to be much more prevalent than not.

The positive feedback was overwhelming, from both the patients and families. It was apparent from early on that I would receive more appreciation from helping people die than I ever would from helping people live. Since graduating from nursing school, I have worked mostly in large teaching hospitals, mainly emergency departments, with two years of intensive care unit experience. Those two years of intensive care work were so valuable in the hands- on application of the concepts in this book. I say this for the most part because emergency departments deal with sudden or traumatic death, while the intensive care units, hospital floors, hospice, and other nursing facilities deal with the longer slower processes of dying.

During those two years in the intensive care unit, I continued to speak openly with patients and family about imminent death and their choices. Amazed, I kept track that within the first six months of intensive care work, I received six boxes of chocolates, two coffee cups, and several cards thanking me for my time and effort in helping a human die with peace and dignity, and in helping their family to deal with that death.

Over the years I have established two rules, or guidelines, from which I attempt to work. I say "attempt," for the pressures and demands of the healthcare field did not always allow me to carry out my role the way I saw fit. My rules are plain, short, and require minimal effort.

Rule #1: The mind is equally as important as the body. If you look at the body as a total system, its primary function is first to supply oxygen and nutrients to the heart and brain, and then to the other vital organs—the lungs, kidney, liver, intestines, and skin. This is important to understand, because sometimes in a situation of multi trauma, it can come down to a choice between the heart and the brain. There is a classic brief professional conflict that I have witnessed several times, a discussion between the trauma surgeon and the neurosurgeon regarding who should take the major trauma patient to surgery first. The argument has no correct answer. Without the brain, the body would not be able to feed itself, keep warm, or protect itself; thus, the body will die. Yet obviously the brain would die without the other organs providing their vital functions. However, the brain is a priority for me because I see the healthcare system in general expending the least amount of effort in caring for the mind. One way I wish to help change this neglect of the mind is first to correct the lack of person-to-person communication between the healthcare staff and the patient or family members. I am proud to say I have been criticized, mainly by other nurses, for spending too much time talking with patients and family members. I am not just "talking" with them; I am caring for the mind and holistically teaching about their disease process. This neglect or lack of priority is why my first principle is that the mind is equally as important as the body. The mind is also where our world is perceived, the mind is where we feel and experience the self and the world around us, thus giving us our "quality of life."

Rule #2: *The family is equally as important as the patient.* The concept of "family" for me includes the "chosen family," as well as the biological family. Over the years, it has become apparent that a chosen family can often provide more appropriate support for the individual than the biological family. <u>Throughout this book I will use the term "family" to include all people of personal support to the patient.</u> There is always room for improvement when it comes to including family. It is assumed that the choices the health care field makes are typically guided by the latest research. Repetitive studies show that patients heal more quickly and experience less pain if their family is allowed to participate in care and/or remain with the patient. Yet visiting hours are often limited or, in some large emergency departments, not allowed at all. These rules do have hands-on patient care needs and safety as their origin, and for the most part are wise and necessary in very large departments. However, there is also a need for a little improvement and development in this area.

In the early 2000s, our department began to allow the family into the emergency room during an attempted resuscitation/CPR, also known as "coding," of their family member. One of us on staff would stand with the family, inform them in detail of what was happening to their loved one, and explain the procedures and outcome they were observing, or lack of response to the procedure or drug. For the most part I found this to be extremely helpful to the family.

They could see we were trying very hard to resuscitate, or save the life, of their family member. They also could see what a violation chest compressions, shocking, and lung ventilation are to the body. More often than not after some attempts, the family would actually ask us to stop and thank us for our efforts. It is imperative that families are able to understand the process and the outcome.

These two rules have been my basic guiding principles and big-picture keys to a giving and rewarding career. They will also guide my direction, style, and intention for how and why I am writing this book. This book is not filled with answers, but with very real information.

Concerning your death or the death of a loved one, I certainly do not wish to influence, but only to inform. Each process of dying and death is an individual experience that should be guided, as much as possible, by that person's wishes. But I do wish for you to be aware of the most difficult parts of dying and death, so you can make your decisions with a broader scope of knowledge. I apologize, and yet I do not apologize, for the frankness of the material. I have always worked to promote the acceptance of humanness. The life and death of our body, our only lifelong vehicle to carry our short, scary, exciting, painful, and amazing journey of ourselves, is a part of humanness.

For the most part, the healthcare field does not believe there is a need to have the family have a true awareness of what goes on when the family is asked to step out of the room, or when the curtain is closed. Except for patient privacy, sterile procedure, or serious protection of some harsh procedures, I think you deserve to know what is happening. After all, it is happening to your spouse, your child, your parent, your close friend, and eventually to you. In the same paragraph, it is not appropriate for many reasons to have family stay during most procedures, but you still have a right to understand those procedures with a broader scope.

My Inspiration for Writing:

I am not by any means a professional writer. I held off for some time in writing this book due to my own self-doubt about my writing skills. But watching the strength of both our health care and our legal systems grow, I felt it too important to get this information to you. I also felt a duty to trust you and openly share this hard to hear information to protect you. I promised this to a significant group of people in the early spring of 1985. The night I graduated from nursing school, I stood with the rest of my class before a hundred people or so—our friends and family. We recited what is known as the "Nightingale Pledge," after Florence Nightingale, the founding mother of my first chosen profession. That oath, to me, called for me to be a patient advocate. An advocate, according to Webster's Dictionary, is "One who pleads the cause of another," or "one who supports or promotes the interests of a cause or group." My nursing instructors taught me that this also meant to teach the patient and family, to keep them informed of their rights and their plan of care. I have always taken this oath seriously. But within just a few weeks of graduation, I found there was a small group of my colleagues that would attempt to stop me from being a patient advocate. A short time later, I also found that the family sometimes would aggressively not want me to be the patient's advocate, but to be their advocate instead.

I remember the first time these two realizations hit me. I was caring for a man in his mid-forties. He had been shot several times in his early thirties. The most damaging wound was in his upper spine; he was a quadriplegic, meaning he could not move or feel his arms or legs. The night I met him he had been transferred to the emergency department due to a high fever. He knew the cause of his fever was sepsis. Sepsis is an infection of the blood, meaning his blood was overrun with bacteria. It is a fatal condition if not treated early in its progression, and early detection is not a guarantee of survival. He was well aware of the seriousness of the condition; he had been septic on numerous occasions in the past. He also knew if we "cured" this case, it would return again soon. Before I give you the two reasons why he was septic, let me tell you a little more about his case. The night this man was shot in the lower neck, which caused his quadriplegia, he was also shot in the abdomen, chest, and genitals.

The wound to his genitals ripped through his urethra (the tube that carries urine from the bladder to the outside of the body), and his prostate gland (which surrounds the midsection of the urethra). There was too much damage to repair his urinary tract, and for over fifteen years he had lived with his urine draining from a supra-pubic catheter (a rubber tube that passes directly through the skin into the bladder several inches below where your belt buckle would rest). His buttock had very large decubitus ulcers, also known as "bedsores" (open sores where the skin has broken down, and in his case, muscle has broken down also; with time they can be very deep and extensive), across his lower back and both cheeks. These had occurred from fifteen years of lying in bed or sitting in a wheelchair. You and I can start to get decubitus in a day or two if we are not turned from side to side every few hours. Now imagine the condition of his decubitus after fifteen years of depending on others to care for all of his needs, except breathing, blinking, chewing, and swallowing.

Since the time of his accident, he had lived in a nursing home, visited infrequently by family, and he told me his "friends" had stopped visiting after the first few years. The two repetitive causes of his sepsis, or blood infection, were the supra-pubic catheter and his massive decubitus, neither of which could be resolved or healed: the supra-pubic catheter because of necessity, the open skin breakdown because of its extent and the unavailability of the high level of care required to heal such a decubitus. He knew all of this all too well. After fifteen years of chronic medical care, he knew more about his medical condition than I did at that point. He told me he was tired. He was tired of being dependent totally on others. He was tired of the emotional pain and isolation. Although he could no longer smell it, he was tired of his odor offending those around him, and he said some people would have to vomit when they cared for his decubitus. He told me he was ready to die. He said this and then told me, "But I can't pull a trigger, and nobody will give me a lot of pills." I had not brought this subject up; he had done so all on his own. I told him the truth; I informed him that he could refuse treatment if he wanted. Yes, he would die if he refused treatment, and he knew that. He just didn't know it was his choice. When I left his bedside, I was immediately, and harshly, informed by a coworker that I had no right to say that to the patient. I was told that I was out of line and that I was never to do it again. This was followed by, "Do you understand me?" I was shaken. It was my first scolding as a professional, or since my childhood. I pondered the situation for days and came to the conclusion that I had upheld my oath and had informed the patient of his rights. I never stopped informing patients of their rights, and I always worked to remain neutral.

The first time I got into trouble with a family was also the first time I was ever called into my nursing supervisor's office and professionally reprimanded. It was not really a reprimand, but more of an attempt at a professional informing. I had cared for and spoken with the family of an upper-middle-aged man who had been fighting cancer for some time. At this point the cancer had spread, known as metastasized, into his liver, lungs, and bones. His body was emaciated, his eyes deeply sunken; he lived with chronic nausea from the chemotherapy, his breathing was slightly laborious, and the pain from the cancer in the bones was extreme. His wife and daughter were "caring" for him. They kept telling him, "You're going to be just fine," and then insisted we do everything we could to keep him alive. He kept saying, "I want to go home. I just want to go home." To which his family would say, "No, now, we're going to stay right here and let them get you better." I knew my following interactions were for the family mostly; I could see he accepted his death, even welcomed it. I asked him if he knew what was going on with his body. He said yes, and that he knew we could no longer stop his cancer and that he was ready to die. I responded by saying, "Yes, that is right." I asked him if there was anything we could do for him. He informed me his pain medications were not working. I told him we would increase his pain medications to something stronger. I informed him that he had the right to refuse treatment, and I asked him if he had a living will. He told me he did not have a living will and repeated his wish to go home. We talked some more, I made him as comfortable as I could including more pain medication, and he was admitted. His family had refused to take him home. I don't know when or where he died, but I'll bet it wasn't at home. I was called into the office and informed that the family had taken out a complaint. They had charged me with telling this man, "You're going to die; there is nothing we can do for you, so you might as well go home." I informed my supervisor of my side. She believed me but informed me it was not my role to talk that frankly with patients and family about death; that was the physician's role.

I pondered that for just a moment and considered my experience with health care professionals in general. I took into account that most health care professionals have little or no training in communication, and even less training when it comes to talking about dying then death. I had two years of academic training, and at that point three years of clinical application, and only two negative responses. I decided to continue, and I informed her that it was my role, and that I would not stop. She told me she knew I would say that, winked at me, and told me to, "Get back to work; it's busy out there." The positive feedback from my colleagues, patients, and patients' families only increased. Maybe every two or three years my supervisors would get a call from a family member who felt I had overstepped my boundaries. A bit more frequently I would have a young resident tell me that I didn't "have the right" or "shouldn't" inform patients that they have the right to refuse treatment. But for the most part I was told, and I saw, that the openness was highly appreciated.

I love my work because I learned to give and care from my heart. Because of this heart-based origin, my work has given to me more in goodness and growth than it has taken from me in mental and physical energy. I went home from my twelve-hour shifts feeling total fatigue, but I had gained. It quickly became apparent to me that I may not always agree with inserting a hard plastic tube down the nose of a ninety-four-year-old man who is trying to die peacefully, but, by staying in the field of nursing as long as I did, I knew at least the tube would be placed gently and carefully. That is one or many reasons why I stayed and gave twenty-one years to hands-on patient care.

The reality is this book will be magnifying the information that I shared with the paraplegic gunshot victim and the man overrun with cancer. It has the potential to upset people in all levels of society, health care, nursing, medicine/surgery (meaning the doctors), and administration. I am taking a risk to share my experience, to inform the public of their choices and what true pain and suffering can often turn into if we do not accept our mortality. I hold much comfort in knowing that I am not necessarily a rebel in the health care field. Many health care professionals hope that when their own death is imminent, they will not have to endure the pain and suffering of "heroic" procedures. "Just let me die" is the call I hear over and over from most of the health care professionals I've ever asked, and most volunteer without being asked. Usually these wishes were volunteered as we watched, and participated in, a patient being denied the peace and dignity of a natural death. I want to share what I have learned from the inside, so you can make your own choices that will allow you to have a faster, more natural, less prolonged, and less painful death, if that is your choice, respected.

In closing this chapter, I would like to answer one of the most common questions I have been asked since first publishing this book in 2007, "Why did you title the book *Suffer Less in Death* rather than *Suffer Less with Death?*" We as a society in general do not want to look at death. We say death is beautiful and natural, but we do not actually treat it that way. We shun the subject and place it on the back burner for another day, hoping that will keep the day from ever coming. I joke, since books on death and dying never make the top ten list, that I think I'll write my next book about orgasms! But here I am creating the second edition, because although the subject is in "black wrapping," it is still my heartfelt gift to you. I use "in Death" as opposed to "with Death" because death is in us and everywhere around us. We are surrounded by death and it is actually in us. Cell degeneration, meaning the decline or deterioration of cells, can be from trauma, illness, or the normal organic aging process. Youth does not negate this process. A simple example is that your red blood cells only live about 110 to 120 days. Those cells are weakening and dying the last few weeks of their life. Friends, family, and acquaintances are dying for all sorts of reasons, and strangers in some of the car accidents we pass are dead or will die. Our beautiful pets, that show us the greatest unconditional love we will ever know—they live lives too short, and we must say goodbye to too many of them in our lifetime. We may not be attending a funeral today, but we are immersed in death throughout our life.

I want to thank so many people over the last fourteen years who told me this book had also helped them greatly to accept the mortality and grief of their pets. I was informed by more people that they loaned it to someone for a pet getting old than for people. I attribute that to the higher level of discomfort about talking of the dying and death of a human loved one. The same choices from pet owners now need to be used with veterinary practices, too. When I was younger, our vets were always very open about end-of-life issues, and euthanasia was often quickly offered. Due to advanced medicine having moved into the field of veterinary medicine, all of this information now applies to your pets also. Chemo and other advanced care for pets was not available years ago. I am a huge dog and cat lover, and I have owned several of both in my life. It is all of our jobs to protect them at a certain point in their health care, and this also requires discernment and courage. Again, that is your call, not mine.

I also want to give great praise and respect to our Doctors of Veterinary Medicine (DVM). They all have both the responsibility of what to offer or not, to guide owners towards or away from futile, expensive procedures. Your guidance is imperative for both expense to owners who may not be able to afford what their heart says "yes" to, and to prevent unnecessary suffering in our beautiful pets that have zero ability to speak for themselves.

Over 100 million of these amazing beings in the U.S. alone provide us with an abundance of love and companionship, prevent isolation, fill emptiness, instill feelings of self-worth, give so much, and are our greatest teachers of unconditional love we will ever know. Such a significant contribution to our society also deserves to be treated with respect and dignity as they die.

A huge part of my heart goes out to you veterinarians for the thousands of times in your careers you will insert a needle and inject the loving purple medication that ends the life of love, joy, protection, assistance, and fulfillment, yet also prevents further unnecessary suffering. I know it wears on a part of your being, your spirit, and your heart. Not only the physical death that occurs so humanely fast, but the shattered owners with powerful shoulders shaking, beautiful tears, sobs, and crumpling of their upright self as their love goes limp to death because your thumb moved the plunger on the syringe forward. You are angels with scars and dark places due to the loving, realistic, and repetitive actions you do for us and our furry buddies over and over. I deeply thank you for taking on that thankless painful burden. Please find a way to safely let it out.

I extend a personal even deeper thank you to all the doctors who came out to my car to end the life of my dogs. Your special action allowed my friends to not have the conditioned response of fear by going into your office, but to die in my lap, being told they are "the best" in my shaky voice, in their car. My tears are supposed to fall on them as the weight of their body pushes out their last breath.

I have heard various renditions of the following quote. Never have I heard an author of the original, and its wording changes from quote to quote, but this sums it up well: "Only by the lifelong open acceptance and review of our mortality and eventual death can we completely experience the joys and exploration of life to its fullest." My addition to that is, "Not accepting your inevitable death is like trying to stop the sun from setting by tightly shutting your eyes and looking away."

CHAPTER 3

TALKING ABOUT TALKING ABOUT DEATH

"Live as if you were to die tomorrow. Learn as if you were to live forever."
—Mahatma Gandhi, 1869 – Assassinated 1948

THE DIG

The hardest and scariest thing I ever started was looking inside myself
Painful raw honesty
Not the surface but hard digging
Starting to not waste life or self

Without skewing my imperfect humanness
Without painting my pictures so they look like I've done it all correctly
Hard cuts and bleeding unearthing my faults and mistakes
Parts of me would rather blame others

I work to suppress that fast easy out
Self-vision becomes too clear—I want to stop the dig
I have damaged others too

Embarrassment follows

Not looking in means I want others to swallow the responsibility
for my failures
Refusing to not waste my frequent stumbles
I bandage then attempt growth from my messes
Never stop the steep march which only ends at the end

There is a second hardest and scariest thing I've ever tried
Attempting to dig every day
Failing often and shocked at the required focus
Look further there is goodness too

Thankfully pride and peace rise slowly too
Committing to tomorrow takes more courage
I could stop but why—everything is getting easier
I and yes you are worth the benefits of my continued painful and
beneficial digging

THE HEALTHCARE FIELD ASKED ME TO WRITE THIS CHAPTER:

Since the first edition of this book came out in 2007, nurses and doctors have been asking me to write this chapter. As we always do in the healthcare field, I studied the pathology of how I accomplish it. I took a look inside myself to dissect not only what I say, but more importantly the deeper work of what I do inside myself to make talking about death easier. It does get easier, but it never gets easy.

I encourage you as the consumer to remember, you are the pilot of your own life's flight—not the healthcare field, nor the textbooks, but you. The world of modern medicine has much to offer, but that doesn't mean you have to accept it all. It is not the healthcare field's fault; it must work from the textbooks to give you up-to-date treatments and to legally protect itself. The good news is, the textbooks are the latest research; you are getting quality care from quality professionals, and good communication on both sides gets everyone through it so much more easily and more informed.

INFLUENCES AND BACKGROUND:

I went to an amazing nursing school, Louisiana Tech University, which is located in the small town of Ruston in the northern part of the state. The instructors were fantastic; they were hard, caring, and informative, and they threw out nonstop tough questions in the clinical setting to make sure our care was both informed and safe. They were all so knowledgeable and professional, but Ms. Pyle and Ms. Murphy told me a few "gems," as Ms. Murphy called tidbits of helpful concepts and information. Many of these gems helped start me on a path of not just doing nursing, but rather practicing nursing as an ever-changing and evolving profession. All of the instructors reiterated and encouraged us to accomplish professionalism in action, not just a list of criteria in print. "Never stop doing your own ongoing research," Ms. Murphy told us, with examples too long to list but most concerning procedures and medication administration. She summarized it with, "What works for one person may not work for another, so observe and ask the patient about the effectiveness of medications after they are given." Ms Pyle once said, "Never say 'I know that ...' or 'That is just the way we have always done it,' because with constant research, medical knowledge is always changing. What we know today may be improved upon tomorrow." She also listed off a handful of examples. One of her examples, which I still use to this day when teaching the concepts of professionalism is the frontal lobotomy, which involved severing connections in the frontal cortex of the brain for psychiatric reasons. One particular doctor did this using an ice pick, and he performed it over two thousand times. This is a procedure that is rarely performed today. Ms. Pyle said, "If anyone ever gives you the answer 'because that is how we have always done it' to a medical or policy question, remind them the frontal lobotomy was also once an acceptable treatment."

Due to this empowering and wise professionalism, early on in my training I found an issue with how we give "IV push" medications. These are medications that are injected directly into the IV tubing, and therefore go directly into a vein, entering the circulatory system quickly. Back in 1984, not all IV tubing had a one-way valve built in, and if a medication was pushed too fast, it could go back up the tubing, even into the IV bag if it was a large quantity. Not having a one-way valve also allowed blood to go up into the tubing if the bag was dropped below the level of the heart. The first time I was being taught this administration technique was at the bedside during clinical training. I was being instructed to pinch the tubing above the port where I was about to slowly inject the medication over a few minutes. I asked my instructor to step into the hall, away from the patient, and explained that the technique just explained to me did not make sense. "If I have to push this medicine in over three minutes with the tube pinched off, isn't that bolus of medication I just spent three minutes to give slowly going to rush in much faster when I release the pinch? Worse yet, it will be undiluted, as opposed to diluted, if I were to instead let the fluid keep dripping?" She raised her eyebrows, thought a very brief moment and said, "You're right!" She had me teach my findings to the class at our post-clinical conference a few hours later.

It happened again right out of nursing school, when I put their two wise and encouraging statements to work again. The first was an issue I could not fix, presenting itself to me just a few months after graduation concerning a drug called aminophylline given via IV for the treatment of asthma. Due to the humidity in the area, and mold spores it produces, we treated so many asthma patients that they had designated a cubical just for asthma patients. Even if I had not been taught to pay attention to what works and what doesn't, it was hard to miss the fact that most people vomited several times after I administered aminophylline.

About six months later, Aminophylline was removed from the treatment of asthma, and I never gave it again. My second application of troubleshooting occurred after I experienced going with doctors to notify families of a death that had just occurred.

I picked the emergency department at Charity Hospital in downtown New Orleans to walk into as a rookie fresh out of school, because I think nurses should also do a residency just like doctors. But since they do not, I gave myself that residency, knowing both LSU and Tulane residents trained there. I also knew the number of patients treated every twenty-four hours, translating to an incredible barrage of learning opportunities. The entire Emergency System consisted of "The Accident Room" that saw all-age trauma, "The Major Medical Room," an adult medical area, and a pediatric medical area. All three combined treated over 20,000 patients per month. The average for each of those departments was over 7,000 treated per month. It was not only the average or five to ten or more penetrating traumas, meaning shootings and stabbings, every twenty-four hours that drew me in. The medical cases were often rather complex, often far out of balance, requiring serious intervention and, yes, finesse to restore homeostasis. Homeostasis is when the body is in optimal balance and all of its systems are working properly to keep it that way. Homeostasis is to the human body as is a perfectly tuned engine. My last but not least reason for wanting high-intensity training was the magnitude of the legal and human responsibility I was accepting to become a nurse. If I have the same responsibility for giving a wrong medication as the doctor who wrote the order, and if I was going to be dealing with human lives, I wanted to learn everything I could. It was a fantastic hands-on orientation that lasted eleven weeks. Thank you to Jill Roy, my orientation instructor, for instilling in me more knowledge and challenging questions in those eleven weeks than I thought would be possible in a lifetime of nursing. That desire to learn never waned.

It was not only medical knowledge, either; she taught me the need for self-protection, care, and preservation. Jill saved my spirit one night, months after I had finished her orientation. We were working a night shift together. Charity Hospital was a massive, archaic, concrete structure that had received minimal updates since that building first opened. It was a huge financial drain on the state, and that is the main reason it was never reopened after Hurricane Katrina. The trauma side did not have suction or oxygen in the walls, and large, approximately 5-foot-tall oxygen tanks were in each room, chained to the walls so they would not fall on you. If they were not chained to walls, they were on large rollers, to be used in the hallways that were filled with patients the majority of the time. When these tanks went empty, we changed them out ourselves. This one early morning, maybe 4 a.m., I attempted to change out the top of one of these large cylinders of oxygen with a rusted old pipe wrench.

But the wrench was stripped and wouldn't tighten enough to remove the regulator from the empty tank. I was getting really frustrated; she saw this and quickly pulled me into one of the two infection rooms we so harshly called "Pus Rooms," directly across the hall from where I was starting to lose it. She first asked me what was wrong, then wisely asked me if I had taken a lunch break, which I had not. I will never forget what she told me, with a furrowed brow and the direct harshness I needed to hear: "Vincent, don't you ever again not take a lunch break; these twelve-hour shifts are grueling physically, mentally, and emotionally. You are working in one of the busiest and most staff-abusing emergency rooms in this country, just like Grady in Atlanta, Ben Taub in Houston, Parkland in Dallas, or Cook County in Chicago.

Nothing, no one in this emergency room or entire hospital, not another nurse, doctor, patient, or oxygen tank, is more important than you are!" I mean, she was so passionately telling me this, I was probably leaning back with a dropped jaw.

Then she stopped, breathed, and asked me, "Do you know why I say that?" For a split second my 21-year-young being was shocked to hear both what and how she had stated that I am "the most important." Then it dawned on me: "Because if I don't take care of myself first, I cannot take good care of these patients tonight or for years to come?"

"That's right, and please don't let me find out you skipping lunch again, or if you need to stop and walk out on that ramp and breathe fresh air, you do it. Seconds and minutes sometimes count, but it's not often you can't care for yourself first. You are close by if we need you and not the only nurse here; walk out and breathe when you need it. Now, don't touch another patient until you have gone and eaten the well-deserved lunch you just told me you missed." She turned quickly and left the room to go back to work. That was most likely one of the wisest pieces of professional preservation and personal self-care advice I ever received.

There were so many special aspects about the 2,680-bed institution of Charity Hospital. First opened in 1736, in a much smaller building, it was funded by the wish and grant of a French sailor and shipbuilder, Jean Louis. He had died a year earlier but wished to help create a hospital for the poor. As I just shared, sadly, Charity Hospital did not remain in operation after Hurricane Katrina in 2005. I hold being a small, three-year part of that long history as the second greatest honor of my career—second only to the honor of twenty-one years as part of a team that helped so many people and their families though injury and illness, whether that illness was physical, mental, or emotional.

Several aspects of Charity set it apart from every other teaching hospital at which I have ever worked. Aside from the sheer high volume of patients was the fact that Charity was, for the most part, a residency-run and self-taught hospital. This hands-on assistance of third- and fourth-year medical students, interns, and residents was not only vital to accomplishing the care of such numbers, but it skyrocketed the graduates of those two schools and residency programs above others in physician patient care skills. These doctors started IVs, drew blood gases, did EKGs with us, inserted tubes and catheters, and even periodically helped us restrain violent patients. I would hear residents in other teaching hospitals complain about a busy night, as they assessed new patients, wrote orders, and went to the next patient but never carried out a single procedure or action in those orders. I would think about what any graduate of LSU's or Tulane's medical school, or a graduate resident of either program that trained at Charity, would have thought, and laughed. I am sure other high-volume teaching hospitals also had that barrage of hands-on training for its medical students, interns, and residents. To the residents that may have felt roughed-up and abused compared to friends and acquaintances they knew in more cushiony residency programs, I say high five and way to go. I also thank you for your special hands-on part of helping make Charity Hospital the rare and special place it was. Twenty thousand people per month could never have received the care they did without your efforts above and beyond most other programs. Nursing alone could never have accomplished that feat. I can also promise you your clinical assessment skills benefited, too.

I was in a Central West Coast teaching hospital in the late eighties. A 20-something- year-old had been involved in a car crash and had arrived a few minutes before my 7 p.m. shift started. I received a report that this person had been cleared of cervical spine injury and removed from the collar and spine board, and their only complaint was of mild abdominal pain. I was looking across the room while receiving this report and saw this patient's bed was slightly elevated and the patient was on their back. By the time I finished receiving a report on all the patients in that room, this person had rolled onto their left side and was now in a fetal position. This is not a good sign in any abdominal complaint, so I went right over to assess after seeing this change that indicated an abdominal injury to me. Again, thanks to Charity training and the development of clinical observation, which taught me we had a major issue in progress.

On assessment, I found what we call a "hot belly," tender to touch, actually feeling firmer and warmer, and the patient did not want me to palpate the abdomen a second time immediately after the first time, and pushed my hand away, which is also a bad sign. This abdomen clearly had rebound tenderness, meaning pulling my hand up from the abdomen assessment hurts more than when I push in, to the extent most will grab your hand to prevent further discomfort. All of these signs indicated bleeding into the abdominal cavity. Two upper- year surgery residents in the room were finishing talking to another patient. I had worked with them just a few times because I was new to this hospital. I was doing travel contract nursing at the time to gain regional experiences, as different parts of the country are slightly different. I went over and said, "I need you two to come take a look at someone right away, status post a moderate-speed MVC (motor vehicle crash), has a hot belly, and is going to need surgery right away." They lightly smirked at me, told me to order a CT scan, and left without going to lay hands and assess the patient themselves. I walked right to CT and talked to the tech about my concern. She told me to bring the patient right over and wait in the hall until she finished the person she already had on the table. I informed the attending doctor, who came and assessed this person also while I started a second IV and sent labs off, including one to the blood bank to hold in case needed. Once the CT was in progress, I walked down to the radiologist reading room, introduced myself to the radiologist and presented the case, and she too promised to go read it right away, and was doing so as we rolled out of the CT room. No longer than ten minutes after getting back into the room did the same two residents and an OR tech come into the room, take down her IV bags, and ask me to grab her paperwork and roll with them up to OR to give a report to the nurse. Off we went to OR for repair of a lacerated liver, meaning the impact of the crash had caused the liver to split open and it was bleeding into her abdominal cavity, thus causing all the clinical signs I witnessed.

Unless the trauma victim is seriously unstable and the surgeons know they have to explore the entire abdominal cavity anyway, it is not at all uncommon to try and obtain a CT in all major trauma patients before rushing someone into OR. A classic example would be two gunshot wounds to the abdomen that keeps dropping their blood pressure even though we are already rapidly "dumping" bags of IV fluids and units of blood to keep their blood pressure up. That situation does not have time for further studies; it becomes a "get out the ED back door fast, into OR, cut them open, find the bleeding, and fix the internal trauma if it can be repaired" type of situation. Otherwise, I get it: Discover via CT scan what the problem is before the cutting, and then repair the trauma. But what made that event stand out was the fact that they literally did not even lay eyes and hands on the patient after I informed them of something so critical. I watched that lack of hands-on assessment continue to be a trend.

A few days later, I saw those two residents again in the ED. They did stop and come talk with me to let me know the patient had had a moderate bleed, had even required a few units of blood to be transfused, and was still in ICU. They asked me my background and allowed a discussion concerning my concern for their lack of a desire to immediately physically assess the patient. They were amazed that when I worked at Charity, it had only one CT scanner that often did not work, as opposed to the many scanners throughout most huge teaching hospitals. They were further surprised to realize that if it stopped working, you fell completely back on assessment skills only. They were open to realizing the need to continue to develop their hands-on assessment skills. I did not know the answer to the following example I used, but they got the point. I said even though during the big earthquake in San Francisco, when all the hospitals most likely remained with power because each is required to have huge generators, how many CT scanners in the entire metro area stopped working due to the extreme shaking? To make it worse and real, I reminded them of the hundreds of major trauma cases that occurred across the entire metro area in only a matter of seconds. Maybe not a single CT scan went down during San Francisco's big earthquake, but they got slightly wide-eyed considering that catastrophic big picture. In humor, and as a teaching moment in professionalism and not judging nurses, I also teased them about smirking at me when I gave them that fast report a few days ago. They apologized, and we ended with laughs and thank-yous all around.

LSU and Tulane, did of course have attending physicians teaching. They were there to oversee the program during the day, and the trauma attendings would often come in at night, depending on the numbers and severity, but for the most part we all taught each other.

Something else that was interesting, wonderful, and rare was that doctors and nurses frequently taught each other in the clinical setting. Doctors and nurses do teach each other some in teaching hospitals, but not on this high level. At any moment, anyone could give a fast little impromptu in-service, often in ink on the bed sheet next to a patient's head, and several nurses and doctors would stop and listen, answer, and ask questions. The giving and receiving of knowledge was at a level I never again experienced in another hospital in this country. It was so prolific that I altered the old saying, "If you only learn one new thing a day, you will fall far, far behind." Although I have had many great clinical teachers throughout my years, one stands out, not only because of the amount and the width of knowledge, but also because of the why—he knew that every one of us made up the team. Dr. Jimmy Ballone, too, was paramount in teaching me on so many levels. Jimmy also helped me become the knowable and humanistic professional that also went on to share knowledge just as he showed through example. My introduction to this amazing man was just a few hours into our first day in "The Accident Room." I always wondered if the name came from the trauma that side cared for, or the condition of the facility? There were about five of us in the orientation program standing near the tiny trauma nurse station. Jimmy had just placed two cervical spine X-rays on the viewing board that was in the hallway a few feet away from where we stood. He saw us standing there and called us over for an in-service on reading cervical spine X-rays in trauma patients. His desire to teach and give great care was equaled by his compassion, bedside manner, and respectful treatment of all staff and patients.

I asked Jimmy one night about his love for teaching nurses and his high level of knowledge. He informed me that he had worked in Charity's emergency department for years as a med tech before and during medical school. He also told me, "I teach nurses for the reasons all doctors and nurses should be teaching each other for their entire career, not just during residency or only in teaching hospitals. First, because nurses are a professional part of this team. Second, because you also have to catch the mistakes I promise every one of us will make. Last but not least, a nurse can be a great nurse amongst bad doctors, but a doctor is only as good as the nurses who carry out their orders."

One rare night there were a few open beds in the medical cube across from the asthma cubicle. Each cubicle in the medical side held four to six beds, depending on the patient load. Jimmy and I were sitting on the same side of one of the beds talking, breathing for a rare moment of calm. The triage nurse was walking a very regular asthma patient back to the asthma cubicle. As they passed us and turned into the cubicle away from us, I regurgitated something I had heard other nurses say. Please remember, I was 21 when I started working there, learning to grow in both good and not-so-good directions, due to the severity of the place. The only food the department would receive, on some days but not all, was a box of small milk cartons and a box of "egg" sandwiches that were nothing more than highly processed "eggs" on white bread. They were a funny color yellow, too, with no mayo, salt, or pepper to cushion the blow. These sandwiches were so bad that we would make quotation marks in the air anytime we referred to them as "egg" sandwiches. This patient, one we sometimes saw twice a day, would always ask if we had any sandwiches left to give him. So after he finished passing, I said to Jimmy, "I'll bet he wants a sandwich, too."

Jimmy slowly turned his head to me and said in an equally soft voice, "Have you ever gone a day in your life without food?" I replied "No" with embarrassment, realizing the big picture. "Then why would you deny him one of those egg sandwiches that have been sitting there all day and you won't even eat? Maybe give him two sandwiches and two milks?" he stated as we both got up to hustle away the rest of our night. To Jill, Jimmy, and every nurse and doctor that shared their knowledge, asked me a challenging question, and gave or listened to one of my in-services, I thank you from the bottom of my heart for the greatest start and maintenance of a professional career I could ever have imagined. Thank you!

There have been thousands of teachable moments in my life for both professional and professionalism growth, starting with my parents attempting to teach me manners, and much of what is now known as executive functioning. Executive functioning is something worth mentioning that school teachers have been telling me is fading the past few generations.

Executive functioning, according to Wikipedia's definition, is "a set of mental skills that include working memory, flexible thinking, and self-control. We use these skills every day to learn, work, and manage daily life. Trouble with executive functioning can make it hard to focus, follow directions, and handle emotions, among other things." Developing these skills in me first came from my appropriately persistent parents, five older siblings, and then teachers instilling baseline guidance to set the foundation. Throughout my life I continued to work with so many people that so generously and trustingly shared their amazing personal experiences of mistakes and growth. Many of these same mentors also showed a personal concern for me and taught me the value of self and peer review without criticism, to point out areas I could also improve and grow. But there is one powerful and life-changing experience that stood out as true professional review and professionalism in how it was carried out.

In 1986, I was invited to an LSU "M and M Conference," which stands for morbidity and mortality, in the morgue's postmortem, also known as an autopsy, amphitheater. From movies and television shows, I knew such arenas existed to allow large groups of medical students to look down from steeply rising layers of seats to watch basic surgery, or for more advanced physicians to observe new groundbreaking procedures. But I did not know they existed for postmortem exams. They only met in this arena to discuss the exam findings; the actual exam had been previously performed by the pathology resident, who was presenting the findings and leading the discussion with the doctors who had cared for the person who did not live.

This is why pathology is known as "The Truth" or the "The Justice System" of the healthcare field. The postmortem exam (autopsy) answers the questions and mysteries the living body does not always clearly share. What I witnessed that very early morning stirred sheer awe and motivation to spend my life studying the concepts of professionalism in action. It was at Charity Hospital that I learned the difference between the title and roles that we wrongly label "professional" and the earned achievement of professionalism. I have known too many people with titles who fell far short of the classic examples we always list for the criteria of a professional. I once went through a drive-thru many years ago to place an order for three people. I was hungry, tired, and confused with my order, but the voice remained friendly and knew that menu like the back of her hand. She even smoothly guided me to meal deals and packages to save money. She did this all with a friendly voice, not put off or rushed, and not so fast I could not hear. At that moment, getting me to the other side of that experience was her only goal. Do not ever think that because someone is in one of the fields we label "professional," such as doctor, attorney, engineer, nursing, or law enforcement, that they are a professional. Nor should we ever assume that the person feeding us at the drive-thru is also not a professional. Being a professional is not the job we are doing, but rather how we do that job.

The M and M Conference started with a medical resident presenting the case, starting with the person's age, their physical complaints of what brought them to the hospital, how long the complaint had been going on, their past medical and surgical history, what was found on their initial exam, what studies were ordered, what treatment was provided, and how that treatment was changed as laboratory and studies returned. The resident then ended with a long list of what changed, what they thought the diagnosis was or what they changed it to, and everything that occurred until the patient died. Then the pathology resident presented the factual findings on the internal exam of the body. Open discussion followed that lasted for maybe thirty minutes, which was highly educational. To this day what amazed me the most was the level of professionalism in that amphitheater that morning. No finger pointing in blame, no throwing your colleagues under the bus, no unnecessary protection of the ego displayed as defensiveness, just a jaw-droppingly articulate, open discussion for the purpose of learning and doing better. No one had done anything wrong, there was no negligence or malpractice, only a failing elderly human body that can never be put in a picture-perfect textbook, who showed multiple conflicting signs and symptoms until death.

I couldn't help but to attend a few more M and M Conferences over the years. This was rare for me, but I was always quiet, in the back, listening and learning—inspired to never stop learning about the human body, to constantly strive to achieve the difference between being a professional by title as opposed to professionalism by actions as well as omissions, such as blame and defensiveness. This all culminated in the realization that the number-one part of me, or anyone, that will prevent the growth of both professionalism and expanding my professional knowledge will be the often unnecessary protection of my damn ego and false pride.

One of the many reasons I spent almost all of my years in public teaching hospitals is because the spirit of those M and M Conferences somewhat prevails through the day-to-day work and collaboration. To have an attending ask before stopping the resuscitation efforts on a dying body, "Can anyone else think of anything we have not thought of before we stop?" is pure professional gold. It is also the great reminder that the care of the human body, just like all of life, is teamwork. No one person will ever know or see anything with 100 percent accuracy, every one of us will make mistakes, and any one of us can catch and prevent those mistakes—especially if teamwork and not competition prevail. What we think is right one day may be shown by research the next day that there is a better way or that the old way was outright wrong. Because of this fact, every medical textbook will soon after publication have information that is no longer accurate, hence the need for revisions and multi-editions of medical textbooks. This is an even stronger truth in the fast-changing fields, such as internal medicine, surgery, and cardiology, to name a few. This book is no exception.

MY FIRST ASSIST WITH A POSTMORTEM EXAM, AND THE NEED TO CUSHION DEATH NOTIFICATIONS:

Warning: The following three paragraphs contain the visual description of the end result of a human body after an autopsy is completely finished, but not restored for funeral viewing.

I had the opportunity to assist in a few postmortem exams during my first few years out of school. Each was so informative medically and also contributed to my desire to soften the blow of death. The first time I turned into the exam room, I received a shocking and beautifully symbolic vision that clarified what I already felt about our bodies. Our bodies are only our shell with many functioning parts that carries us and keeps us alive; it is our vehicle, but not who we are.

I was walking down the basement hall, headed to assist with an autopsy, not knowing that it would mean holding organs out of the way while others were cut out, and then weighing those organs. The door to the postmortem exam room was to my left and open. As I stepped closer and the door angle increased, I could see the first table in a row of empty stainless-steel tables. Then I see another to the left as I enter the door frame, then another in front of the door, and as I U-turn into the door there is a body on the last table to my far left that has just had an exam finished.

I admit for a moment it was shocking to see that indeed our body is not our being, nor does it define us past our physical features. I was looking at a human body empty of all vital organs. To carry this message home further, the face was not visible, for it was covered by the underside of the scalp that had been cut from ear to ear across the back of the head, so that in a funeral viewing the incision would not be visible. The scalp had then been gently cut off the skull and pulled away from the back and turned inside-out, completely covering the face from the top down, so the skull could be cut open and the brain moved. This allowed the skull to be returned, the scalp rolled back off the face to recover the head and sewn back down, and the casket can then be opened at the funeral. But my first vision was a wide-open chest and abdomen without a single vital organ, with no face but only a solid sheet of gray subcutaneous tissue, and with an open empty skull. The body was truly a shell.

That alone was a harsh but highly reaffirming life lesson in furthering my already-high acceptance of all humans. Except for birth defects, we are all the same human being; only the external pigment of our skin, the cultural and ethnic views, actions, mannerisms, approaches to life, and the guaranteed strengths and weaknesses of each of our brains separates us. But I realized in that moment that one empty body had something to tell me about the thousands of humans that have been examined after their death in this basement room, which hosted its first postmortem exam in 1939. I realized that we as humans have far more in common, bonding us together, than the surface appearances and issues we use to separate us. Every dead body that has ever laid on a morgue slab across the entire face of this Earth, although from different socio-economic situations, with different skin colors, ideas of social order or religion, had actually shared commonalities of much greater depth and bonds than those few I just listed that we allow to segregate us.

First I thought of our common emotions: fear, joy, insecurities, happiness, grief, and hope. Then I thought about the bonding questions we all share: of self-worth, spirituality, reasons for the tragedies we have all experienced in youth and adulthood, not to mention the big question of what and why to our existence and life in general. Then I returned to life tragedies, for every one of us has experienced life's abuses and tragedies, whether childhood trauma, acute or ongoing abuse, or neglect, to those of us who have seen war, whether abroad or the daily war of life that occurs in our homes and streets every day. Don't ever think one has to get in a military uniform to experience war; ask any front-line worker from emergency departments, to EMS, fire, police, to the thousands of people who work with child and adult abuse daily. Every land in this world has its battles occurring in everyday life; the only difference is the domestic warriors are watching it happen in their front yard to their fellow citizens and family members. No matter who you are, what you do, how dark or light your skin is, your political beliefs, or your social status, we are one. Each of us is a human being in a human body made nearly the exact same, carrying a human soul or spirit, fearing, healing from our past, questioning life, and hoping for the same things in life. Yes, those thoughts flooded my mind as I looked at my first human shell.

The morgue attendant rolled out another body and moved it onto the next table. The pathology resident took a very short break and went back into personal protection equipment, I did the same, and then we started my first postmortem exam. I absorbed what I was being taught and seeing like a sponge. Why don't nursing students get assigned to go assist with postmortem exams? I had seen the inside of too many bodies upstairs in the trauma rooms already, but still, why was this not bothering me? Was I that callous already, or had I already turned into a total scientific clinician?

I was definitely in the moment of listening to directions and drinking in the knowledge the pathologist was sharing with me. But for some strange reason, I could not help but think that in the past twenty-fours this person's family had been informed of this death. I was also thinking about how poorly so many of those notifications went. As I helped open this body without being freaked out, it dawned on me that we in the healthcare field may be used to and comfortable with a barrage of death before our eyes. We may be used to placing dead bodies in plastic sheets and then tying them off with thin rolls of gauze, as we did at Charity; body bags were used in every other hospital I worked in. We even are used to sliding those bodies onto a morgue tray, then closing the refrigerator door, and we may be comfortable in talking about death with each other. But the people we are treating and their families are not "used to" or comfortable with death. We are used to it; they are not. It was in that morgue that I also realized we talk to patients and family members about death in the same low tone and volume we talk to people who have just been sexually assaulted. Appropriately for the setting, I told myself I want to study the "pathology" of death notification, to attempt to lighten the load on both the informer of the bad news and somehow attempt to decrease the shock of one of the worst moments in our lives to the family that must receive the devastating news.

First, I evaluated how those far too many times in such a short time span that I had been a nurse, I had gone with a resident to notify a family. Any time we knew a death was about to occur, we would move the family into this tiny little yellow painted room off the main waiting room. This "yellow room," as we so uncreatively referred to it, was also used for sexual assault exams, and it contained an OB-GYN bed, one rolling exam stool, one chair, and a medical equipment case. I was told the case did not have glass because families being notified of a death had over their years broken all the glass. These death notifications did not always go as one would hope; I pass no judgment, as doctors are taught for years to save lives, not to accept death and learn to communicate about it. Some residents were great, but the majority were so vague, with such low tone and low volume, that even though they had in a very roundabout way told a family member their loved one had died, the most common question after some of them finished was, "Is my wife going to make it?" or "Will he live?" Residents, and the nurses who accompany them, on several occasions had even been hurt by accident or direct assault after informing families.

As I looked back at that brief whirlwind of a first year of experience, I discovered the biggest observation to help identify negative contributing factors to these families' reactions: No one wants to talk to these families when they know their person is not going to live.

Families only hear, and I had told families the same thing: "We are very busy; there are several people working with your mother right now, and someone will be out to talk with you as soon as possible." The healthcare field may be well seasoned to look at death and accept it on a realistic level, when trauma or illness tip the balance too far from homeostasis to recover, but none of that makes communicating with someone about their dying and their death easier. The same goes for their family members. However difficult, communication is our job, and the subject of death is not an exception. Our communication concerning death and the dying beforehand is where the opportunity for professional growth is present. If the team knows that death is in the minute to minutes of the final countdown, then the first real information the family receives should not be the full force of what might be the worst news of their lives.

WHAT I DID AND SAID TO DECREASE THE SHOCK:

It was shortly after that realization that the family of patients being resuscitated were avoided that I found the courage to walk away from a "code," as the medical field calls a resuscitation in progress, of a man who was very old and was not going to survive, so that I could go and talk to the family. I was about to create what I call "cushioning time," and I was scared beyond belief. My chest started to burn with every step. I started to fear maybe I was overstepping a boundary as a nurse—what do I say, how do I say it? The door is now just around the corner and open with a room full of people. I feel like I'm hyperventilating; I actually start to have a ringing in my ears. Breathe, Vincent, breathe; there has to be a better way.

I took a huge breath and stepped just inside the door, completely closed it, and somehow said pretty close to what I ended up saying for the next twenty years. I made sure to speak in a normal tone and volume, which was not easy because I expected my voice to be very shaky. I introduced myself, asked the name of the patient they were here with to clarify the right patient to family, and asked how they were all related. His wife was seated with family members on each side holding a hand. I took in one more big breath looked at his wife, and using that one breath I said, "I am going to give you an update on your husband, and I am going to speak openly and directly out of respect for all of you, because the more you know, the better you can deal with something, and you, your family, and your husband's situation deserve that level of open respect. OK?" I asked to get permission and make sure she was truly present. I looked around the room at each face and asked the group, "Is that OK with you all, too?" I think the magnitude of asking such permission creates a bumped-up bond of both respect and gentleness immediately. I pulled in another breath and used it to finish. "Ma'am, your husband is in critical condition right now; he is not breathing on his own, and his heart is not beating on its own. He has an entire team of people working with him right now. But every minute we have to breathe for him, and every minute we have to compress his chest to move his blood, his chances become worse." Breathe, Vincent. "I am going to do nothing else right now but work with you to update you; I'm going to go see how he is doing and come right back out here." I took the extra seconds to make eye contact with each person before I left. I cared, and I needed even a minimal relationship with each one, for I was their bearer of a nightmare. I did just as I stated and returned just a few minutes later. My breathing was getting slightly easier as I walked back to the yellow room and informed them, "He is still not responding. We are still doing CPR; remember, every minute we have to do it for him, his chances of living decrease." The family had been visibly upset since my first statement, but they were quiet, calm, and supporting each other. After this second update, I asked if they had any questions, and again made brief eye contact with each. I don't remember their questions, but I remember they were appropriate for the magnitude of the situation. After brief, simple answers, I again told them, "Let me go check for you. I'll be right back out," and one more time I did, and one more time I went back out to them. The only thing I added on the last update was, looking directly at his wife before I left again, I said, "It has now been a very long time that we have been doing CPR. I want you to prepare yourself." When I went back into the "crisis cubicle," as it was called, they had just "called the code," as the medical field refers to ending a resuscitation effort. He had died.

I wish I could remember the name of the third-year emergency medicine resident that night. He and I had a great working relationship, and he also loved teaching. I told him the family was in the yellow room, and that I had been keeping them well informed, and could I please give them the notification. I remember he looked at me with a suspect raised eyebrow but said, "Sure!" We walked into the door, but not into the room, and they looked at him but then returned their eyes to me with a higher level of fear to see the doctor arrive with me. I said nothing and slowly shook my head. There were tears, moans, and heads dropping, all with a calm I had never seen. They were hugging each other and crying harder, and he and I said nothing. The wife spoke first about two long minutes later, "What do we do now?" He answered by saying, "The only thing you need to do when you are ready is contact the funeral home of your choice, and I do have a few questions for you for some paperwork I need to fill out." He asked and answered a few questions, and I said I was sorry for their pain and thanked them for allowing me to be there with them. We walked out of the room and back through the double doors into the Major Medical Room. No sooner than the double doors closed behind us did he stop me and pull me into this little treatment room behind the secondary triage desk and said with excitement and wonder, "How the hell did you do that? "All you did was shake your head. You didn't say a word, and will you please do that every shift I work until I leave here?"

I very quickly caught him up with what I have already shared with you above. We had a fast, short discussion on what I actually did and said to get them prepared, and he greatly thanked me before we went back to work. When he said he had no further questions for the family, I went back out to tell them they could leave. That was the first time family members ever gave me a hug.

Although I most often let the doctor state the actual notification of death, I did this simple caring act hundreds and hundreds of times over the next twenty years. Yes, it takes a few minutes to do during an often painfully too-busy shift, but that moment is not about me, and it's not about how many charts are in the rack with orders waiting to be carried out. It is the worst and most painful moment in most people's lives, and it is holistic, loving, caring, and compassionate health care in action. I may be comfortable with death as a seasoned provider of critical care, but that family of a human life that ended just lost their wife, husband, mother, father, sister, brother, grandmother, grandfather, or worse yet their child. I think we can find the courage and fifteen to twenty minutes to soften the painful blow their lives are about to hear and feel to the core.

It is a rare day in an emergency department that a Band-Aid at triage can send someone out the door without starting paperwork and an actual registration into the system. Pulling off a newly attached tick and teaching the person what signs and symptoms to look out for in case they have been exposed to a tick-borne microbe may be one of the few times I did not start the paperwork and bring them into the system. This is because your healthcare team always wants to find the origin of the issue and attempt to cure that, not just fix the issue's visual outward signs and symptoms. Have you ever worked with a boss or had a friend or partner that was constantly trying to fix big, late problems that, had they spent less energy sooner, would have prevented the larger later problem? As if they have never heard Benjamin Franklin's famous saying, "An ounce of prevention is worth a pound of cure"?

If I only shared with you the words and technique of "cushioning time" without telling what work I did inside to make it easier, I would be doing you an injustice, and that is not how the professional scientific clinician works. What is the pathology of the problem? What initially caused the problem? What were all of the contributing factors to the issue? If a child comes into the triage area with a dime-sized scrape, I still need to dig a little before I place a Band- Aid on them and send them back out. OK, I have to confess, I am almost laughing thinking about the upper administration, or department heads, reading this and thinking, "NOOooo, you can't place a Band-Aid and send them out the door; we could be sued! There's no documentation; we can't bill for the Band-Aid! Yet worse, you definitely cannot remove a tick that has only been on for a few hours with no redness and the head not yet embedded; you have to check in a tick bite. What if it gets infected; what if they sue us? There's no documentation; we can't bill them." Don't worry, guys, except for us older nurses, most triage nurses will check everything in, but it would be an interesting reversal of liability if someone sued a hospital for excessive care and billing for receiving a

$2,000 bill for the emergency room general charges, doctor's fees, and a sterile tweezer to remove a few-hours-old attached tick.

Sorry for the diversion, but it is a great example of the complexities of potential liability exposure of protecting a hospital versus realistic affordable health care. The reality of this is real; yes, I have had numerous people come in wanting us to remove a tick. This is highly cautious, yes, yet appropriate for some who read or heard the tick's head can stay on and get infected if deeply embedded in the skin or not removed correctly. For most it was their first attached tick. Hospitals have been sued for less, and yes that nurse would hold some liability exposure for having made that choice if a lawsuit followed. Of course, a hefty bill would be paid by the patient and insurance company for that tick removal.

Now you all know why I could never give a TED Talk; as moderately comfortable as I am with public speaking, I could never remember fifteen to twenty-five paragraphs in order. This is not to mention the many rabbit holes my attention deficit issues, and my need to interject supporting information, create. I have such respect for the knowledge and speaking skills of the presenters of TED Talks.

As I was sharing, I easily provided the simple technique and ballpark wording of how I prepare people for highly probable imminent death in minutes in the health care setting. But before I can place a Band-Aid and send someone on their way, the standard of the entire medical field is to dig deeper first. Am I placing a Band-Aid on a kid who fell off their bike 10 minutes ago and then rode up the ED to ask for a Band-Aid, but who also wants to know where the soda and candy machines are? Or is it an adult that has a dime-sized ulceration with no trauma and several areas that are not healing, and definitely needs a further workup to find the deeper origin of the problem? That is what the following information, and the style of this book, is based on: ingrained training to find the origin of issues, seeing big pictures to find more encompassing answers, and to not just place Band-Aids. I am a digger for what is causing an issue. Is Mr. Franklin correct; would you rather spend an ounce now or a pound later? In the case of talking about death, the ounce is spent looking inside yourself and finding tools to make it easier.

The majority of people I have worked with are compassionate, humanistic, and caring spirits; I have met very few who are not. Although I did work with a nurse once that I asked about their consistently short abrupt answers to peers, patients, and families; "I was hired to accomplish nursing tasks, not to be nice" was his answer, but this is not the norm. My mother used to share with me a theory when I was a little boy that I actually watched develop into reality over the years. She was a teacher and a social worker, and she was very attuned to the bedside manner of physicians and staff, after both working in hospitals as a social worker and then having six kids. The irony of that is she did not always have the greatest "bedside manner" when it came to working with the wait staff in restaurants when something wasn't going her way.

My mother was in many ways an out-of-the-box, forward, non-linear thinker. She greatly cared about the well-being of children and actively worked to raise awareness about child abuse, had four degrees past a bachelor's degree, and ended with her PhD at the age of 58. I remember her saying several times throughout my childhood that we should not take all medical and nursing school applicants from the sciences. She felt strongly that a large percentage of those accepted should be from the humanity fields. Her reasoning made complete sense, for you can teach a person the sciences, but you can't always teach a person to be humanistic, compassionate, and deeply caring. I really appreciated my relationship with residents, and I loved asking them of their backgrounds, and more and more told me of backgrounds in other careers and studies from the humanities. Great healthcare people come from all walks of life, but I could see more compassionate, well-rounded communication from both those entering as a second careers as well as those with stronger humanistic backgrounds. With time, I began to work with more and more nurses and doctors from the humanities. I share this because I found in order to accomplish this open, direct, normal-volume conversion with the dying and their families, I was definitely coming from a holistic and caring place.

However, and I mean a big however, the interesting duality was my realization that it was this exact holy grail holistic and caring emotion that was preventing me from delivering a clear, heads-up, strong-voiced communication about dying and death in the first place. We know all too well that death is forever, and being informed of terminal illness is a painful and emotional blow to the receiver of the information. So naturally to show respect, and even to not appear clinical, flippant, or cold, we speak softly, we bow our heads, not to mention our own emotional baggage around death that pulls us inward and downward from the inside. All of these legitimate contributing factors are multiplied times ten when you are looking at and talking to the person that is actually the one dying, or to someone about to lose their loved one to a rapidly approaching death. My loving, emotional concern for others was actually hindering me; it was part of my problem. I admit, I also did not want to talk to the family of the person we were coding because it is really hard, painful, and emotionally stirring to feel in myself, and to know the anxiety, fear, and pain the information is going to cause them.

Without going to the cold, hard, and calloused side, I learned to move away from my emotional thought process and into my rational, matter-of-fact thought process to talk about death and dying. Yes, is it our role to be holistic and caring; I have been told that to a fault. The two most common complaints I received about my work from my fellow ED nurses was, "You are too nice to be an emergency nurse, and your discharge instructions are too long." I would thank them for the input and go back to work. Yes, death, whether in five minutes, five days, or five months, will be a terrible blow to self, and all that felt love, respect, or appreciation for who is close to death. Yet at the moment I am answering their questions, or giving them hard-to-hear-and-digest information, that very moment is about their deserved need for appropriate information to help them deal with eventual death. The chances are fairly high they are already in crisis mode, which does very little to help with memory and big- picture vision. So by bringing your voice back up, steering clear of vague answers filled with euphemisms, and giving the clearest, most straightforward, and honest answers you can, you are actually given someone a higher level of humanistic, holistic care. At that moment it is not our role to protect them from painful information, but rather it is our role to make sure they hear and comprehend that painful information.

To give another harsh example, this same technique works when we are going to start an IV or any pain- or discomfort-causing procedure. Infants and children are of course the hardest patients on whom to practice this "blocking out pain" that I preach. In this case we are talking about actual physical pain, not emotional pain. At the moment I am about to insert an IV catheter, or any needle or tube, I actually block out the pain that I am about to inflict. Yes, that infant hopefully is stable and alert enough to scream and cry at full lung capacity; yes, IVs are painful; yes I care–but my job is to get that IV hopefully on the first stick. Adding in the magnitude of inserting a needle into an infant is not going to help me, on top of the already difficult job that it is. The frequency of misses on IV starts for me went way down once I started practicing this. It is hard enough to get an IV into those tiny little veins on a dehydrated infant, and adding in the pain and straining cries does not help. I am not being indifferent to tell myself such an apparent uncaring statement; I am increasing my chances of only having to inflict pain once.

Pulling all this internal awareness and work into application at the moment I am about to talk about dying and death looks like this. I tell myself they will have to go through the pain and misery of their grief, whether I answer their questions or not. I again go into the rational, not emotional, part of my being, and I hold my head up, I breathe a little deeper, and I talk. I greatly care about their fear and pain of grief, but that is not the topic. The topic is their terminal illness. Giving information clearly and having it comprehended and retained is the only task at hand at that moment. They need to hear as much as they can from you, to the best their ability at that dark moment will allow, to be able to make informed and self-confident choices for someone they have that responsibility to, or for themselves. They will need your patience and answers to maintain that same high level of understanding. Our ears may not ring when discussing death, but theirs may be starting to.

I want to give you a beautiful example of an acute notification of someone's approaching death. I was once caring for a patient only in his late sixties; they had already had several repairs of aortic aneurysms, which is the weakening and then distention of the major artery that comes out of the heart that feeds the oxygen-rich blood to your entire body before smaller vessels branch off to do the final transporting out to the far reaches of the body. This person presented to the ED late one night with vague complaints of chest and abdominal pain. After we had ruled out a cardiac issue and completed a chest and abdominal CT scan, vascular surgery was consulted. I had worked with this vascular surgery resident for years, starting as an intern in the ED. A sharp, well-rounded resident, he had operated on this person less than a year ago. After hanging up with his attending, he brought me over to the CT screen, showed me the huge long aneurysm, taught me the history and surgeries, and sadly told me all the reasons this new aneurysm could not be repaired. He informed me he had a great rapport with this patient but wanted me to witness the talk anyway. He sadly looked at me and said, "I'm sending this patient home to die when it eventually ruptures." Rupture, meaning it will eventually break open and spill out the body's blood supply in the chest and/or abdominal cavity. I have heard so many great nurses and doctors give such wonderful, caring talks with patience about critically fatal situations, and this one was no exception. We walked in that room, and he talked to this person with his head and voice up and presented the situation clinically with a perfect mix of respect for the magnitude, yet not a word was minced. We easily spent twenty minutes there as he fed him every angle he could think of for this person to go home and live life to its fullest until the aneurysm ruptured– including, "Enjoy all the ice cream you want but try not to cough, sneeze, or strain too hard for any reason, so to keep the pressures down in your blood vessels." He answered this person's questions directly without dancing around the answers, the hardest being, "What will my death look like, and how long will I take to die once the aneurysm ruptures?" He had no trouble saying, "I can give you an educated guess, but I cannot give you a definite answer to that type of question," and he went on to do just that. This older couple I am sure was scared and screaming on the inside, but they remained attentive and continued asking questions, as if mirroring this doctor's approach. Knowing they had just burned up a huge amount of simple energy reserves, first due to spending hours in the ED without fluids because I did not know if surgery would be required, but then to hear and have a conversation of that extreme level, the only thing I could think of to help was to bring them both a ginger ale. Followed by a slightly firm request for them to finish it before getting dressed and heading home, I then left them alone to process this horrible news and support each other.

TALKS UNRELATED TO DEATH NOTIFICATION:

Most of the talking about dying then death should be done long before the actual death occurs. Respectfully, I get it; this is just outright painfully tough for a huge percentage of us. Being from South Louisiana, I often wonder if there is not a little superstition thrown in there, a little voodoo fear, as if talking about death will jinx us. Whether healthcare professionals or a couple learning each other's wishes, it is indeed a damn hard subject. "But again closing your eyes tightly and looking the other way will have zero effect on preventing the sun from setting." I might be sharing gems with you to make it easier, but it still takes a tough percentage of me to get going, too. I figure if I care for another, personally or professionally, I am showing them the greatest love or professional respect by having the conversion with them. Trust, too, that most people can have the conversion, but always respect, "I don't want to talk about that right now." Over the years I have definitely refined my abilities to have these painful talks, yet at the same time they will never get easy, and I wouldn't want them to. It would mean I stopped feeling the pain and fear of others. Several basic concepts have walked through all these years, and I think each has made my sharing more respectful and appropriate and less traumatic for both myself and the other person.

Shortly after moving to the bayous, I met a large family that lived one street and a bayou over from us. It was a neat family, funny and to the point, and their grandfather lived with them. It was the home and family where the kids in the neighborhood would gather. Even a kid could appreciate the value of the kitchen table talk and not feel a need to jump up and go run and play. The grandfather taught me a few tricks about gardening, and we had a few little talks over the years. I was really young, but I remember him sitting on a cool little stool while he worked the weeds near daily up and down the rows of his garden. It was a raised bed made of railroad ties. The matriarch of this huge force of a clan was pure gold on every level, humorous, challenging, with massive maternal instinct and life experience, and grounded with a common sense that shone. If you shared something with her about your life that she knew did not fall into the category of her grounded common sense and experience, she wouldn't try to steer you in a different direction. She would not say "You should...," as so many so freely do, but only squint her eyes a little and say, "Ya, how's that working for you?" Over the years I visited her a few times when I went back to the region. As I would catch her up on my life, I would dread her interjecting that question. Answering her simple, wise "Ya, how's that working for you?" usually did the trick for me, and I would do my own steering in a new direction.

I was in my rookie year of nursing when I heard the grandfather was in the hospital closing in on his death, and I went to visit him. I drove the hour or so to the hospital. I walked in the room, and he was awake and sitting up in bed. He was even more deaf than I remember, despite his lack of hearing being an ongoing joke in this colorful family. We were practically screaming at each other to communicate. I had to help him remember me. After saying my name several times and a few stories he might connect to me, he said, "The little skinny kid with more hair on his arms than I had on my whole body, right?"

Yep, he remembered! He had the short, abrupt style of communication that ran through the entire family. This family was real in how they handled and saw the trials and failures of life. I got even closer and brought my volume up even higher to a near yell, "How are you doing?"

He said, "They tell me I'm dying, and I think they're right." A second passed and he yelled, "Feels like it too!"

Way loud back, I asked, "Are you ready to die?"

He said, "No," a lot more softly.

"Why not?" I asked him.

"I'm scared to die. I think I'm going to hell."

At that volume, I'd bet the nurses station could hear us. I asked if he ever murdered anyone or intentionally hurt anyone. After he answered no to both, he added "But I made a lot of mistakes that hurt people."

I replied, "Who hasn't made too many mistakes that hurt someone else, and why do you think you are going to hell?" I had rarely talked to someone getting that close to death at this point in my life, but I can promise you it was the highest-volume one I ever had.

"Everything the damn church scared me with." He started to cry, and I did too. I remember being kind of mad that this dying, not-half-bad man was scared to die because he was scared of going to hell. I reminded him of the good but grumpy man I knew him to be, I reminded him of the gardening tricks he taught me, and of his regular weekly visits to church, and hollered a few more good things I could remember about him. I remember inappropriately near-screaming, "The only thing you might go to hell for is making too many fruitcakes at Christmas!"

He looked at me with surprised wide eyes and chuckled. Whew. He calmed down further, and we talked about the house and garden, and I asked to tell me about all of the dogs in his life. That home always had dogs; if their doorbell ever broke, they would not have known it.

I share this story because the main subject I have always worked to stay away from, unless the other person wants to talk about it, of course, while talking about dying and death, is religion. This man, who kept trying to give away his fruitcakes at Christmas, was far from the last dying person who shared their fears with me around their religion or spirituality as their death rapidly approached. I want to be gentle and respectful concerning this subject even as I write, so I will not give direction. Instead, I will only ask a few questions. The first is the most important.

If someone doesn't bring up religion or spirituality, should you? These are highly personal subjects. Some may have spent a lifetime becoming wonderful people with or without religion or spirituality. Perhaps they are healing from their religious past, sexual abuse, or a parent or partner that would control, manipulate, or suppress using religious ideology. As the grandfather, having chosen and embraced a path, but still fearing the afterlife, he had brought it up, not I. Two more questions: Would you want your lifelong beliefs questioned or to be told they were wrong or dysfunctional as you neared your death? Are you cautious to not have an ethnocentric view of others' established beliefs? I completely respect the magnitude of this subject for many, and I will stop there.

When talking to another about their dying or death, attempt not to share what you would do. This is a big one for two reasons. The first is obvious: it is not your dying and death process; it is theirs. It is only a slightly different story if they asked for your opinion, but even then, I try to redirect back and ask what they would do. In my personal life, I am a little more comfortable answering this one, but not much more. The reason for this is because dying then death is so individualized not only by choice, hopes, and fears, but also in how the body responds. Anything past sharing my knowledge and observations is just not my place. I will tell you what I do know about a medication or procedure, but I will not tell you to take the medication or have the procedure. It's not my place. It is equally important to be able to say, "I don't know, but I will try to find out for you."

Last but not least, take full breaths often while discussing painful subjects, and use that full breath to get the hard sentences out. I used it unknowingly by chance the first time I walked into that yellow room alone to talk with the family, and I have used it hundreds of times since concerning more subjects than death. It's a great way to start the talk with a person about your own wishes around death. Pull in a big breath and maybe try, "I know it's a hard subject for anyone to talk about, but I think we should talk about our wishes concerning our eventual death and get our wills and paperwork in order." Pull in the air, and commit to getting the subject on the table; hold your head and voice high, and let it out.

THE HARDER BLOCKS HINDERING PRODUCTIVE COMMUNICATION WITH SELF AND OTHERS:

Mostly I hear really positive things from people who have had recent hospital admissions or personal health care encounters of any type. But I know many others, and from my own experiences when I am not in scrubs, just how tricky, temperamental, and frustrating it can be. I too am guilty of having to deliver poorly wrapped communication at times. I hated when I was truly dealing with the "every second matters" situations to save a life that forced me to be more abrupt than I would have liked. Yet, two-way communication is the vital link to quality patient care and can also be wonderfully educational for both sides, as well as productive and rewarding.

Whether the doctor is unable to return calls or the nursing staff is spread too thin and pushed too far, many of the causes of this breakdown in communication are legitimate reasons, but they should never be excuses. The great majority of our healthcare field is pushed to the max, both individually and in the entire system in general. The estimated population of the United States, before the final 2020 census is completed, is now 330,000,000, with only an estimated 220,000 primary care physicians. The ratios and proportions of emergency departments, home health agencies, and hospices are equally critical.

Above I mentioned "reasons" versus "excuses." If I make a mistake and say or do something wrong, although I also fail at what I am about to say, I work to accept the responsibility for my part and apologize. My apology may include the reason, "I am sorry I said that; it was a tough day, and I had not eaten in hours. That was wrong of me." As opposed to an excuse, such as, "Well you bit me first, and I was just trying to finish my sentence." Knowing the difference between those two is critical for professionalism, avoiding arguments, self-growth, and to help increase one's acceptance, tolerance, forgiveness, and understanding. I have always found those four extensions of the self to be the main pillars of peace with self and others. I will humbly tell you the reason I find it easier and easier to extend acceptance, tolerance, forgiveness, and understanding to others. As time passes and my internal visions become braver in self-honesty, my ego is kept in greater and greater check and balance. I am able to admit that almost every day of my life, I most likely will say something I should not say, or not say something I should. The same holds for actions; daily I may do something I should not do, or not do something I should. Therefore, I know each day from one person or another I will silently or outwardly beg pardon and hope to be shown acceptance, tolerance, forgiveness, and understanding. Since I acknowledge that by human limitations, I am filled with hypocrisy and double standards, then why in the world would I not actively attempt to extend those pillars daily to others?

Although I am speaking of the reasons to be patient with each individual in the healthcare field, I want you to know that I do realize, it is really the healthcare field's job to show you the acceptance, tolerance, forgiveness, and understanding in communication and not the other way around. For you are the patient or family member, and you are the one sick, injured, scared, or in crisis. It is our job to get you through your crisis. Although it is not your job to get us through a painful, busy twelve-hour shift filled with tragedy, violence, and even the verbal and physical abuse we all too often receive, your cooperation and assistance will help you be care for quicker. The fewer small fires that must be put out the faster all will be cared for. Other than meeting our basic needs of food, fluids, elimination, and safety, from the time we walk into the building's door and leave eight, ten, or twelve hours later, caring for you and your family should be our only focus. Sharing our knowledge and skills to heal, support, and educate, keeping our egos in check when conflicts do arise, listening to you and not sharing our life's problems unless asked, and offering some appropriate humor if the situation allows, is what your health care experience should look like. We will fail at times. Please forgive us; we are human first then our titles second. Every single one of us, patients, families, and staff, are all limited to humanness, and we all have a faulty, imperfect mind, just as the rest of the over seven and a half billion people on the face of this Earth.

Because no two human minds have the exact same strengths and weaknesses, expecting anyone to align with your thought process and expectations is a near-guaranteed setup for failure. It has become one of the pitfalls of our society: throwing people, groups, cultures, or businesses away completely because of a behavior or view that does not line up with our own. This also unfortunately usually walks next to unchecked hypocrisy and double standards−, harsh but true. I strongly believe that not one of our imperfect minds is powerful, consistent, clear, or self-honest enough to always be and act outwardly as we believe we are in our thoughts.

Although this theory is indeed hard to hear, it has the ability to greatly increase our own internal peace and create more peace around us. We get a choice, we can accept this shared human condition of imperfection, and we can be open to finding and attempting to minimize our hypocrisies and double standards. Or, we can let our ego win in their powerful attempts at self-deception and never catch them. But finding the courage to admit and look out for them is another power tool to professionalism in life, not just in our career. Completely eliminating these internal to external inconsistencies is not humanly possible. For example, while driving, the person who thinks they cannot cause a crash or fatality is much more dangerous than the more cautious and aware driver who realizes they, as every human, can drop their guard and commit an error that can kill. As well, the nurse or doctor who admits to themselves they are capable of making an error decreases their chances of making one, because they are constantly looking out for their potential to make a mistake. How many times have we been upset with someone moving into our lane, correcting within inches of contact, yet immediately asked forgiveness when we did the same to someone else?

I bring this up because we have become a society of blame rather than one that strives to be solution based, and it is a horribly self-perpetuating vicious cycle. Highly appropriate self-preservation comes into play when another person is trying to get us to accept their percentage of a mistake or breakdown in communication. Be gentle in both directions, and remember self-defense mechanisms are naturally ingrained protective measures will all have. But when we overflex our defensiveness and attempt to accept zero responsibility in the breakdown of communication, rather than accept our portion of the blame, we are lying to ourselves and heaping abusive blame on another.

Again, I know this is harsh, and not always easy to accomplish, but I share to attempt to prevent communication conflict in the hospital, which does happen. No one likes to be reminded that we are all capable of being a part of the problem, but I too must show constant vigilance for the frailties of my imperfect human mind that can potentially contribute to the breakdown of communication. Each of us will fail periodically, hopefully less and less with time and greater self-awareness.

One reason is that emergency rooms can be such violent places due to so many factors. In the early nineties, I became an instructor in a course that taught techniques to de-escalate violent behavior. I taught that course for about thirteen years to departments in the hospital that had to deal with higher levels of anxiety, anger, and aggression to attempt to keep staff members safe. Areas such as psychiatry, all registration clerks, billing or accounts receivable, emergency and clinic nurses, and hospital police all sent their staff to this training. To summarize, the sixteen-hour course, aside from some hands-on techniques to restrain violent people, was about recognizing and dealing with anxiety.

Although anxiety has evolved from a simple definition into a diagnosis first printed in the DSM-3 in 1980, the simple definition of "fear of the unknown" still sums up anxiety well. Meeting an anxious person's needs and eliminating their unknown to the best of your ability also sums up the course. The main emphasis was on early recognition of low anxiety levels and prevention of escalation by communication and redirection. Above, I jumped to the point about keeping our ego in check and balance because ED nurses are to-the-point people. We have to be a fair percentage of the time. But without saying so directly, that is what the sixteen hour class was teaching: Don't blow up to aggression initially, unless their level of escalation already requires immediate staunch direction or physical action to keep you or someone else physically safe. Again, the key to being able to do that was to check your ego and defensive verbal responses at the door, and meet the crisis person's needs early to calm them and avoid further issues.

The times I have had to be blunt, to the point, or even aggressive with a patient or family member had legitimate reasons, such as use of alcohol or other intoxicants, and after they had not responded to rational direction, or they were escalating quickly in verbal and/or physical abuse towards staff or family, and higher redirection was required. Although that is a reason to advance the verbal force continuum, or if we had to go hands-on to restrain for the safety of all, those would never have been an excuse for me to be rude or use excessive force. It is important for the recipient or witness of physical force being used to understand the difference between excessive force and exceeding force. There is rarely a need for excessive force unless death is the immediate threat. Yet at the same time due to the basic laws of physics, when restraining someone, exceeding force must always be used. Otherwise the restraint and safety of all will not be achieved. That line can become blurry at times to the recipient or witness.

There are often behind-the-scenes events going on that make your calmness and patience even more appreciated by the staff and will actually allow us to get to you more quickly. If the medical staff appears not to be at a peak level of professionalism, including regarding how quickly you are being attended to, your patience and tolerance may at these times be needed the most. Every emergency nurse who has spent at least six months in practice has been in situations such as the one that follows. One moment I walked out of a trauma room, having just placed an infant killed in a car crash into a body bag after sitting with the parents while they cried over the body. The next moment I walked into a room to assess someone who became angry for one reason or another and punched a wall or a window and broke and/or cut their hand. Then I walk into a treatment room to care for a patient who needs eight stitches after dropping a chef's knife on their foot while at their restaurant job. This patient barks, "It's about time! What the f*#k took so long—did you decide to finish your break?" Painfully being "mf'd," as we refer to it, should actually be written in the job description of all emergency personnel, including fire and EMS: "The role requires a willingness to remain professional during the times you will be inappropriately labeled, verbally abused, and physically assaulted."

I do completely respect how hard it can be to wait long periods when you are in pain, intoxicated, frightened, injured, or acutely ill enough to be looking at the ceiling of an emergency department. I have been that waiting person, too. Calmness, patience, and tolerance improve almost any already not-so-pretty experience, whereas inflaming a situation only adds layers of difficulty and delay in numerous directions. When asked about the wait time on busy nights, I would validate and compare. "I am so sorry for how long it is taking for you to be seen, but I want to share a different angle of your wait with you. You are most definitely unlucky to have ended up in this emergency department tonight, but you are lucky that you can wait. You are lucky that you are not the car crash victim we just took up to the OR with bleeding into the brain, and you are lucky that you are not the person having an active heart attack that we need to get to the cardiac cath lab right away, and you are lucky you are not the person sedated having the piece of steak removed from the esophagus on the other side of this wall. However, I can see you are in pain, so let me quickly present your case to the attending and fill out an order sheet for her to sign, so I can order your X-rays and get you some pain medication. Are you allergic to any medications? Can you hang in there a little longer while I attempt to work on that, if nothing else more critical comes up before I accomplish that?" The response is usually one of new grounded acceptance that indeed they are lucky in their unluckiness. I have also validated their long wait and pain, and I have also taken action to move their care along. To avoid violations of patient confidentiality, I will often use past cases not actual cases happening in the department at that moment.

By title and role, the healthcare staff is made up of doctors, nurses, nurse aides, laboratory phlebotomists, radiology technicians, nutritionists, and physical therapists, clerks, and receptionists, to name a few. What the healthcare staff is really made up of is individuals, human individuals. That human factor, in all of us, creates a limited capability and fallibility.

For every year but my first (before this awareness came to me), I have worn a name tag with my first name only, my title, and with one special addition. No matter what badge or tag I have worn, I have written or taped the initials "HB" after my name and before my professional title of RN. Once or twice a week someone would notice and ask about that "HB." I would reply with pride and seriousness, "It stands for 'Human Being,' and the reason it comes before the RN is that my nursing abilities are limited to my human abilities." I then follow that with, "It is just as much a reminder to my colleagues as it is to the patients and family members." Every person that you talk with concerning your health care or your loved ones is limited to their human ability for that given moment, as is the case with you and everyone we meet in life.

You will find "professional" and "unprofessional" behavior on all levels of the healthcare field, as in all career fields. There are several criteria that should be met to call someone a professional, and many fields meet this criterion. The reason I put the quotation marks around the "professional" and "unprofessional" is because I feel one's behavior is very much a part of that earned and worthy title. I have known surgeons who have wonderful, mild bedside manners with patients and family, but literally throw tantrums and objects in the operating room if a nurse hands them the wrong instrument. Now that a few nurses have brought assault charges against them, if the thrown instrument hits them, these periodic unnecessary unprofessional emotional lack of control behaviors are quickly becoming less and less frequent. I have seen nurses who would rather argue to be right, than to be calm and understanding and treat the patient and family members with flexible, professional respect during their momentary crisis, which has left them not at their best abilities. I have seen staff members place their ego before their professional responsibility, and those who inflame patients or family members to the point of verbal or physical violence, resulting in the patient or family member being arrested, restrained, or escorted from the emergency department or hospital. Unfortunately, once human behavior passes a certain point it becomes a no-win situation for everyone involved. Again, that loss no-win loss could be physically, mentally, emotionally, or legally.

The problem I see that causes the most damage and distance between the healthcare staff and the patients and family is the failure of the healthcare staff—remember, I mean individuals—to meet the needs of the patient and family before the needs of self or the department. Of course departments have policies and procedures that are wise and appropriate to keep things moving and to keep all safe, and these need to be adhered to as closely as possible, if possible. Setting clear and appropriate limits for unacceptable behavior is one thing, but getting into a power struggle is another; it is a futile waste of time and only destroys any functional working relationships. Health care recipients in acute care settings are under heightened stress, have often completely burned up their blood glucose levels, and are running on low reserves of basic energy and tolerance, add on top of that anxious, fearful, and with very little control of the powerful happenings around them. Literally offering a glass of regular ginger ale, not diet, with some informing communication, validating their complaint if appropriate, and expending some energy to expedite their care will go so much further than reacting to impatience or aggression. Upset patients and family all too often have respectable and understandable reasons for their behavior. The mind is equally as important as the body.

But this really is no different from any communication with anyone. In observing how my colleagues respond to communication from patients and family, I can give you a few keys to success. Always attempt to communicate through asking non-challenging, information- seeking questions, such as, "What do I need to know about the length of wait before we are seen by a doctor?" "How can I prevent and care for bedsores?" "What should I do if the doctor has not returned my page by ten o'clock when my loved one tends to wake up in pain?" "Is there something I can do to help?" "Why is there so much nausea with this pain medicine, and is there one that works as well or better without so much nausea?" I greatly encourage you to ask the question again if you don't understand the answer. There is nothing wrong with stating, "I still don't understand; can you please explain that to me another way?" You have a right to ask, know, and walk away empowered with the knowledge to fully understand the cause, care, complications, and potential outcome of the disease process with which you are dealing.

Studies show that as many as 20 percent of return visits and readmissions to doctor's offices, clinics, and emergency departments could have been prevented with complete and understood discharge instructions. I am proud to say that I too have been criticized by other nurses for my spending too much time at the bedside teaching. Appreciate the healthcare professional who ends teaching with, "Is there anything I just shared that you don't understand, or do you now have any new questions, even if you're not sure how to ask them?" Throughout my career, I have been so grateful to have learned to ask that question. It is amazing the number of times something was misunderstood, or an important follow-up question was asked. The information we teach as the professional may be basic to us, but to the patient or family member, it can be difficult to comprehend. When stepping into your healthcare system it can be easy to feel surrounded by an overwhelming environment, and it can be hard to remember your questions and remember all the information provided.

I encourage every healthcare professional who thinks they do not have the time to achieve more complete teaching to reconsider the above research: If 20 percent of all return visits to the healthcare system could be prevented with better patient teaching, then by not stopping to take the time to educate, you are increasing your workload by 20 percent down the road. Respectfully, I have never understood why we will follow the research in every aspect of our care except this one.

One of my favorite doctors, and to this day a dear friend, whom I worked with for years, told me of also being criticized for taking his time with communication. One night I walked in the back door to get ready to start my regular weekend twelve-hour night shift. He was sitting at the tall attending desk facing the ambulance bay door. As I turned to go back to thelockers, he said, "Hey, Vincent, come here; I want to show you something. I want to frame this and hang it in my office. It is a negative comment on an evaluation of me by a third-year resident." Every year the residents graduating from the program get to evaluate the attending physicians who have taught and guided them the past three years. The evaluation read, "Spends too much time at the bedside." I looked up and he was smiling huge and wide, his grin was even up to and into his eyes, and he beamed, "Pretty good, huh?" We high-fived, and I congratulated him on such great, negative, fantastic, horribly, wonderful criticism. We then had a short, fast discussion about how telling that is of the new generations of doctors, and we both hoped we were wrong.

Another important trick for better communication in the healthcare field is to pre-plan when you can. Write down your questions before you get to the office visit or as they come to you during the waiting periods, even if sitting in the ED. Even if you're not sure how to ask a question, or are embarrassed to ask, make the attempt. Maybe the answer to your vague question will actually answer your question, or will get you a little closer to what you are looking for, or will guide you closer to asking the more specific question you could not word. Try to also pre-plan for physical and technical needs, such as getting medicine prescriptions refilled before they run out. So ask about having medications on hand for nausea, diarrhea, and pain before the need arises. Most doctors will not have an issue with this in small quantities, especially with a terminal patient. Remember the paperwork. Have your legal paperwork in order and in hand. It does a lot of communicating for you. Actually, it takes away the need for a lot of unnecessary communication around the concept of treatment and cardio-pulmonary resuscitation. Keep copies at the bedside or taped to the refrigerator; I also kept a copy in my glove compartment for my parents.

At the same time, please be respectful for how busy the healthcare professional is, their time is spread so thin. But ask your questions, because according to that 20 percent, you may be keeping yourself from needing to return to the office, emergency room, or clinic just by walking out the door more informed.

Don't let the white coats, scrub suits, and years of schooling and experience of the team intimidate you. Your question is too important of a matter not to ask. Make sure you don't find yourself not asking questions or expressing concerns because of embarrassment or shame caused by the subject or your lack of knowledge. Again, that doctor, nurse, technician, or specialist is human first and their title second. You know the saying, "They put on their pants one leg at a time, like the rest of us." Let us take that a step further. They have bowel movements and urinate, and if not, that means they have a colostomy. They may have had cancer, or their family members have. They have had mastectomies and they have had children die. I know I have literally wrapped the bodies of their children and siblings. They have had fears and concerns just like you. Yes, they are very smart in their field, which is their job. Use their experience to learn from, not to be intimidated by. They have faults and failures, and, just like you, can make mistakes or not always be up to par in their communication skills. But I promise you, for the most part they very much want to hear your concerns and needs, and to help alleviate them by sharing their knowledge. At the same time, try to always be mindful of their time, too.

If major personality conflicts do occur that cannot be resolved with open communication, one can always ask for someone else to take over the care. You have that right; if it is nursing, they may have already changed the nurse assignment. It is a standard in nursing in every teaching hospital I ever worked in, if staff is available, to send in a more compatible personality. We gladly do this for each other, too; it happens to every one of us at times. A professional nurse teammate will even volunteer if they see a conflict brewing, "I'll trade you, your room seven for my room nine. I had that person a few weeks ago. We got along OK; let me try." It can be a little harder to change doctors, but that also is possible. It is always a good idea to find a doctor willing to take over your care before relieving the first one of your case. If you are admitted in a hospital, that is pretty much how it has to happen anyway. It is not uncommon for doctors to want to write a professional letter or share a phone call to each other before officially transferring patient care. This is mainly a professional courtesy; physicians do so to be respectful to each other's practice. Depending on the circumstances and state, transferring patients between institutions is most likely governed by law. These laws are designed to protect both you and the institutions. I don't recommend you do this too often, for it may lead to doctors not wanting to pick up your care.

I encourage you to get second opinions if you feel the need, but don't discharge a doctor's opinion just because they have the appropriate professional courage to be honest with you about painful, bad, or poor outcome news of your disease. Respect that honesty. Although painful, it shows they have respect for you. The more you know, even if it is painful to hear, the more you will be able to deal with. That is why I didn't dance around the subject when writing this book. Again, I use myself as an example. So many disease processes and physical ailments can be prevented, decreased, or alleviated if we would just lose weight. I constantly fight weight gain and have to work too hard to stay just above my appropriate weight. After 40 it got even harder. Sometimes it goes higher than "just above" my appropriate weight. I thank every person who cared enough to be honest with me over the years, whether doctors, my fellow nurses working next to me, friends, and family. I do have moderate knee issues, and I do not want to tax my cardio-pulmonary system twenty-four hours a day by forcing it to work harder than it should, as that leads to heart failure. Nor do I want diabetes due to my love of that damn sugar, or to hold excess weight in my abdomen, as both contribute to eventual diabetes.

Bad news does not always have to be completely bad for you. Even if it is cancer, attempt to not become your disease by choosing not to weigh and define your life by your illness, your ailments, or your appointments. Your life is not over; remain you, as no one gets a guarantee. Even if you just received a diagnosis of liver or pancreatic cancer with a poor prognosis of only six months to live, I could still die before you tomorrow as I travel underneath a green light, and someone may fly through the red. I have worked with people in their forties having major strokes, and I once cared for an 18-year-old having an actual heart attack. Every day is a lucky day, and that is a percentage of what our longevity is bound by: luck, not age. Attempt not to give one day away voluntarily to your terminal illness, or your chemo and radiation therapies; they will steal a few on their own. Life is hard and painful, yet an amazing exciting experience. Argue less and laugh more. Worry, judge, and fear less, yet explore life more. Don't give your days away to the fear of your mortality; it is whittling them away without your help as it is.

CHAPTER 4

GUILT AND DEATH

"Dying is easy; it's living that scares me to death."
–Annie Lennox, b. 1954

Not Be Will

I should not be
Ashamed of my attempts
Throwing more shoulds
Sitting in my irretrievable past

I should be
Forgiving myself
Giving myself credit for getting close or accomplishing
Cautious with my incomplete perspectives

I will
Forgive
Silence my critical criticizer
Forgive accept and be

This chapter was not included in the first publication because I did not realize there was such a need. In my clinical years, I talked to hundreds of people at the bedside about dying and death. After writing the book I began to have more conversations with people about their past experiences. The subject of guilt is not really something that is discussed in the clinical setting in great depth, mainly due to time constraints. However, once I began talking to people about their experiences with a loved one's dying and death they began to share with me extreme, often admittedly suppressed, feelings of guilt. It was quickly apparent there is a strong need to talk about guilt. I had no idea so many people felt either responsible for a death directly, guilt over having allowed someone a natural death, guilt over not allowing someone a natural death, or for the dying feeling guilty about the life choices they made or how they treated people.

There are several basic definitions for guilt, such as Merriam-Webster's third definition used as a noun: "A feeling of deserved blame of offenses." I personally really like the broader definition given by *Psychology Today*: "Guilt is aversion and, like shame, embarrassment or pride—has been described as a self-conscious emotion, involving reflections on oneself. People may feel guilty for a variety of reasons, including acts they have committed (or think they committed), a failure to do something they should have done, or thoughts that they think are morally wrong." An example: "*If I had just been faster/closer, my Dad would not have fallen and broke his hip.*"

This statement and its variations are the overall themes for how people tell me they feel responsible for someone's death. This is not something that I have heard just a few times; it is a very frequently stated feeling of guilt. Failure to prevent a fall from bed or an unassisted late-night attempt to make it to the bathroom is another common reason for guilt. My own mother's demise to death was from a very early-morning fall in the bathroom. Telling the medical team to continue or to stop once death is imminent is right behind falls for the cause of guilt. There is no question—fall-related death and end-of-life decisions are the most frequently admitted subjects of guilt that I've encountered in the past fourteen years of post- clinical conversations.

Right out of nursing school, I went to work in one of the busiest emergency departments in the United States, Charity Hospital in New Orleans. I began wrapping more bodies in plastic morgue sheets than any 21-year-old kid should ever have to see and touch. Some hospitals have morgue transport workers, but, in many other hospitals, transport of these bodies often fell on the nursing staff. We kept track of the deaths in composition books; I use plural because at the end of my first three years, there were several of these composition books. I was leaving to start a few years of contract nursing around the country, and I was curious how many deaths had I witnessed. I counted the lines on a page, the pages in a book, the number of books, and then divided by four because we worked twelve hours shifts. To make it a more accurate rough estimate, I subtracted one hundred to make up for days off and not working every resuscitation effort. Five hundred was the number. I had been a nurse for three years and had been present at the last breath of five hundred people. I estimate that the majority were traumatic and younger-aged people than the lesser number of older non-traumatic deaths. I stayed in nursing for eighteen more years. Although I worked in very large, high-volume departments, I never saw that volume of deaths in so little time again. I feel deeply for the intense volume of deaths the world experienced in the first year of the coronavirus pandemic, that hit it so hard in 2020.

From the moment "the water breaks" and we begin our journey to leave the warm, watery, protective, and floaty environment of the uterus, we have to fight gravity. Even in our sleep, our chest wall must fight gravity to expand our lungs to breathe each breath. But at the moment of death, gravity wins its final victory. It will win many times before someone dies of old age; from the numerous times we fall learning to walk, gravity has an impact on everything from our skin sagging to our height decreasing. I once read, "Gravity is not only a good idea; it's also the law," referencing Newton's law of gravity.

I don't care how much we try, or want, to protect our aged or weakened loved ones, falls are going to happen. In some way it is a blessing and good for the spirit that a fall can occur. It means a person still has the spirit and drive to be independent, to stand and be mobile, or to attempt it. It denotes the healthy drive that is two of the ten characteristics of life that all living organisms share: The Will to Live and Mobility. I have fallen in my past many times and, unless I die tonight, I will fall again. On the same note, I didn't want my mother's fall to lead to death. But, if I look at the bigger picture, I am also grateful she fell and died when she did, exercising her independence. I find that comforting, and I hope I follow in both of my parents' footsteps: to die before chronically bedbound.

My mother was a strong and willful person. She lived in an assisted living facility and did not require assistance to walk, although she did use a walker after her hip fracture. Well, no assistance beyond her walker, which her ego did not like, but she eventually accepted.

She also told me she would rather die than lose further mobility than the walker. Her dementia was slight but slowly and steadily increasing, and her pulmonary function and aortic stenosis (hardening of the aortic valve in the heart) were also getting worse, noted by her increasing shortness of breath. Supplemental oxygen was next, but she did not want that, either. My mother accepted her aging and death and often stated, "Aging is not for wimps." I will share more with you about my mother's death later, but I want you to know her fall was inevitable. Hers just happened to occur at a timely point in her 90th year of life. Some could argue that she should have been on a "walking with assistance" status, but she would have fought that big time, gotten up by herself, and fallen anyway. I have a saying that I chant often in life: "Everything is as it should be."

But sometimes I modify it a little, as is the case with my mother's traumatic fall: "Everything is as it should be ... damn it."

If you are experiencing guilt around not preventing a fall, I encourage you to back up and look at the bigger picture of gravity and fragility. We are going to fall, and gravity is going to win. Even if you had gotten around the car faster to help a parent not fall stepping up on that particular curb, gravity was going to keep after them. Besides, if we can place ourselves in another's shoes, how many people want to be coddled on that constant level anyway?

There are those that age with high levels of acceptance. Then there are those who have high levels of fear, who will accept constant help, and I respect that wisdom too. But overall, most people wish to retain some level of independence. I have also found that people want to attempt to make the home of the aging "fall-proof" by removing all the rugs from their home. That type of action has its merit, but I personally would like to be asked if I want my rugs removed or not. In both humor and seriousness, I would rather trip and fall on a rug, rather than trip on nothing and fall on a hard floor. I am going to trip and fall, and so was your loved one; you are not responsible for the powerful constant of gravity.

Guilt over past choices we have made involving the death of a loved one is another common origin of guilt. I have heard both directions many times: "I feel like I should have told them to keep trying," or "I wish I had accepted their death and let them die sooner." In 2007, when I started public speaking, I quickly started to include a side note about not feeling guilty over past end-of-life choices made for another person or pet. People would hear my talk and tell me during questions and answers, or afterwards in private, that they felt maybe they had made the wrong decision for a parent, loved one, or pet. I encouraged all to realize the body has an amazing ability to protect itself at the moment of death. I am going to share a harsh graphic reality I have witnessed, which I hope brings you as much comfort as it has brought me. Let us allow someone else's extreme trauma to be another poorly wrapped gift for us.

There have been a handful of occasions in my career where a person arrives awake to the ED with extreme unsurvivable trauma. The few times I have witnessed this unfathomable awake state during that extent of trauma, not once did the person say a word. There was no screaming, no request for pain medicine—only looking around before dying a moment later.

This is a rare occurrence. Yet, to see such a mangled body yet awake, and no complaint of pain or even a sound made, to see only peace in their eyes as they look at us, has always been reassuring to me that the body and spirit take exceptional care of themselves during death. I share this to assure you whatever choice you made or will make, all is as it should be.

One last helpful way of releasing guilt came to me many years ago and has also been most helpful in assisting with decreasing my own harsh self-judgment. I once heard that unless one has a mental health condition that distorts or removes one's conscience and remorse, most people don't make choices thinking, or knowing, it is the wrong thing to do.

This means that for the most part, we don't say to ourselves before an action, "I am going to do it this way because it is the wrong thing to do." Most of us at any given moment make our choices to the best of our ability. Hindsight is a different discussion, yes; I can look back on my life and admit that I painfully made too many wrong choices. Yet unless I did not learn from that hindsight and I keep making poor choices, I do not have to feel guilty for doing what I thought was right at that moment. One could stretch this further to the concept of blame, and the frequently unnecessary assigning of blame to another. It is not easy to hold the authority of a medical power of attorney. Making an end-of-life choice for another is one of the hardest things we have to do in our lives. Not to mention the compounded factors of how stressed and worn down we become during these critical periods of our lives. Please be gentle with yourself, or with someone making that choice, whether you are reviewing past choices or you have to make these calls now or in the future.

I do encourage you to take one question into consideration at the time you have to make decisions for someone in an end-of-life dilemma. It applies whether or not they can make their own choices—whether you are accepting the dying person's choice or making it for them. Ask yourself: Are you making the decision for yourself or for the person dying?

Always keep in mind that you are not the one approaching imminent and inevitable death. Remember that you are not the one being stuck a few times a day for laboratory draws or new IV starts, or the one with tubes in their body, or on a ventilator. Think of how sore your body becomes if you stay in bed too long, or have an illness that takes your strength for a few days. Now add in months of inactivity and being bedbound; the body has its limits. I also encourage you not to make decisions for another that is near imminent death because you do not want them to die, or you fear the pain and grief of their absence from your life. Please remember this book is only about imminent, inevitable death, which means you will be going through the pain of grief soon no matter what. I respect the difficulty of these moments; please do not think I am cold and callous to such decisions—to this day I miss my parents.

I placed this chapter towards the front of the book to help alleviate second-guessing yourself as you read. Please work to let go of guilt you may have about-life-and death choices you had to make in the past, or will make in the future. At the moment you made the decision, you did the right thing for that moment, to the best of your ability. Yes, please, be very gentle with yourself, for I know about wanting someone's pain to be over, and I know about wanting one more day.

CHAPTER 5

THE GENERAL BASICS OF WHY WE DIE

"As a well-spent day brings happy sleep, so a life well used brings happy death."
−Leonardo da Vinci, 1452-1519

According to the World Health Organization, in 2019, there were over 55 million deaths worldwide. Ischemic heart disease, meaning a heart attack, and stroke remain the two leading causes of death, totaling approximately 15 million deaths. This is followed by what is referred to as "lower respiratory infections," also known as pneumonia. The fourth leading cause of death remains chronic obstructive pulmonary disease, or COPD, also known as asthma, bronchitis, and emphysema. Other disease processes that remain in the top causes of death are tracheal/ bronchial/ lung cancers, Alzheimer's/ dementia, diabetes, and road injury. It is important to mention that diabetes, dementia, and road injuries all have sadly shown significant increases since the turn of the century, only twenty years.

Only through the unfiltered awareness of the processes that occur to the body when it is dying can we be realistic about what to expect. In the big picture, if death occurs slowly, it is a complex process. But in the smaller view, it is really quite simple;

the short definition of death proves this. Total body death occurs when all functions of the vital organs—heart, lungs, and brain—have stopped. Yet with the complexity of modern medicine, there are other types of death that can preclude this definition of dead. Parts of the body can die separately. This is where the question of what death is becomes a bit trickier; therefore, what to do concerning partial death should become a matter of individual choice.

What *causes* all death is also fairly simple to answer. All death is caused by the body's inability to provide vital levels of oxygen into the cells, known as hypoxia. This can be expanded slightly to include the inability to get food into and normal metabolic waste out of the cells. Although these two issues do not cause the body to die immediately, as it would if deprived of necessary oxygen levels, if the nutrient/waste problem is not corrected, then death is inevitable. Another aspect and reality of partial death is when the brain dies and the rest of the body continues to live. This is an important issue because our emergency medical system, meaning first responders and paramedics, now have very advanced equipment and knowledge. In the past, before these advances, if the brain died, then the breathing would stop, and the heart would eventually stop when the oxygen within its own tissue ran out. The greatest recent contributing factor is many technologies, skills, and procedures that were once only in hospitals are now in the field being started earlier by paramedics.

First, let us take a look at the basic causes of poor or total blockages of oxygen to the cells. If you have taken a cardiopulmonary resuscitation (CPR) class, you are aware of the ABCs of the CPR process on someone whose lungs, heart, or both have stopped. "A" is for airway. Oxygen must first be able to move through the mouth, throat, down the trachea (windpipe), and into the lungs. The most common cause of airway failure is some form of blockage. A wide variety of things, such as food, cancer, blood, a pen cap, or asthma can cause a blockage. A blockage can occur from narrowing of the airway from smoking, asthma, or chemical exposure; from a stabbing or gunshot wound that causes neck swelling from internal bleeding capable of squeezing the airway shut; or from an allergic reaction to something such as shellfish, peanuts, or bee stings.

"B" is for breathing. Oxygen must be able to move through, or be pulled into, the lungs, and the waste (carbon dioxide) must be able to exit, or be pushed out of the lungs. The causes of breathing failure are many—mechanical, neurological, or from fatigue, poisons, or intoxicants. The movement of the muscles around the chest, back, and the diaphragm (the wall of muscle that separates the chest from the abdomen) does all the work of moving the air in and out. An example of a neurological issue would be trauma to the upper spinal cord or brain; this would stop the "breathe" message in your brain from getting to the chest wall. Or an enlarging cancer on the spine or brain could also slowly cause this problem. A stroke, which is bleeding into the brain, or a major blockage of the blood flow into the brain, also can stop the brain from sending the "breathe" message.

Mechanical issues can come from a few different problems, all decreasing your ability to fully expand your lungs. For example, if you were to take a simple piece of cellophane from the kitchen, hold it open, up to your lips, and pull in air to create a suction, it would form firmly to the inside of your mouth. Your lungs are basically held to the inside wall of your chest through this exact same negative pressure situation. With this cellophane analogy, we can illustrate the three basic situations that can go wrong with the mechanics of breathing related to that negative pressure.

If the chest wall cannot create suction due to any penetrating trauma creating an opening. This would correlate to a stab or gunshot wound, or any other injury that would cause an opening in the chest. I have seen this happen from nail gun injuries, a puncture from a stick from falling out of a deer-hunting stand, and, yes, once from a kid who was running with scissors. That opening would equal a hole in your cheek, which also would prevent you from being able to create negative pressure, and the cellophane again would not form to the inside of your mouth. This is why the lungs "collapse" once the chest wall has been penetrated, it cannot hold the negative pressure required to keep the lungs expanded.

If the chest wall itself were greatly damaged and multiple ribs were broken, this could also cause a mechanical failure in breathing. This type of injury could prevent the chest from expanding fully, or the sharp ends of a fractured rib could puncture the lungs. This would equal a puncture hole in the cellophane itself. Even if you could create suction, the cellophane would not form to the inside of your mouth if it were punctured. A hole in the lungs can occur because of trauma or for no apparent reason at all. Cancer could eat a hole through the lung, holding your breath for a long time could force an opening, or a serious force injury like a fall or car crash could rip the lungs.

"C" stands for circulation. Once absorbed into the lungs, the oxygen must be circulated to the body, and the carbon dioxide waste must be circulated back to the lungs. Circulation troubles are numerous but, again, if I use an example, you can get the bigger picture. Your body's circulatory system is like a water pump and garden hose in an orchard. Except, in your body, the water must return to the pump after it waters each tree; the trees will represent each cell in your body.

Your blood circulation system is made up of three major parts: the heart, which we will correlate to the water pump; the blood vessel system, which we will call the garden hose; and the blood, which will be the water. So there are three systems that can fail in the circulatory system, which carries the life-giving oxygen into the cells and body-killing waste back out of the body. The orchard analogy works twice, both to explain the entire circulatory system of the body, and again to explain a heart attack and some strokes. Just as a water pump needs fuel to work, so does the heart. A pump in an orchard needs only one type of fuel—gas, electricity, or diesel. However, the heart requires many fuels at the same time, some of which are oxygen, glucose, sodium, potassium, magnesium, and a few other elements. Aside from a fuel problem, the heart could have mechanical or electrical difficulties. If the valves do not open and close correctly, the blood will not move. If the electrical system fails, the pump again cannot function. Your heart also has an electrical system that controls the rate and timing of the contractions of the heart's four pumping chambers.

Last but not least, if the water pump or hoses have a hole in them, well, can you imagine how fast the chest fills up with blood if the heart or major chest vessels are torn, shot, or stabbed? I'll give you an idea. A healthy heart can pump an average of 2 to 4 liters of blood every minute, and upwards of 20 to 25 liters per minute or more if excited or exercising. That means your heart is filling one to two of those 2-liter bottles of soda every minute of your life. A person who weighs 150 pounds has about two and a half of those 2-liter bottles of blood in their body, approximately 5 liters of blood.

One more general pump requirement is pressure. Just like a water pump, the heart is designed to work within a minimal low- and a maximum high-pressure range. The heart, and all organs, require this optimal pressure range to function. This is what your blood pressure represents. Problems with the garden hose have to do with either the amount of fluid, pressure, a blockage, or a leak. If the hose is too small or there is too much fluid in the lines for the pump, the pressure will be too high. Likewise, if the hose is too large or there is not enough fluid in the lines for the pump, then the pressure will be too low. What causes the blood vessels to constrict or dilate (get smaller or larger) are too numerous to list, but some reasons are good and some are very bad. Sometimes it is easy to correct, and sometimes it will be impossible. Of course, if there is a hole in the hose (or blood vessel), the system would empty and run dry. Blockages of the circulatory system are just like frozen ice in a garden hose; nothing can get to the other side. This is basically what happens in a heart attack.

What is a heart attack? This most common killer of the human body is known as a myocardial infarction (MI) in the medical community. Myocardial means heart muscle, and infarction means blockage. So a heart attack is when the flow of blood to the heart muscle is blocked, causing oxygen to be deprived to the cells, and heart muscle dies.

Let's go back to the orchard, but now the hoses represent the coronary arteries (the blood vessels that are on the outside of the heart, and that supply the blood flow to the actual heart muscle). Even though the heart moves all that blood through itself every minute, the heart muscle gets none of its oxygen from this blood being pumped through the inside of the heart. The coronary arteries start at the top of the heart, just as the blood is pushed out of the heart to again circulate through the body. Such a wise design—the body feeds the heart oxygen first, just as the re-oxygenated blood leaves the heart/lung, also known as cardio- pulmonary, system to circulate through the entire body. As the oxygen-rich blood moves down the outside arteries of the heart, the coronary arteries continue to branch off into smaller and smaller vessels, and feed more and more of the heart muscle with oxygen. We have three major coronary arteries that feed the heart. If these were the three main hoses in the orchard stemming from one pump, each would continue to fork into smaller and smaller hoses until each fruit tree had one little tiny hose that dripped water onto it. This is how the estimated 2 to 3 billion cardiac cells, and 37 trillions cells in the average human body, are fed oxygen.

A heart attack (MI) can be correlated to a blockage in that irrigation hose. If the blockage occurs low in the system, then only a few thousand fruit trees die. But, if the blockage occurs at the halfway point in one of the three major hoses, maybe one-sixth of the orchard could die. When you hear of someone having a "massive heart attack" or "coronary," one or more partial or total blockages has occurred very high in the heart's irrigation system, which means maybe one-third of the entire heart was deprived of oxygen in one instant.

Blockages also can occur in the body's circulation system. These can cause partial or complete death of the organ on the other side of the blockage, such as the brain, lungs, kidneys, or an entire extremity. Examples of this are the one of two types of strokes caused by blocked blood flow to part of the brain. Another circulation blockage is known as a pulmonary embolism, which is a blockage of blood into the lungs for re-oxygenation, and these can vary in size. Renal failure, caused by blocked blood flow to the kidney, is yet another major circulation blockage issue. The causes of these blockages range from fat/cholesterol, blood clots, calcium buildup, or of build up of dead cells from burns or electrocution.

Other potential troubles with the water pump system come from the blood itself. The body can have either a quantity or a quality problem with the blood volume. The liquid in the vessels consists of not just red blood cells; it must also contain nutrients, waste to be removed, water, white blood cells, proteins to expand the blood and help it clot when needed, and other elements. The hemoglobin on the red blood cells carries the oxygen to the organs from the lungs. Hemoglobin also carries the carbon dioxide back to the lungs to be expelled from our bodies every time we exhale. White blood cells fight infections. In a healthy person, water makes up about 60 percent or more of the total body, with the heart, lungs, and brain being an even greater percentage. Many different conditions can create too much or too little blood volume. Bleeding from, or into, the body requires no explanation; the hoses will run low or dry. The main cause of too much blood volume is the kidney's inability to get rid of the water buildup that occurs from everyday food and fluid intake. This occurs for two basic reasons: Either the heart and/or lungs are creating pressure that is too high or too low to filter the blood appropriately through the kidneys, or the kidneys themselves are not functioning. It is not uncommon for someone to lose kidney function, also known as "renal function," after prolonged resuscitation efforts that have revived the person. This occurs due to the lack of pressure and oxygen flow to the kidneys during CPR. This condition can correct itself with time; however, short-term or permanent dialysis may be required if kidney shutdown does occur. Dialysis is a life-sustaining machine that most require two or three times a week to have their blood volume cleaned and decreased. "Artificial kidneys" sums up dialysis, and it is a life saving procedure.

The quality troubles we can have with the blood in our circulatory system are also too numerous to count; doctors known as hematologists even specialize in only blood problems. But for the purpose of informing, I will use broad categories again. Poor quality of the blood can be a problem with the blood cells, as in the case of sickle cell anemia (cells are shaped like quarter moons and clog the vessels), or leukemia (a type of cancer that affects the blood). Or there could be the old problem of waste buildup where, again, the kidneys or the liver can be the cause. Some other causes of poor blood quality that usually lead to other organ issues include HIV/ AIDS, hepatitis, and a host of other organisms and viruses, from ebola, to polio, to rocky mountain spotted fever. The list is long. Infections are bacteria or viruses that overrun a part or all of the body. Most infections are not initially life threatening, unless left untreated. However, infections of the brain/spine, such as meningitis, some heart infections, and lung infections, such as bronchitis and pneumonia, can cause death much faster. When an infection enters the blood and overruns the entire body, again known as sepsis, if left untreated or caught too late, it will cause death.

Cancer should also be mentioned as a general category for why our bodies die.

Cancer can, and does, cause many of the above-mentioned complications. Cancer is defined as abnormal cells, very strong and fast growing, that are not a normal part of the body. These cells are so fast and strong that they require a large amount of the body's oxygen and nutrients to live and grow. Because cancer is strong and powerful, it takes what it wants, and slowly starves the rest of the body.

This general overview of what can go wrong with the body to cause it to die will be greatly built upon in the following chapters while I explain what the healthcare field does to attempt to save a life. There will be some overlap, but the layers of information will be most helpful in understanding not only "why" some procedures are performed, but also the idea that "why not" should sometimes be considered.

Being able to accept death when it is imminent and inevitable, and allowing the body to die peacefully with respect and dignity, is the ultimate goal.

CHAPTER 6

NATURAL DEATH

"Death is a challenge. It tells us not to waste time. ... It tells us to tell each other right now that we love ...."
—Leo Buscaglia, 1924-1998

Natural death occurs when the dying process is not prolonged by medical procedures and/or interventions. These procedures and interventions will be the subject of the next chapter, which discusses procedures that attempt to postpone natural death. This chapter deals with what may occur during the very final stage of life, known as the end stage of dying. Death, the last breath or functional heartbeat, is the final moment of the end stage of dying. The total process of dying, as opposed to the end stage, is a much broader subject. Many wonderful books are available on this subject and can expand your understanding of your own and others' inevitable death. This book is more about the harsher realities of choice in the critical moments of whether a procedure of intervention should, or should not, be performed.

I would also invite you at some point in your life, when you feel it is appropriate, to volunteer to help a person in the end stage of life with comfort and companionship. This could be volunteering at an assisted living facility or hospice, which is an organization that helps people who have accepted their death and are in the last few months of life. Or by making a commitment to visit with, feed, rub the feet of, or even bathe a friend, relative, or an acquaintance two or more times a week until they die. I encourage continued contact to experience the bigger picture of dying and, if appropriate, maybe even to return and stay when the moment of death nears. I recommend starting with an acquaintance or even a stranger, through volunteering. Those with strong fears or even phobias around death and dying, or issues with abandonment, may have a more fulfilling learning experience without the attachment of it being a close loved one who is dying. There is nothing wrong with seeing a counselor for a professional sounding board through the experience either, or even after reading this book. Reading this book from cover to cover is capable of seriously stirring some of our deeper, darker hidden storage. Allow the stirring, and don't hide the shaking it may cause. I don't care if you have been an ED doctor or nurse for forty years, or you are helping in the presence of dying for the first or first few times; all human tragedy will go inside you and it will affect you. You can attempt to guide the experience towards positive benefits to yourself and others, separate from the grief you will feel. But if you think it is right, I invite you to experience the benefits of this gift of love to someone rapidly approaching their death.

Through this gift, you gain an experience that is richly rewarding. Most people, including myself, think the perfect death would be to simply go to sleep and not wake. That likely is what will happen to most of us. But how and why we go to sleep will vary, as will what we do during that sleep. To be semiconscious or unconscious alone is not a painful state; to watch someone in these states can be much more difficult. "And the living suffer," has been a term I have used for most of my life.

The very moment of death itself appears to be a painless moment. This is not saying that the process of dying will always be painless, but what I really want to clarify here is the process of dying and death are two different things. Dying can indeed be a long, painful experience, physically, mentally, and emotionally.

The caregivers as well endure these same strains, from the obvious mental and emotional pain, to back pain and insomnia to general fatigue, to name just a few of the physical strains. Dying for many is not painful; aside from some light grimacing I noticed when I rolled my father during his last few days, he did not seem to experience pain. Death is often welcomed at this point, the end of a long chronic disease or long fatiguing terminal pain, and an experience through which one can personally grow. I have had so many near death tell me they have enjoyed catching up with so many people to say goodbye and to review their own lives.

Dying is a process that takes a lifetime, no matter how long or short that life may be.

We all complete another day of dying each time we go to sleep, just as the sun gets a minute closer to setting even as it is still rising in the early morning to its highest point in its day. It is when we are informed of a terminal disease, or sustain serious trauma, that we often become aware or conscious of the process of dying. Death, on the other hand, is a clear and not-so-drawn-out stage of life. Having observed the death of so many, I feel it is safe to say that understanding four potential events will assist in the acceptance of the natural death process. Acceptance is the keyword here, as acceptance of these events at times may be very difficult. But not accepting them, stepping back into the mainstream healthcare field, will often set into motion a death involving medical interventions that, once started, are not always easy to stop. Yet, never hesitate to return to hospital if you feel it needed or appropriate. Being prepared to accept what one may feel or witness during the natural death process may at times be helpful to allow a natural death to occur. It is important to remember that the alternative to natural death includes tubes, needles, procedures, loss of privacy, and loss of environmental peace and personal dignity that so often occurs once the modern healthcare system is brought into the picture. Without the proper understanding, awareness, and legal paperwork to control, contain, and work with the modern medical field, a natural death cannot occur in the hospital setting. It is an across-the-board understanding in hospitals, if your DNR paperwork is not in order, resuscitation attempts will almost always be carried out. The healthcare field must protect themselves from liability, as DNR issues are a big percentage of lawsuits against hospitals.

Of the four potential processes that may occur during death, only bleeding is not related to low oxygen levels, although the less blood there is, the less oxygen that can be circulated. Bleeding can be external or internal. External bleeding does not require an explanation, so let's talk about internal bleeding. This bleeding can be caused by cancer eating away at tissue, or general thinning of the tissue due to illness, medications, heavy use of alcohol, natural advanced aging, and many other factors. Internal bleeding is often from the GI system (gastro-intestinal), the lungs, or other locations where the bleeding is not visible.

Internal bleeding could be from a ruptured aneurysm (weakening and tearing of a blood vessel). Bleeding into the abdominal cavity can be painful if the person is awake or still conscious. This is caused by blood, and maybe even the content of the intestines, spilling into the abdominal cavity. This causes irritation and inflammation of the lining of the abdomen and other organs, leading the abdomen to feel a burning or cramp, to become firm, extremely painful, and can even get hot to the touch.

Other internal bleeding, or blood flow blockage, may occur to the brain, which is known as a stroke or CVA (cerebral vascular accident). Whether from blockage or bleeding, a CVA may cause one or more of the following: headache, nausea, vomiting, slurred or absent speech, heavy sleep with heavy snoring, weakness on one side of the body, confusion, aggression, and/or eventually a loss of consciousness. These signs and symptoms occur either due to a severe decrease in blood flow or an increased pressure in the brain due to bleeding. This pressure occurs because the brain is the only organ that is completely surrounded by the non-expanding hard skull.

Therefore, when bleeding or swelling occurs into the brain, it has nowhere to move to accommodate the space the blood is now occupying, and the pressure builds. If the pressure is great enough, it stops the brain from telling the lungs to breathe and respirations will stop. The other type of stroke I mentioned is a blockage of an artery in the brain. This is the opposite of bleeding. Just as with the description of the heart attack, the same thing happens: The brain cells on the other side of the blockage stop receiving oxygen and start to die.

Bleeding from the lungs can also be a fatal issue. Depending on which part of the lungs is weakened or traumatized, bleeding from the lungs may be internal or external. Bleeding into the lungs causes blood to accumulate into the airway, resulting in the person coughing up blood. In extreme bleeding, choking or total filling of the airway with blood may occur. If bleeding occurs from the outside of the lungs into the chest cavity, shortness of breath will most likely follow, and a burning or pain with movement may occur. Bleeding internally may also cause the chest cavity to lose its negative pressure that is required for the lung to remain expanded properly with each breath. Either blood building in the chest cavity or the loss of negative internal pressure causes increasing shortness of breath, a sensation of tightness, chest pain, and if not corrected, air hunger.

Bleeding into the GI (gastro-intestinal) system, which includes the mouth, throat, esophagus, stomach, small and large intestines, and the rectum, is a rather difficult type of bleeding to deal with for many reasons. It is visually upsetting, and it most likely will require vigilant attendance and effort to deal with the potentially large volume of blood coming from the body. The odor can be very potent. Bleeding from the mouth, pharynx, esophagus, or stomach can cause vomiting of bright red blood and potential airway complications. All of these symptoms make this a great obstacle to allow an at-home, natural death to occur.

Planning, preparation, supplies, people to help, and a general safety of knowing how to deal with body fluids are all extremely helpful tools when dealing with a GI bleed. If the person dying has AIDS, COVID, hepatitis, or many other diseases, this knowledge goes past "extremely helpful" into the "essential" category, due to possible transfer of disease to caregivers. There are certain things to expect with a heavy bleeding situation. In the upper GI system, the esophagus can bleed at an alarmingly fast rate. Most esophageal bleeding is caused by heavy alcohol abuse over a long period of time, long term gastro-esophagel reflux disease known as G.E.R.D. (this is when the stomach acid is pushed back up into the esophagus, commonly known as "heartburn"), or cancer.

The following is applicable to all upper GI bleeding; however, all bleeding is not this severe. Heavy upper GI bleeding causes vomiting of bright red blood, or older blood may look like coffee grounds. If the bleeding is heavy, two or three receptacles may need to be rotated to keep up with the vomiting of blood. Although the person may be able to hold their head up to vomit at first, they will weaken or fatigue quickly with this level of bleeding. So after a short period of time, expect to move the person onto their side to protect the airway as best as you can. Once the person is moved into a flat position, the bleeding may become heavier and may flow almost freely from the mouth. A product known as "blue pads" or "chux" are helpful to control this potentially large volume of fluids. These pads are normally 2-foot by 3-foot thin pads that are absorbent on one side and plastic on the other, much like a sheet of diaper material. Eventually, this blood begins to pass from the rectum also, and again blue pads and diapers are helpful to control this fluid once it is outside the body. Boxes of non-sterile gloves will also be required. If the person has AIDS, hepatitis, or any fluid-transmitted communicable disease, then gowns, mask, and even a clear face shield may be required. Other disease processes may also require this level of self-protection. Consult a physician or nurse with any and all questions concerning safety or tips for dealing with body fluids. Bleeding from the intestines, if it continues, turns into a dark black or dark maroon odorous diarrhea.

As bleeding continues, the person weakens and moves through a semiconscious state into unconsciousness. This bleeding may or may not include any or all of the signs and symptoms of decreasing oxygen levels, which are described shortly. Although GI bleeding involves a lot of difficult work for the caregiver, the person bleeding will basically die in their "sleep," meaning unconscious.

The second potential process that may occur during death is an altered mental state. This could present as confusion, inappropriate words or actions, aggression (which is rare but could even be violent), restlessness, or a decreased level of consciousness or awareness.

This occurs due to decreasing levels of oxygen to the brain, which can be caused by less oxygen in the blood, and/or less blood or blood pressure than is required to get oxygen to the brain. Increasing levels of the body's waste building up due to liver or kidney failure can also contribute to an altered level of awareness.

Giving supplemental oxygen may or may not help this stage, depending on the reason. It is of paramount importance to understand that providing oxygen, even just one or two liters per minute via that little nasal cannula that goes around the ears and under the nose, will almost always prolong the actual process of dying, which could possibly sustain or increase suffering. I once cared for the father of a dear friend during his last few days. During this restless phase of decreasing oxygen, he would frequently wring his hands for a few minutes then stop. He had been a surgeon, and my friend quickly realized he was probably scrubbing up before surgery in his semi conscious state, since he had done it thousands of times throughout his life.

The third potential process is a change in the skin color, temperature, and even texture from dehydration. The skin is one of the first organs the body will move its blood supply away from when blood pressure or blood and oxygen levels are decreasing. This is why we can become pale and sweaty so quickly. The body does this as needed throughout life, but this can be rather pronounced the closer death becomes. The color changes in the skin vary from reddish, to whitish or pale, to eventually a bluish silver-gray. A combination of any of these colors may occur no matter the original skin pigment. As the blood flow to the skin decreases, the person may also become pasty and sweaty. Extreme sweating is not uncommon in the beginning stages of decreasing skin blood flow; in the latter stages it will often remain dry.

Other than preparing to see and feel these skin changes, a towel to dry the skin may be needed. The body cools quickly with moisture on its surface, and the person may experience chills.

Please remember that when the body has a fever, it basically becomes confused and tells us we are cold. Fever and "chills" often cause us to cover up, but if the body has a high temperature, this is the wrong thing to do. I cannot tell you how many times in the ED I was called a "mean nurse" for removing the nice warm blanket an aide had given a patient complaining of being cold, and removing their socks, after I checked their temperature and discovered it elevated. I would do this, only to check on them fifteen minutes later and have them tell me, "Thank you; my chills are gone. I'm sorry I called you names." Please remember and consider this for all fever and chill situations of all ages, and consider if it is right for the situation. Too often we make fevers and chills worse by adding layers when someone complains of being cold with a fever. This action traps even more body heat on the person, rather than removing layers to get the heat away and cooler air circulating, allowing the body temperature to go down.

Unrelated to the body's temperature, many people feel very hot and restless as their oxygen level decreases and their carbon dioxide levels increase. An example of this hot sensation, as it relates to high carbon dioxide levels, is how you feel hot quickly if you pull the bedsheets over your head. Of interest, the other reason you become hot so fast is you are exhaling warm air trapped around your body underneath the sheets. There were very few occasions—I repeat, very few—where I would place an open second gown over their face for two or three minutes when I so "cruelly", as some would label me, uncovered their body to get their fever down. This would still allow oxygen airflow, but slightly raise the carbon dioxide level to help them "feel" warmer quickly. Their actual shivering would usually stop faster also.

The fourth and final potential process of dying is also a difficult one to deal with. "Air hunger" is the term used to describe the actions of a body experiencing the normal decreasing oxygen levels of near death. I have witnessed two stages, "conscious" and "unconscious" (I use quotations around these words for their use in the stages of air hunger only). For the following explanation these words will be synonymous with "aware" and "unaware." Flexibility using these words is required, for I have known people to experience low levels of oxygen yet be awake or talking, but later tell me they remember none of the events. This information is based on my clinical observations and from talking with people who have gone in and out of these stages. It often can be unclear when one moves from an aware to an unaware state.

The reason I have seen people enter this unaware stage then return to a level of weak conversation is family intervention. It can be difficult to observe air hunger, and families at times will request the person in this final stage of near-death be returned to supplemental oxygen. Although starting supplemental oxygen may postpone the moment of death, they most likely will go though the same stages even with supplemental oxygen. There have been several times that giving oxygen has returned the person to a level of consciousness that allows them to answer my questions. I share this because all the information I relay has been told directly to me because of this return to supplemental oxygen. It is also the reason this point of view can be respected on an even greater level; it came from a person experiencing it, not just me telling you what I witnessed.

Air hunger is the body's instinctual drive to seek oxygen and decrease carbon dioxide levels. It is the reason you yawn when you are tired, the reason you surface in a pool when you can no longer hold your breath, and the reason you will fight if someone ever attempts to choke or suffocate you. The initial stages of air hunger in a person who is awake can be anything from calling for help, to pulling at sheets, to grabbing and fighting someone so strongly as to cause injury. This concept is much the same as when the actions of a drowning victim cause the rescuer to drown also. In my experience, I have seen this extreme type of air hunger most often caused by a sudden or fairly rapid decline in oxygen levels, rather than the slow, more chronic oxygen decline of terminal illness or advanced age. I also cannot recall seeing this extreme reaction in a major trauma patient, even with low levels of oxygen. I believe this has to do with the level of shock the body experiences in severe trauma.

However, in the near-death, terminal person, some level of agitation may occur as the oxygen level decreases. The breath rate initially increases, and then begins to decrease as the body begins to accept its imminent death. The heart may also go through these same two stages, initially increasing in rate then slowing.

From what I have been told, from those I have been able to ask, they do not remember more than the first part of the air hunger. If they did have a period of physical anxiousness, reaching for help, pulling at sheets, or not wanting to stay in bed, they expressed that they did not remember this or the events that followed. This brings me personally much comfort, in that it seems our bodies have an ability to protect us from our own fears, and to provide us with comfort at this moment of transition and death. I find having been told this directly several times very reassuring, both for my dying then death, and for those who observe this stage in loved ones.

The breathing may pass through various stages. The breath may speed up for short periods then slow again over and over. It may stop completely for periods of time—ten, twenty, even forty seconds or longer; this is known as Cheyne-Stokes breathing, and the breathing can even stop for one to two minutes. Cheyne-Stokes can even occur when you and I sleep and, if significant, it is diagnosed as sleep apnea. Kussmaul breathing also may occur, and this is a deep and rapid breathing that is attempting to balance the increasing acid level that is normal in the end dying stage. Kussmaul breathing is more common in healthier, or non-end-stage people, attempting to "catch their breath," such as after sprinting a mile, whereas the more frequently witnessed Cheyne-Stokes breathing may occur as we near our death.

Other signs of nearing death are increased weakness and fatigue, eventually decreasing to little to no movement. Fluids can start to build up in the back of the mouth and throat once we become unconscious and no longer have the swallow reflex. This fluid buildup is commonly known as "the death rattle," and it can be a rather loud and concerning gurgling sound with every breath. There are drugs that can be prescribed to help decrease these secretions. Even with the drugs, rolling of the entire body to the side will allow gravity to drain it from the mouth and throat. Frequent rolling may be required, and it is a good time to use those fluid collection pads mentioned earlier.

Urine output will slow, become concentrated, then most likely stop altogether. This is normal due to both dehydration and decreasing kidney function with lower blood pressure. Urinary incontinence, which is the inability to hold urine in, also might happen. Swelling of the feet and any area below the heart may occur. This too is due to the kidneys not removing fluids, to gravity, and to some other more complex changes that are occurring. The person's head may roll from side to side. They may yawn. In the final stages, the mouth may even attempt to grab a breath, much like a fish that has been out of water for a period of time. The jaw will often relax open and stay that way. Although these are clear signs of imminent death, how long this period lasts can vary greatly, especially from the point at which the breathing is starting and stopping. If the person is receiving supplemental oxygen, be prepared; this stage is very likely to last.

I would like to remind you there are no hard and fast rules to how an individual dies. If we look at textbook signs of nearing death, most all state a loss of appetite occurs first due to the GI system shutting down. This is so important to know, because feeding the dying person may seem like the right thing to do, but it may actually cause more issues. The intestines may already be slowing down for days or weeks before actual death. Narcotic pain meds greatly slow or stop the intestines' normal movement, known as peristalsis.

I once helped care for a man nearing his death in his home, and he summed up this appetite demise well. He went into a rather harsh, yet funny (through his inflections and facial gestures) monologue about people pushing food on him the last few weeks. He stated, "That damn casserole of love, they bring it to me and tell me to 'Eat, you have to eat.' I don't want to eat. I'm so constipated it's not even funny. They say 'eat,' then they go home and poop one or twice a day, whereas I hope to poop a little every few days if I'm lucky. You want to bring me something from love, make it a bran muffin with Ex-Lax icing— THAT I might eat!" I will never forget him calling it, "That damn casserole of love." He was a gentle, aware man, who knew the gesture was indeed from love, rather than actually helpful.

Although this is a raw story, it is one of value and appropriate irony since, after his casserole monologue, he happened to be on the commode when he made his final choice to accept death. At his family's request I had been with him a few days. He was weaker by the day and had accepted my companionship and help. To stay alive this long, he had required a blood transfusion monthly for some time now. It had been well over thirty days since his last transfusion because he knew he was dying with or without them. I had just lifted him, with minimal strength assist from him, from his wheelchair to the toilet. He had lost much strength quickly in the few days since I started staying with him. He was too weak to leave alone, so I remained at his side but turned away, attempting the little privacy such a safety situation can allow. No luck, no bowel movement. After a few minutes, he sighed and started a conversation I will never forget.

I wouldn't forget this conversation not only because in all my years I had never had a death talk with someone on the toilet, but also because of its realistic, to-the-point, no-nonsense, let's-put-all-the-cards-on-the-table directness. "Is this the end?" he asked me.

"That's not my call, it's yours," I said.

"Is everything going to get harder from this point on?" was his next question.

"Most likely, yes," was my reply.

"Then I'm done. I quit. I don't want to not accept the fact and have everything just get worse and worse by being unrealistic." He said the last line with a sureness and force that matched the casserole monologue the day before. He asked me, "Will you stay with me until I die?"

"Yes, of course; I'll stay in that bed right next to yours," I said as I squeezed his shoulders. He died two days later in his own home and in his own bed.

It is not only the intestines shutting down that can cause issues with eating the closer one is to death. Difficulty with swallowing without choking or coughing and food going down the airway is another concern with passionately encouraging food in the last stages. The ability to swallow can be compromised for several reasons at this point. As with my father, I could see it was hard for him; he periodically choked or cleared his throat a little. This is the other reason I wouldn't push. I would softly encourage him but never said, "Come on,

Dad, one more bite." I only said, "Would you like another bite?" and not say another word if he turned his head.

As a general rule, until someone gets within minutes of their moment of death, it is hard to say exactly how much longer someone will live. Questions such as, "Should I call this relative or that relative to come?" or "Will they die in the next 24 hours ...?" are often hard to answer for the healthcare professional. This may be because talking about death is hard for them, but mainly it is because even the unconscious person's body still has the shared characteristic of all living organisms known as The Will To Live. The physiological drive to survive does not know cancer has overrun this body, or that the person has end-stage liver disease, so its many check-and-balance systems continue to correct the system failures and imbalances. The body's drive and abilities to constantly rebalance imbalances are amazing and highly persistent, until that imbalance tips too far. A nurse or physician may say someone won't live twenty-four more hours with confidence, in many situations it is safe to say, but in an equally respectable percentage it may not be correct. When the family hears such a timeline it creates a hypervigilance that is very hard on them, often leading to a constant last-breath watch and fear. At the same time, that type of statement can appropriately prepare a family for the imminent and inevitable death. Answering that tough question of "when" is one of the toughest questions we are ever asked, unless it is in the last few minutes of life.

Death occurs when both the heart and lungs no longer function. Once the heart stops, the body may take a few more breaths, but this will not last more than a moment. Likewise, at times the heart may continue a short period longer after the breath has stopped. This continued "beating" of the heart is really not a beat at all, and most often does not have a functional pumping action; a pulse will almost never be felt. These final beats are the last consumption of oxygen and electrical activity of the heart more than an effective pumping action. Depending on your personal, spiritual, and cultural beliefs and practices, the heart and lungs ceasing to function may not yet be the time of spiritual death or death of the being.

These are personal and cultural subjects that vary for each individual.

This chapter, as all the others, is to prepare for, to give an understanding of, and to lessen fears about our own death and the death of others. I again encourage you to help at least two people during their dying. It will be the greatest gift you have ever received or been given, to the dying and to yourself. No, it's not easy, but it is rewarding, loving, and giving.

This experience can help you see that death is a rather peaceful moment, and that much of what I have described will not occur and we just die. This chapter was written while keeping in mind the old saying, "Prepare for the worst, but hope for the best." Observing what I have described is so much harder than living through it, or should I say dying through it. This is why I believe death is so much harder to watch than to do. It is why I so repetitively say "And the living suffer," whether through watching the end stages of dying or experiencing the pain of post-death grief. The pain of watching the last breaths of a being, person, or pet, and the core shattering pains of grief that follow, deserve to be validated.

CHAPTER 7

PROCEDURES INVOLVED IN ATTEMPTING TO POSTPONE DEATH

"For thousands of years we suffered cruelly from a lack of
medical knowledge; now we suffer from knowing too much."
A summarized quote from *Great Medical Disasters*,
Dr. Richard Gordon, 1921-2017

This chapter may be even more difficult to read due to the
graphic nature of the material involved. We in the healthcare
field have been trained, from multiple directions, to protect the
public from much of what this chapter will share. Yet this
information is important for anyone who will be treated by our
modern health care system. I will share what goes on when the
curtain is pulled closed or when the family is asked to return to
the waiting room. Television now portrays so much uncensored
material that some of this information is not new to the public.
However, TV attempts to have the viewer focus on the drama;
the intention is to captivate. My wish for you is to focus on the
recipient of these procedures. If we shift the focus away from
the interest of drama, we will see the pain and suffering of the
procedure, and often its futility when death is imminent.

Remember, I am writing from the perspective of the end stages of dying. These procedures, unrelated to terminal states, frequent routine procedures that are truly beneficial, and the recipients go on to lead full lives because of them. Many procedures are necessary before, during, and after some types of surgery. Some are required for those who have sustained trauma, such as from a car crash, fall, shooting, or stabbing, so they may live. I share this information not to induce fear, but to encourage open awareness, and ultimately to help decrease fear. The more you know, the more you can handle on a more rational and less emotional level, with a wider range of knowledge and resources from which to draw. There are many interventions, tests, and procedures that postpone death, or are done to legally protect the hospital and staff. Remember that not allowing these events in the hospital, or totally preventing them by staying at home, can prevent pain, suffering, and a violation of dignity. One can never force the healthcare field to do something, but you almost always have the right to say, "No, thank you." This right to say no unfortunately is all too often met with resistance and judgment. However, always hear the health professional out, as they may share information that appropriately changes your mind.

I had just this situation occur several times with my mother, including the morning she fell and had an obvious complete fracture of her left upper arm. The assisted living facility nurse had given me a complete report when she called and informed me of the fall a few minutes earlier. Sadly, even though my mother was enrolled in hospice, with hospice pain meds in her medication drawer at the nurse's station, the nurse could not give her pain meds without the doctor seeing her first. This was facility policy. There were no doctors in the house full time at her facility. I arrived the same moment EMS did, and we walked into the front door together. I introduced myself, told them she had a complete fracture and that no pain meds had been given. As I led the way to her room, I further introduced myself and said, "This is your scene, I'll help if you ask me, but please give her some pain meds right away, and please don't push it too quickly, so she doesn't vomit." The paramedic thanked me for the fast update and started her IV and gave her pain medication immediately, but slowly. I stayed out of the way and didn't say another word except "Thank you" as they closed the door of the ambulance to transport her to the emergency department. The ED doctor barely introduced himself to me and did not listen as I introduced myself back to him—an introduction that always includes "twenty-one years of emergency and intensive care unit nursing, in level one teaching hospitals across this country." So when he said he was ordering an EKG and head CT scan for my mother, I responded, "Let's hold off on the head scan and EKG until we see the extent of her arm fracture." He started to attempt to override me. I calmly informed him, "She was just placed on hospice for aortic stenosis and is starting to show increasing signs of dementia; further tests may not be necessary." I don't pass judgment on him, because he didn't know her history, but I did. She also stated she had not hit her head, and she clearly remembers falling from dizziness, not "passing out," which could indicate a cardiac issue; thus, the EKG was also an appropriate order. He smirked and left to order just her arm X-rays. The department was moderately busy for six in the morning, but everything happened quickly and efficiently, including more pain medication on arrival; I was impressed.

She returned from her X-ray, and the doctor asked me to come take a look at the X-ray with him. Before it finished loading onto the screen, I said, "Well, you can't put screws in cork, dammit," before he had said a word. Now he turned his head, looked at me with a raised eyebrow, and said, "Tell me again what you did?" I reintroduced myself, and he treated me as a peer after that. My mother's humerus, upper arm bone, was severely fractured with both ends having slipped past each other. One edge was pointing up angled out towards her outer arm, with jagged edges that will be causing her great pain with any arm movement. My "cork" statement came from an extremely weak, porous, low-calcium-content bone. On her X-ray, her humerus looked more like frail cork webbing, and nowhere near as "bright" in whiteness as a healthy calcium-rich bone looks on an X-ray. Normal hard bone can have a screw placed into it and it will hold, but weak, crumbly, 90-year-old cork cannot hold a screw, and even with a cast it would not have held. It is well known that exercise helps keep calcium in the bones, and her life of zero exercise was evident on the X-ray. In twenty-one years of looking at hundreds of X-ray fractures with physicians, my mother "won", or I should say lost, as I had never seen such a low-density X-ray in all my years. Most 90-year-old people's bones are not this frail and weak, but my mother had advanced osteoporosis, decreasing bone calcium density, leading to weak bones and fractures. The physician shook my hand, apologized for questioning me, and for the fact the healthcare field could really do nothing for my mother except provide comfort. He also asked my full name so he could document that I was the one with her medical power of attorney, and that I had said no to further studies. I presented the copy of her medical power of attorney I kept in my glove compartment and confirmed that I was refusing further tests for her. The clerk made a copy for their record. He also nicely ordered her another round of pain meds and asked me if I wanted her admitted or if I was taking her back to her care facility. I told him I'd take her back, and he told me he'd arrange the transport right away. He came back five minutes later to make sure she had received more pain meds already and to tell me transport was minutes away.

Granted, I did have an unfair advantage in that situation over the non-healthcare person, but I encourage you to always understand what is being told to you. If needed, ask to have something told to you "a different way." You have every right to fully understand. In this case you can clearly see why I refused the other tests until I knew what we were working with. My mother chose to not have her aortic stenosis corrected years ago, nor did she want oxygen down the road, and she had been telling me more and more the past few months she was tired and wanted to go see Dad. So now you can see why the EKG and head CT scan were unnecessary; nothing was going to be treated anyway. The doctor talked with her, I talked with her, and she said, "Well, then, let's go home."

Patients enter health care institutions in one of three ways: EMS (emergency medical services) is called by the patient, family, police, or bystanders; patients are placed in a car and brought to an ED; or patients are seen in another hospital, doctor's office, or clinic and then transferred and admitted to a hospital. No matter how this action is started, it is as if a very large, heavy ball has been set into motion down a hill; once it is started, it is not always easy to stop. Without a medical power of attorney, being the legal spouse, or being the parent of a minor, it is not guaranteed that you will be able to control the care process. This chapter is about what may happen if these brakes and legal controls are not applied. Always remember that choosing to stay at home is the ultimate prevention of these procedures and the only way to ensure control.

EMS is not just the ambulance that brings you to the hospital. It has become a system of highly trained and skilled professionals, whose actions are determined by strict guidelines or by communication with a nurse or physician in the ED. Many modern EMS systems give the paramedic (the highest trained of the three levels of emergency medical technicians, or EMTs) the autonomy to make many critical decisions. But for the most part, your local EMS personnel's actions are guided by protocols based on their observations of the patient. An example: If your complaint is shortness of breath and/or chest pain, you usually cannot choose the hospital to which you would like to be transferred. EMS personnel must take you to the closest hospital. Now, if you are about five minutes from two hospitals, they might give you a choice. If they do not take you to the closest hospital, the EMT or transport company could be in trouble, fined, or sued because of their request to bypass the closest hospital. Numerous other actions are guided by protocols, such as when oxygen, drugs, or fluids are given, when IVs are started, whether or not plastic neck collars and hard boards are used to immobilize the spinal cord in the case of trauma, or even if CPR is started. Riding in the back of an ambulance unit is not a comfortable event. The stretcher is hard and very thin, and it can feel unstable when being rolled, even though it is not. The transport is often rough, fast, and shaky; you will tilt at turns and you will be facing backwards. IVs are much tougher to start under these conditions.

Whether you are brought to the ED by private car or ambulance, the amount of time one waits to be seen and treated (at times two very different things) will vary. After a total of nineteen years in emergency nursing and two in the ICU, I know that the reasons one has to wait to be seen are almost always out of the control of the people who are staffing that department. Triage is a French word that means "to sort or prioritize." Triage is not isolated to nurses in the front rooms of emergency departments deciding where and how high your priority is to get there. Triage is what all healthcare professionals are doing every minute of every shift. Whether working in the ED, ICU, hospital floor, office, clinic, or at a county 911 dispatch office, every healthcare professional must evaluate and prioritize the needs of those around them. This is where the anger and frustration of patients, family, and staff alike come into play. I can promise that ED staff wish they were not dealing with the high level of human tragedy that keeps them from seeing you quickly, for you might be unlucky to be in the ED, but still be lucky enough to be low on their priority list. The number of patients arriving, how sick they are, how badly they are hurt, how cooperative they are due to intoxicants or psychiatric reasons, whether or not it is a holiday, or even such an event as a hurricane approaching a coastline two hundred miles away affects wait time. Yes, patients being evacuated from coastal hospitals hundreds of miles away can affect your wait time in the ED a few hours inland. Hospital events contributing to wait time range from whether or not the department is understaffed due to flu, or to factors like budget cutbacks, the number of beds available in the hospital, how "backed-up" the ED is, how many operating suites are up and running, the number of CT scanners available as well as techs to run them, or even how many people are staffed in every department throughout the entire hospital. Every department affects this, including registration, admitting, central supply, nursing, laboratory staff, X-ray, and more. Often in the ED, this waiting is done in the waiting room, not in a bed inside the department. It is not the desire or preference of the triage nurse, or ED staff, to have a weak, tired, pained, or nauseated person wait in a waiting room. But if an ED is truly stressed to capacity and staff availability is tied up dealing with multiple traumas, with active cardiac trouble, or with a child who has been hit by a car and is not breathing, at that particular moment, what else can be done? If every bed is full, and every nurse and doctor is working on truly critical patients, again, what else can be done?

When a person near expected death, meaning someone with cancer or other terminal illnesses, arrives at the ED, vital signs are taken, including a pulse-oximeter reading, also known as pulse-ox or oxygen saturation. It measures just that, the oxygen saturation in the body tissue. This is most often done by projecting a special beam of light through the finger. By measuring how much light reaches the other side of the finger, oxygen levels can be determined as a percentage. If this reading is low, oxygen will be given, or increased if the EMS has already started oxygen. Oxygen is most often given by a nasal cannula, or by face mask if higher levels are needed. The nasal cannula is the thin plastic tube so often seen on television; it has two little plastic open prongs that rest just under or slightly into the nose. This little plastic tube is a major deceptive culprit of long-term lingering before death. Even the smallest amount of oxygen given by a nasal cannula, just one or two liters per minute, can cause the breathing and thus the body to go on for hours, days, or even weeks. It is amazing the number of times I have seen how fast the body will die, once the family has been informed of this fact and has chosen to take off the oxygen, or to have artificial ventilation discontinued. I call this nasal cannula oxygen system the "little culprit" because so often it is given or started to "help" the patient as a "comfort measure."

As I stated earlier, not one patient who I have ever placed back on oxygen and who then came back to consciousness has told me they felt discomfort during a period when the family thought oxygen was necessary. More often than not, during the final stage of dying, oxygen is given to the patient for the family, not for the patient. I will tell you from personal experience, even hospice will push oxygen, for low oxygen saturation levels or "for the patient's comfort." They were relentless to give my mother oxygen, even though I knew for a fact she had told me over and over, "No oxygen!" I had even given the hospice doctor, and Mom's primary hospice nurse, a first-edition copy of this book. Yet, they still tried to make me feel like I was doing the wrong thing and that I was heartless. Hospice requires your attention, too; they will also want to bring in their hospital bed. This can be a great offer, as it helps everyone save their back while caring for the dying person and prevents falls from bed, but it is still a personal choice of the dying. I am glad I got to ask my parents about their wishes around that issue long before they ever needed the bed. My mom said she didn't care, but my dad asked me to teach him the difference and chose his own bed.

The most basic requirement to keep the body from dying is the ability to breathe, and thus to move oxygen. The ventilator (some regions and countries call it a respirator) is the machine that accomplishes this task. Before the ventilator can breathe for you, an open airway must be started and maintained. This airway is known as an endotracheal (ET) tube, and the procedure is known as Intubation. An ET tube varies in size in relation to the size of the patient but is approximately the size of your pinky finger or larger. It is inserted through the mouth, sometimes through the nose, and into the trachea. The trachea is the middle part of your airway or "windpipe." An ET tube has a balloon, like a doughnut or ring, on the outside of the part that rests down in the trachea. This balloon is inflated to prevent air from escaping around the tube and to prevent the secretions from the mouth and stomach from spilling into the lungs. When someone has an ET tube inserted, they will not be able to talk. Voice and sound are created by air moving across the vocal cords. But with an ET in place, the air now moves through the tube, so the vocal cords can no longer create words. Also, when on a ventilator, your hands are tied down to the side of the bed, either until you are well enough or awake enough to move them, or you are so very sick that you no longer move. If this restraining is not done, instinctive reactions cause us to reach up and pull out the tube.

A note of comfort: When a person is intubated, drugs are given to sedate, calm, or even completely paralyze the person. Patients are paralyzed for several reasons. The two basic reasons are cooperation and to allow the ventilator to do its job without the patient "fighting" the ventilator. Victims of serious car crashes or trauma often need to be paralyzed on arrival to the ED, most often due to either a high alcohol level or a head trauma, which can cause patients to be uncooperative at a time when their lives are truly in danger. Also, patients who have some breathing function left may attempt to breathe against the set pace of the ventilator, again "fighting" the ventilator. This not only causes the patient discomfort, but it jeopardizes the breathing safety of the patient.

The ET tube itself is fairly firm; I have had patients describe the feeling as a tree branch constantly stuck in their throat. Many have shared that most of the discomfort is felt where the tube increases the pressure on the back of their tongue and the back of their throat. Almost all have told me for the first several days any movement of the head, and especially the frequent deep suctioning, greatly increases the discomfort. Once someone has adjusted to the tube's general discomforts and inconveniences, there is still one more great, and repetitive, discomfort that is required as long as an artificial airway is in place. The lungs and trachea do not adjust to this foreign tube. The tube's presence causes an increased production of mucus, or secretion. These secretions will block the airway, thus preventing air movement in and out of the tube. Therefore, this tube must be suctioned frequently at first, and periodically thereafter. Even a tracheostomy tube or airway that has been in place for years requires periodic suctioning. Stop and think how uncomfortable it is to swallow just one drop of liquid down your windpipe. Now imagine a tube about one-fourth to one-third the size of your pinkie going through the ET tube and all the way into your lungs. It usually requires two or three insertions of this suction tube to open the airway each time, near hourly, for the first several days or longer to keep the tube from clogging. Keeping that airway clear becomes second nature to ED/ICU nurses; that is how frequently suctioning occurs.

Depending on the patient and the reason for intubation, suctioning may be required three or four times an hour, though usually not that frequently. All patients who are intubated require suctioning. Someone who has been intubated for a long time may require suctioning only two or three times a day. These are usually people who breathe through a tracheotomy, which is a hole in the crevice where your neck meets your chest bone, or sternum. The most common complication of an ET tube is an infection in the lungs, also known as pneumonia or bronchitis. Bronchitis is an infection in the bronchi or larger upper airways, as opposed to pneumonia, an infection actually down in the lung tissue. Having a tube in your lungs and the frequency of suctioning greatly increases the chances of infection, which is the unwanted growth of bacteria or virus.

Pneumonia is a frequent complication for elderly and terminal patients. It greatly increases the rate at which the human body dies, and many people near inevitable death will choose not to treat pneumonia, or even a urinary tract infection, with antibiotics. The lungs can begin to bleed internally from the frequent suctioning. If an ET tube has to stay in for an extended period of time, the cells underneath the doughnut-like balloon can begin to die.

These areas of necrosis (meaning any area of dead tissue in the body) can also cause bleeding, infection, or even a hole to open through the bronchus into the chest cavity. Pneumonia is fairly common, but the rest of these are all rare but major complications, leading to the need for more and more procedures, interventions, and eventually a tracheostomy.

I have never been intubated, but it has been described to me as "uncomfortable," to "feeling helpless," to "hell on Earth." I have never met a person who has been intubated, no matter how many times, who does not have fears and reservations about allowing it to happen again. Most say, "Only if it is truly necessary," and a fair number say, "Never again." People who say "never again" are often in the terminal state of their illness, though some will, and do, change their minds when the air hunger becomes strong. For deserved balance, thousands of people are intubated every day for surgery without complications or even remembering the experience, except for being groggy and maybe having a slight sore throat. Anesthesiologists and nurse anesthetists are really good at what they do.

Be prepared, though: When this form of life support is turned off and the person is allowed to die, a few different breathing outcomes may happen. Sometimes there will be no spontaneous respirations and death occurs immediately. At other times there may be some breathing that may last for minutes or hours. Even more rare, the body's drive to breathe will increase once it realizes the ventilator is not there to help, and breathing can continue for longer periods. The body "realizes" this as oxygen levels drop and carbon dioxide levels increase, which is a natural occurrence in all of us before death. There are rare cases where the breathing continues, but this increase mostly just prolongs the inevitable death and does not mean the person's overall wellness will improve. I have had numerous family members tell me the spontaneous breathing gave them a false sense of hope.

As stated, the use of a ventilator to breathe for patients will be applied to the dying person unless the legal paperwork necessary is in place to stop the artificial intubation/ventilation. Once placed on a ventilator, it becomes a little more medically and legally difficult to take someone off. Remember, if certain laboratory tests are done, the failure of the respiratory system, which is a natural primary cause of death, will show results that would indicate a need for intubation/ventilation. These are the critical moments to have the personal knowledge, and legal control, to stop this if indicated, offered, suggested, or already done. Once placed on a ventilator, and/or given the stronger drugs to keep the blood pressure up, the patient must be admitted to an intensive care unit (ICU). ICU nurses are fantastic at fine-tuning and correcting the imbalances of the dying body. If death is imminent due to a terminal disease process, this fine-tuning of imbalances will only prolong time to death, not prevent it. Critical care and emergency nurses, especially in teaching hospitals where nurses and residents work and teach as a close-knit team, become very skilled and knowledgeable at the finer points of keeping the human body alive.

The ventilator and ET tube are without a doubt first-action, life-saving measures. I started with oxygen, airway, and ventilation because they are the "A" and "B" of the ABCs (airway, breathing, and circulation) of cardio-pulmonary resuscitation. I will return to the discussion on circulation at the end of this chapter, but for now I will cover routine procedures that may cause discomfort and prolong life. These procedures are also lifesaving, but for the most part do not save the life immediately, as artificial breathing, heart measures, and circulation restorative measures do. My reason for this order is the airway and breathing are always the healthcare field's first evaluation, and the moment the heart stops is most often but not always termed the time of death.

The nasal-gastric (NG) tube, which is passed down the nose, sometimes down the mouth, and into the stomach, is placed for several reasons: sometimes to help with a diagnosis such as bleeding, sometimes to prevent or solve a distention problem in the stomach or upper GI system, and sometimes to give medicines or nutrition for short periods of time. Almost all major trauma patients will receive an NG tube in order to empty the content of the stomach, check for bleeding, remove air forced in from artificial reparations before the ET tube was placed, and give medications. The NG tube is also inserted if someone is vomiting blood or passing blood from the rectum. A similar tube is also placed to give nutrients, but that is a much smaller and more flexible tube, known as a "feeding tube." Feeding tubes can also go through the mouth, if the nose is not indicated, or can be surgically placed directly through the abdominal wall. Those are the basic reasons for this tube's placement. I allowed a NG tube to be placed in me in nursing school so I would know what it felt like. I had to concentrate very hard to overcome my instinctual response to reach up and block it from being passed into my nose and down to my stomach, or to not pull it out. Once in place it felt like a rock was stuck in my throat, not to mention the overwhelming desire to gag and vomit. I have been told that after a few hours or days, "You get used to it." I have also been informed, just like the airway tube into the lungs, that irritation is increased with head movement, talking, or swallowing. This tube, if left in place for an extended period of time, will cause soreness, irritation, skin breakdown, and potential bleeding.

A "catheter" is almost any tube that is passed into the body. There are many different types of catheters. Urinary catheters pass urine out of the body. Heart catheters check for and repair cardiac artery blockages. There are catheters to measure pressures in the brain, and those used for tests, studies, or surgery. A urinary catheter is a latex and/or rubber tube that is passed into the urethra and continues into the urinary bladder, where urine is stored. The urethra is the tube between your bladder and the outside of your body; it is the tube from which urine leaves your body. Once the tube is fully inserted and there is a flow of urine, a balloon located at the end of the catheter is inflated with sterile water. This is done by injecting the fluid through a "port," or opening that is on the end of the catheter on the outside of the body. Once inflated, the balloon is what holds the catheter in place, for it can no longer slip back out of the bladder, unless yanked out by accident. This tube is placed for several reasons, either to drain and obtain the urine, to watch hourly how well the kidneys are functioning, or to help with diagnostic studies.

Following the discomfort of the actual urinary catheter insertion is a phantom sensation, or the overwhelming desire to urinate. The reason it is only a phantom sensation of a need to urinate is that you are already urinating. Because the catheter is now in place, as soon as your kidney makes urine, it passes out of the tube. It is the presence of this catheter in the urethra, and the balloon putting pressure on the bladder where the urethra exits, that creates a physically and mentally annoying feeling that the bladder is full, not an actual full bladder. So I would tell patients, "It is just a sensation that you need to urinate—you actually are urinating constantly into a collection bag hanging here on the side of your bed," and I'd lift that bag and show it to them. At which point the patient usually says again, "But I need to pee." That is how frustrating the sensation of needing to urinate is the first few hours, some patients have described the sensation as "maddening."

It is very important that this tube is immediately secured to the leg with several pieces of tape or one of many devices designed to secure this tube. I inform you of this need because too many tubes are not secured correctly or at all. In my experience I have found that many smaller and/or private hospitals do not secure these catheters, as I discover on the patient's arrival after transfer for more advanced care. I have seen too many catheters accidentally yanked from the body because they were not secured with tape or a device. Slow and right is always better than fast and wrong. Such a simple action prevents so much pain and complication. If a urinary catheter is accidentally yanked from the body, it means the balloon containing ten milliliters of sterile water was pulled through the urethra, and through the prostate gland in men. It is also important to secure this tube for general comfort reasons. Like other types of tubes or catheters, any movement increases the pain or discomfort, for the first few days especially.

The discomfort to men on insertion is usually greater, because the urethra is much longer, and the catheter also must pass through the hard, walnut-size prostate gland.

Removal of this tube is also normally more painful to men, also due to length of the urethra; the prostate, and with time the urethra and prostate, will "grab" it and hold on to the catheter. This "grabbing" is the tube sticking to the urethra the longer it is in, and the prostate will often swell and also hold on from inflammation from the catheter's presence. A great rule of thumb: The body really does not like foreign objects to remain for long. Even basic sutures to close a small external laceration will show some tissue inflammation, because the body is rejecting the foreign material.

The longer a catheter remains in, the more discomfort may be felt when the tube is taken out, unless daily "catheter care" is done, which includes manipulating the catheter slightly so "sticking" does not occur, as well as some special cleaning. Once removed, the overwhelming desire to urinate often returns. Even an inability to urinate can follow its removal; this is again more common in men, but women can experience this also. One trick is to attempt to ignore the sensation of the need to urinate for at least one hour, allow the bladder to fill with some urine, then attempt to void. Remember, the bladder is empty at the time the catheter is removed. Thus it is again only a sensation, but also an extremely frustrating one. I explained one seemingly weird, but effective, trick to my father after having a catheter: the use of cold water. He had the catheter removed in the doctor's office and went home. He was told to return if he did not void within a few hours. He listened to me and didn't try for the first hour, but then a few hours passed, and he still couldn't go. I lived away from him, and I was checking on him often by phone. So he was getting worried and the pressure was building. What makes most of us need to void? Cold water! I told him to stand at the sink, slash some cold water on his penis, and just go in the sink if it starts. He called me back a few minutes later thanking me as if I had saved his life. I remember telling him, "Just send me the $250 emergency room copay and we'll call it even."

The greatest complication of the urinary catheter is infection, especially in women because the urethra is so short, and in the elderly. Urinary tract infections often lead to sepsis (an infection of the blood), especially in the elderly. Again, once the body becomes septic, the rate at which the body dies greatly increases.

The rectal exam, another diagnostic procedure, is when a gloved, lubricated finger is inserted into the rectum. Most often it is to check for blood in the stool. It is also done to trauma patients to make sure the rectum squeezes the finger, which it cannot do if there are certain neurological injuries. In men, it is also done to check the size and location of the prostate. Other than a total invasion of personal privacy, it is a minimally uncomfortable procedure that lasts only a few seconds. Depending on the complaint, of course, rectal exams are a routine part of a complete head-to-toe emergency room exam by the physician.

Intravenous (IV) catchers are an extremely basic procedure. Their level of discomfort, as well as importance, is often taken for granted. I may start five, ten, even fifteen IVs a night, but because I have had them myself, I never forget just how painful they are. The healthcare field will warn the patient of a "sting," or "pinch," but to me it has always felt more like a vice grip squeezing a hunk of skin. I have received one a few times to let students or new nurses practice; if that is a "sting" or a "pinch," it's a whopper of one! An IV is started to draw blood for tests, to give fluids, and to deliver medications or blood products. If dehydrated, the vital signs will often show a low blood pressure, an increased heart rate, and other visual indicators. IV fluids will help correct this and often will increase awareness or level of consciousness of the patient. If the patient is able and conscious, sips of water to hydrate the mouth will increase comfort without really correcting dehydration. Of course, even in the hospital setting, IV fluids can be withheld. If death is imminent, IV fluids, just like oxygen, are capable of adding hours or days to the last stage of dying, and possibly to the patient's suffering and pain.

If you do allow tests to be sent—and yes, you can request lab tests not be done—IVs may be suggested to correct any abnormalities. Potassium is the most common electrolyte to be abnormal, and it is most often low unless kidney failure is present or the patient is on a potassium supplement. Depending on the stage of major organ shutdown, intervention via IV may or may not delay death. If the choice is made to die in the home, all of these stressors and decisions would not be added to an already extremely difficult time. Lab tests may also show a potential infection indicated by the number of white blood cells found. If this is the case, antibiotics will be given or offered. Infections in the weakened or elderly body are a common natural occurrence, and cause of death.

For thousands and thousands of years before antibiotics or the ability to give IV fluids, infections and dehydration were the two most common causes of death. Untreated infections, as previously mentioned, will often lead to sepsis. Sepsis is when bacteria enter the blood system, and the total body can be overrun with bacteria. There are stages to sepsis, but an end result is hypotension, meaning a very low blood pressure. If the family does want this treated, IV fluids will solve the low blood pressure for only a short time. Eventually strong medicines will have to be given to keep the blood pressure up.

These powerful drugs, known as dopamine, levophed, and a few others, are at this point advanced life-saving measures. These drugs work by causing the heart to pump a little stronger, but mainly by causing the blood vessels to constrict and get smaller, therefore increasing blood pressure. Dopamine has a limited ability to do its job; once the body's dopamine receptors are saturated, the drug often stops working. Then Levophed is used next. Levophed is so strong in its ability to constrict vessels that the fingers and toes often will discolor, die, and then blacken, all from the extreme loss of blood flow.

The ability to give medications is the other main reason for starting an IV. If an IV is in place, medications can be given directly into the vein rather than continuing to stick someone with a needle or continuing to give pills. It is not uncommon for pills to cause nausea and vomiting in many very sick people. IV medications often work more effectively, and always faster than pills or medicines injected into the muscle. At times IVs cannot be placed in the arms. In long-term illness, the arm veins may have been "used up." This means there are no further sites in which to start an IV. Or some medicines, such as cancer medications or long- term steroid use, will "burn" or weaken the blood vessels. This is why IVs are sometimes placed in the legs, or other access areas. A central catheter, or "central line," which is an IV placed in the neck, chest, or femoral vein in the groin area can be used. Major large blood vessels are located at these points.

A very common first alternative is a peripherally inserted central catheter, or PICC line. A PICC line is a great alternative and provides access for any long-term care situation. It is a very thin, very flexible, long catheter, which is most often inserted in the bend of the elbow but can be placed in other areas. It too is for infusing fluids or medicines through a long thin tube that extends up to the shoulder area reaching the vena cava. The vena cava is the last and largest major vein before entering the heart. Infection and becoming clogged or blocked are the two most common complications of a PICC line. I highly recommend this type for long term care; however, it is important to learn its proper care to avoid the potential complications. Some types of

IV catheters are used for continuous blood pressure monitoring if inserted into an artery. There are other types used to help know what the blood pressure is in the heart or the large blood vessels that lead to or from the heart. These central lines and all IVs have the potential for infection, as well as blood clot formation. Blood clots have the potential to form blockages both in the blood supply to areas of the body and to the blood return system back to the heart and lungs.

Once the initial pain of the insertion is over, the IV will normally continue to cause a dull, achy discomfort. IV medications can cause burning, itching, or dull, achy pain at the insertion site or up the arm. Slowing the infusion rate, or diluting the medication further, can most often decrease these discomforts. Most medications should be diluted and given at a steady rate to avoid pain, burning, or irritation in the vein. In the hospital setting, laboratory tests are taken from almost all patients at least once a day. Depending on the seriousness of the illness, blood tests are sometimes drawn more frequently, even as often as every hour or less. The reasons lab tests are drawn so often are to allow the nurse to closely track if the illness is getting better or worse and to fine-tune medications.

Blood is often taken from an artery to check the pulmonary function, meaning the oxygen, carbon dioxide, and acid levels of the blood. This test is known as an arterial blood gas (ABG). If not drawn from an arterial catheter that is already in place, an ABG can be a painful test. Most often a needle is inserted into the same point of your wrist where the pulse is checked, and this is a very sensitive area. If a natural expected death is imminent, or a "do not treat" situation is present, then this test will most likely not be offered.

Drug administration is also considered an intervention. This is an area that I could write pages and pages about, as the pink pages of the *Physicians' Desk Reference* list more than one thousand drugs and drug variations. But I can narrow the discomforts caused by drugs down to a few general categories. Most chemotherapy drugs used to treat cancer, some antibiotics, and protease inhibitors can cause extreme fatigue, nausea, and vomiting. I use the word "extreme" because these side effects can be debilitating. I have known too-many-to-count patients who have chosen to let a second or third relapse of cancer not be treated because they did not want to relive the side effects of chemotherapy drugs. The most graphic description I ever received to describe this drug-induced nausea and extreme general horrible feeling was from a woman undergoing chemotherapy for breast cancer. She told me to "Imagine the worst nausea you have ever felt, multiply it by ten, run it through your whole body, not just the belly and head, and then live with it, because it doesn't go away." The fatigue has been described to me as anything from "the flu" to a feeling of "partial paralysis."

There is a double-sided sword to medication-induced nausea. There are medications that help the nausea and vomiting, but rarely does a medication take it away. Patients have told me that marijuana greatly reduces, and sometimes completely takes away, nausea. But it is still illegal in many states. When a healthy person is nauseated, it is usually the body trying to get rid of something it doesn't want. But people with medication-induced nausea either have nothing in the stomach to start with, or they would really like to keep the little bite of food they worked so hard to get down from coming back up. Nausea and vomiting are not a sign of the body wanting to get rid of its stomach content, but a side effect of the medicine triggering the body and brain to feel nausea and an unwanted need to vomit. This nausea and vomiting must not be overlooked as a consideration to decide to end treatment. So many terminal patients have told me the reason they are choosing to accept their death and stop treatment is due to the nausea and vomiting.

Steroids are given for a variety of illnesses, frequently for chronic lung disease, but any disease process that causes inflammation of a body part can be treated with steroids.

Steroids can also produce nausea, but patients most often complain of the mood swings. Some people experience increased energy and feelings of happiness at first, but that can turn into moodiness, depression, or anger. It is not uncommon for patients on long-term steroids to feel or act out suicidal thoughts.

Many medications produce side effects that play out as body sensations. The feeling of skin "crawling" is one of the more common body sensations caused by some medications. Patients have also described extreme tiredness that is felt as heaviness or fatigue in the arms and legs, clumsiness, itching, or even a sensation of an arm or leg feeling "on fire" in response to various medications. Respect for the fact that no two people are alike when it comes to medication-induced side effects needs to be emphasized. One person may or may not have the same side effects as another person. What works for one to alleviate discomfort may not work for another. One person's nausea on a medication may be described as mild, whereas another person of the same size, age, and dose of the same medication may experience unbearable nausea. Any medication has the potential to cause any sort of side effect in an individual. Both family and the health care staff need to respect these subjective descriptions. It is difficult enough to experience an uncomfortable side effect in response to a medication or procedure, but it is much worse not being believed or to be told, "It is all in your head." This must be hard for someone already knocked over with illness, and it damages the trust and respect of any relationship.

Side note: I know for a fact I did not always say the right thing to patients and family members. But, I was constantly attempting to evaluate what I was about to say, and even reviewed how I had said something to attempt to improve. I am not "bashing" the medical field when I write of the harsher moments that I have witnessed or more frequently been informed of by people dealing with the healthcare field. My intention is to provide humanistic review in both directions, as all communication between us humans is both sent and received by our imperfect minds. It is an opportunity for basic human peer review, to keep us all with checks and balances, and an opportunity to improve. To this day I fail frequently, but to this day I continue to attempt to improve. Just ask my siblings if you want a comical reply to this side note.

"Scope" procedures include any procedure that is done by passing a fiber-optic tube into the body. A bronchoscope looks into the trachea or bronchi, which again are the tubes that move air into our lungs. A gastroscope looks into the esophagus, the stomach, and part of the small intestines, also called an upper GI. A colonoscope is passed into the rectum and up into the colon, also known as a low GI. Many other procedures are now done through this scope method, including numerous types of abdominal surgeries, bone and joint surgery, heart bypass surgery, and stent placement in blood vessels (a stent is a metal straw-like tube to open blood flow in narrowed, clotted, or damaged vessels). Scope procedures not only look at or diagnose a problem, but they can also be used to correct a problem or take a sample. A scope procedure can be used to remove a piece of meat stuck in the esophagus, which is the tube food passes down after you swallow. Meat is the most frequent food lodged in the esophagus, so please take smaller bites and chew a little longer. A scope procedure could also be used to take a sample piece of cancer for pathology review.

Dialysis is not necessarily a procedure that causes pain, and it is without a doubt life saving. Dialysis is a machine that filters and cleans the blood when the kidneys fail to perform their full function or have completely stopped functioning. Most patients who require dialysis receive it two or three times a week. I include this procedure as it may be offered at some point to the dying patient, or they may already be receiving the treatment. This too must be considered on an individual basis in relation to quality of life and imminent death. It does cause fatigue during and for a short period after. Often those receiving dialysis will choose to stop just because they are "tired of going" and living a life with great restrictions. Many do return back to dialysis on their own due to increasing complications that cause discomfort and shortness of breath. I pass no judgment; the will to live is a powerful, near-constant, deep and instinctual drive. Shortness of breath is a powerful motivator.

Providing nutritional supplements is the act of feeding the body. This procedure can basically be done two different ways. "Tube feeding" is the process of placing "food," meaning a nutritionally rich liquid, into the stomach or small intestines. This is done through a plastic tube that passes directly into the stomach through the abdomen, or that goes down the esophagus through the nose or mouth. Hyper-alimentation is the process of slowly disseminating nutritionally rich sterile fluid directly into the blood. Both provide the body with the nutritional requirements to live. The family of a near-death patient sometimes chooses nutritional feeding to alleviate their feelings that the person is "starving," because they haven't eaten in days or weeks. People in this state of near-death have often told me they were weak, tired, and/or in pain, but "hunger" or "starving" is a sensation that has never been expressed to me by someone in the very last stage of their life.

Cardiac resuscitation, or attempting to restart the heart once it has stopped, is the last and most graphic procedure to share with you. I saved it for last because it is normally the last procedure done to the body before death is "pronounced" by the physician, or by a paramedic with that authority. There are four parts to cardiopulmonary resuscitation: compressions, artificial respirations, electrical shocking, and drug administration. If cardiopulmonary resuscitation (CPR) is performed on a human body where death is imminent, whether because the heart or the body can no longer sustain life, it can at times for short periods return the heart to a pumping condition, postponing inevitable death by a few minutes, hours, or days.

At the time of a non-pumping cardiac condition, drugs are given to assist the heart in regaining the correct electrical activity, as well as to stimulate the heart in general to want to pump correctly again. Drug administration cannot assure that when the heart restarts, it will restart in a pumping condition. Electrical shock actually shocks the heart into stopping completely for a brief moment in the hope that when it restarts, the electrical sequence will have returned to the correct electrical pathways required for a functioning blood-pumping heart. The heart's four chambers, which are controlled by electrical activity in the heart, must contract in a specific order or the heart does not actually move blood. Thus the heart does not have to "stop" for death to be imminent, though the heart will stop shortly if the non-pumping heart activity is not corrected.

Shocks to the body are measured in an electrical measurement known as joules, pronounced "jewels." The shocks to the body are given in increasing increments according to the heart's response to the previous shock. Although newer defibrillators that use fewer joules are replacing older ones, for the longest time the first shock has been 200 joules, the second shock 300 hundred joules, and the third and following shocks 360 joules. Newer biphasic defibrillators use between 120-200 joules. These shocks are directed through the heart in one of two ways: Large electrical pads can be placed on the body so the heart is directly between the two pads, or hand-held electrical pads can be held onto the chest, one on the right upper chest and the other well below the left armpit. Here is what happens: Before each shock is delivered, the person discharging the shock loudly states "all clear," visually scans the patient and bed to ensure staff is not still touching the patient or bed, glances one more time at the cardiac monitor to make sure the rhythm has not converted back to normal on its own, then delivers the shock. The shock does not only pass through the heart; it travels the entire body. Often the arms of the body will jerk towards the center of the body because the electrical current stimulating the heart also causes the muscles to contract. The jerking of the body during these shocks becomes more pronounced as the joules of energy are increased. As minutes pass, if these efforts are futile and unavoidable death quickly approaches, this same jerking inwards of the arms during shocks will eventually become less pronounced the further off balance the body becomes chemically. Repetitive shocking sometimes causes mild surface burns to the skin.

The chest compression part of resuscitation is done by compressing the sternum, also known as the chest or breast bone, which is directly over the heart, approximately 1 1/2 to 2 inches with the palm of the hand and the weight of your body behind the compression. If you have never seen compressions in progress, be prepared; it is harsh to see. We attempt to compress at a rate of one hundred or more times per minute. It is estimated that under the best of conditions, this circulates only about 30 percent of the heart's normal blood flow, and carries a much lower percentage of oxygen.

When we perform compressions on a mannequin while learning CPR, there is something very real that cannot be experienced. The first few compressions, especially in the elderly or someone who has been bedridden for a long period of time, will either break the ribs or separate them from the sternum. This can often be heard, and felt, by the person doing the first few compressions. Once again, the entire body slightly and rhythmically jerks or moves with the one hundred compressions per minute. These last few heroic procedures are called a "code" situation in the healthcare field. Most code situations, the compressions, drugs, and shocking of the body, will go for five to twenty minutes, depending on the situation. Coding someone can go on much longer in a younger person, or if the person has a very low body temperature, depending on the age, circumstances, and medical history.

I know that I mention the various angles and reasons why I wrote this book frequently. I admit part of my need for that is to push myself to continue to remain bold and open with you. It is not easy for me to tell you these raw facts, mainly because I know for many it is hard to hear and visualize. I keep telling myself it is to inform and empower, and that passion comes from the barrage of pain and death that touched my being for so many years. I have taken part in this so-often-unnecessary abuse of the assured immediate death, or already dead body, easily more than a thousand times in my twenty-one years in teaching hospitals. There are times when these measures indeed work immediately, and restore the heart to its normal function, and the person goes on to have a normal life, or near normal if their brain did not go too long without oxygen. But in the terminal and elderly, more often than not it is futile. If the heart does restore to a functional pumping action in these groups, it usually does not last, creating repetitive false hope cycles for the family, only to have the person die a few hours or days later, and to receive more and much larger bills.

If the healthcare field is not informed in the appropriate and legal manner of a legal DNR, or "do not intubate, do not give compressions, and do not give first-line drugs" order, you or your loved one will spend the last moments before death naked, in a room full of people, having tubes placed into the body, chest compressions done, drugs injected, and electrical shocks sent through the body. Too often I have felt that the individual would not have wanted their body treated this way at an otherwise peaceful, beautiful, and magnificent time of transition.

Now you have a graphically firmer understanding of what CPR entails, and the magnitude of what those three little letters really mean. Almost all counties, or parishes in Louisiana, in the United States now have a means for the patient or family to stop the EMS system from starting CPR. This "out-of-hospital DNR" is special paperwork that is different from other DNR paperwork. Most EMS systems will start CPR unless you can present their county's "out-of-hospital DNR" form. It must be obtained, filled out very accurately according to county or state requirements, and in hand when EMS arrives, or CPR will most likely be started if the breathing or heart stops. I kept a copy of my mom's at the bedside, on the refrigerator in an envelope, and in my glove compartment.

If death has not occurred en route to, or in, the ED, and the patient will not be going back home or to an alternative care facility, then admission to the hospital will occur. The choices for "in house" admission are to a floor bed, a step-down unit, or an ICU. Step-down units are not the high level of care of the ICU, but nor are the nurses spread as thin as on the floors. Being admitted during end-stage dying can be helpful or the hindrance you are learning about now. The hospitals are there for good reason; just use caution and choice, with paperwork all lined up and in hand. If the caregiver is unable to continue providing care for one reason or another, this is a valid reason for hospital admission if there is an acute issue, or direct placement to a secondary care facility if not. I will cover this more in the chapter on stress on the caregivers. Personal touches can be provided in the institutional settings on some level. I've even sneaked dogs into hospitals so goodbyes could be shared. But there is no replacement for the personal comfort and amenities of home.

Before closing this chapter, there are two more subjects I would like to cover. Although one may not think this is possible, to some readers these may be even more sensitive or controversial than those already covered. Yet I feel this is both the appropriate time and place. These actions are both procedures and procedural even though death has occurred.

The first, known as post-mortem care, is the care and placement of the body following death. There is a great difference in what happens to the body in the hospital as compared to what happens in the home. In most states, all deaths that occur within seventy-two hours of admission to a hospital are considered a "coroner's case." This means the coroner has the final decision on whether or not an autopsy is performed, and when the body can first be moved. The coroner basically has total legal control over all bodies, until the point the coroner "releases" the body back to the family and funeral facility. Death in the home is also a coroner's case. However, if the death is a known or obvious terminal patient, or an elderly patient, the coroner will most likely release the case directly to the funeral home.

Except in very small hospitals where the body is left in the room or ED until the funeral home transports the body, most bodies in the hospital setting will be transported to the hospital's morgue. The body is first wrapped in a plastic body bag, then taken to the morgue on a regular hospital bed or a metal scoop-like stretcher without a mattress. Once the family has contacted the funeral home, the funeral home's staff will then transport the body away from the hospital's morgue. This interim transport and storage of the body in the institutional hospital setting is avoided if death occurs in the home. Depending on the state, county, patient's age and history, the police, coroner, or justice of the peace may come to the home. Again, if this is a clear-cut case of old age or terminal illness, this will only be a brief formality and the body will be released to the funeral home. If a detective does show up, which will happen a little more frequently if hospice is not involved, show them the out-of-hospital DNR and a letter from the primary doctor. Most doctors will write a short note stating an in-home death is imminent and they will sign the death certificate. This will help the detective see this was an expected death. I have found if hospice is involved, law enforcement rarely shows up.

The topic of expenses may seem the coldest to you, and it is difficult for me also. I have addressed healthcare economics lightly only because so many non-health care people talk to me about it in general and in reference to the bills they received after the death of a loved one. I am also not one to remain silent when there is an elephant in the room. One of the many reasons I spent my twenty-one years of nursing in public teaching hospitals is, although they also send you a bill, for the most part money is not their first objective.

Encompassing health care and education should be their first goal, and yes, a profit is required to remain in operation. Unfortunately, many of my doctor friends around the country tell me the upper administration of their hospitals, who come from financial backgrounds—not four years of medical school, one year of internship, three to five years of residency, and then must pass a state board-certified competency exam in a specialty—like to create policies that direct the physician on how to practice medicine to attempt to increase profit margins over safe research-based practices. I have known many exceptional doctors who have left the clinical setting because of this upper administrative influence. Again, this is a subject I do not like to get into, but again feel I should, mainly because so many do not have insurance, and health care is skyrocketing in cost. Even with insurance, being responsible for 30 percent of a $100 or $200 thousand hospital bill is still $30 to $60 thousand. Add this onto funeral expenses, and this quickly becomes a debt that will break the average-income family. Now, even public hospitals will turn over no- or late-payment collections to an agency that will destroy a credit rating and often forces families to file bankruptcy.

The percentage of all U.S. health care dollars spent on the last six months of life is a serious reflection on several aspects of our society's and our healthcare field's beliefs and fears. It is a reflection of our allocation of funds, our fears of death, our legal system that forces healthcare to protect itself from lawsuits, and our unrealistic expectations of modern medicine to keep the irreversibly, near-imminent-death patients alive. Or perhaps it reflects our unwillingness to allow those dollars to be diverted into early detection, health education, and preventative programs. Health care institutions are getting much more aggressive about nonpayment, and some are even bringing civil action against debtors. They may not expect you to be able to pay the total if you lose the case, but then they have secured your debt.

I wish you great peace, acceptance, and serenity with the choices you make about what procedures and interventions you do or do not allow. These should always be your choice to make for yourself, so do it while you can. Although difficult, your choices can provide a greater level of respect and dignity to you and your loved ones, as well as helping control skyrocketing health care costs in every direction. To do otherwise, and to not plan or fail to document these choices into writing, is completely leaving your care up to an undesignated relative or the uncontrollable and appropriately self-protective choices of our modern healthcare system. That physician left with your unknown decisions may completely know, respect, and accept that your appropriate natural death is now, but must code you anyway. I absolutely will not tell you what choices to make, as that is not my place, but I and hopefully all will accept the choices you make. But I do highly encourage you to make them, assign the right person for your medical power of attorney to respectfully carry out your wishes and not their own wishes or beliefs for you, and control your own end-of-life events and death.

CHAPTER 8

EMOTIONAL AND PHYSICAL STRESS ON THOSE SUPPORTING THE DYING

"There are only four kinds of people in the world. Those who have been caregivers. Those who are currently caregivers. Those who will be caregivers and those who will need a caregiver."
—Rosalynn Carter, b. 1927

I AND ALL

When I was young
I knew so much
I've got this

Then time
Then tragedy
Then more thens

I fell backwards
I fell on others
It was others to blame

I sat and looked
Out not in
New for me

Everyone is hurt
Everyone is healing
I and all hold the blame

Look both in and out
It's an amazing view
Then reach in then out

I have been told that mother lions, during times of famine, will aggressively keep their cubs away from a fresh kill until they have fed first. She is not being selfish; she knows if she doesn't care for herself first, she will not be able to care for her cubs tomorrow. This is not always the norm for human caregivers. I have repeatedly seen people confuse care for the self with selfish behavior (I am certainly guilty of the same), believing that self-sacrifice translates into love and caring. Pulling long vigils in the hospital, or not keeping self-care paramount while caring for someone in the home, is detrimental on many levels to all. It is self-damaging first and foremost.

I realize we are in times where being gender-specific is not politically correct, but my first two years in sociology have made demographics a large part of how I see the world.

Various demographics also benefit from research and awareness. It is a completely different situation when demographics are used for prejudice, manipulation, or exclusion.

Women, by deeply ingrained natural instinct, are often highly devoted caregivers. I have also often found the equally devoted son, father, or husband who also needed the advice inherent in this analogy, but it is statistically significant that many women tend to shy away from giving self-care. It is considered one of the reasons women are slower to seek medical attention when actually having an active heart attack than are men; they feel they don't have time to seek help because they have too much to do. Quickly, just to educate: Another reason women delay medical attention is 50 percent of women past the age of 50 having an active heart attack will not have the "classic" cardiac signs. Women have been taught from the time they were small children to put the care of others before ourselves– learned behavior from our families, the media, religions, society in general, our partners, and out of fear of feelings of guilt. Thank goodness this long history of women putting others before themselves has been rapidly changing over the past several decades. It is not healthy or right for anyone to expect women partners to put others ahead of their own well-being, nor is it a healthy model to continue to teach young women. While this is unrelated to any woman or man who chooses to be an active primary caregiver, which is at its foundation the most noble and important role on Earth, it only relates to improving deserved and necessary healthy self-care.

Ultimately, we do not give optimal care to others if we are not at an optimal level ourselves. In the hospital setting, this played out in the form of the uninterrupted vigil at the bedside or in the intensive care waiting room. On many occasions I have seen it go as far as a caregiver refusing to eat or go home to shower. "I can't leave him," is the chant. I think the movies get some of the blame for this one. We see the husband in the intensive care unit from a heart attack or car accident, or maybe we see a cop who has been shot, and the wife doesn't leave until he awakens from the coma one or two weeks later. We forget it was a movie made over a period of months, and that the actress had breakfast and lunch, went to a fine restaurant, then slept the night away in a hotel bed. She even had breakfast again before getting made up to look like she slept the night away in a hospital chair. In reality, it tears people up to attempt this type of vigil; they literally pass out, or can't comprehend information, and thus can't make decisions to their fullest potential. Periodically they are brought down to the ED for care, when all they needed was rest, food, and fluids to prevent their near or complete unresponsive state. This type of behavior is not only a great disservice to the self, it is also a great disservice to the patient, who needs their loved ones to be strong and clear.

Whether caring for someone in the hospital, a care facility, or at home, taking care of your own basic needs is essential.

Again using myself as an example, I want to share an excerpt from the journal I kept while caring for my dad during the last two weeks of his life. This entry was written on day four of my role as his primary caregiver (I had already spent two days and nights with him at the care facility), and it illustrates how I was already aware of the toll it could take on me if I didn't take care of myself:

Yesterday my family decided to take my dad out of the Alzheimer's care facility and bring him back to his home, which he left only six months ago. He and I are sharing a bedroom that has two double beds. Three of my sisters live here in town and continue to make sure I know they will give me breaks. I have set a plan for self-care and committed to myself to stick to it. I plan to walk daily. It is July in the South, and I am looking forward to a slight sun-cooking during these walks. Although this house is filled with junk food, such as bite-size candy bars and cakes, I have strong (OK, a little shaky) intentions to stay away from those temptations and eat healthily. My body, mind, and emotions do not need the sugar highs and lows that sweets give me. No more coffee than my usual one or two cups in the morning. I refuse to turn off my sense of humor; I will need it. Every day I will ask one of my sisters to relieve me for a few hours so I can drive away to spend some time alone. We will see how this plan pans out.

The stressors on caregivers are so multi-faceted. First, life does not go on hold because a loved one is dying. Jobs, kids, and financial and personal needs do not and cannot be put on hold. Then there is the stress of the care task itself. All this is enveloped by the mental and emotional storm of the dying and near-death of a loved one, be it a friend, partner, parent, or, so much worse, a child. Needless to say, you're not going to *feel* clobbered; you are going to *be* clobbered. Don't sacrifice yourself. No self-care plan is going to be perfect.

Not everyone has family or friends available to help and/or give relief for breaks. The dying may need to be left alone while you go to work or care for your child or yourself; this one is a tough call with much to consider, depending on the needs of the person staying alone. It may not be possible. Sweets and coffee may be how you care for or spoil yourself, although I highly encourage moderation. You may see that your self-care time is only fifteen or twenty minutes when you lock yourself in the bathroom to take a long bath, instead of a four-minute shower. If this is the case, halfway through that bath, turn on the hot water again, and spoil yourself by refreshing the temperature. Maybe it will float away another ounce of stress and rejuvenate another ounce of energy.

Care of the self does indeed involve the mind, body, and spirit. The care of a dying person greatly adds to the wear and tear on all three. Let me start by briefly touching on the spirit aspect, which you may call your heart, soul, or spirit. I will keep this brief because I do not in any way want to place a religious or spiritual spin to this book—that I leave to each individual, and I fully respect what works for each person. So when I use the word spirit I mean no tone or direction of any specific religion or sect. I understand that losing someone we love does tear our spirit to bits; to this day I miss Ken, Mathew, my mother and father, and Dave, and tears still form. But, I also recommend trying (I say "trying" because I am realistic) to go to a place of understanding within yourself that helping someone die can build your spirit as well as drain it. Giving this type of care and support to someone dying will be physically and mentally draining. But, it can also give you something amazing. It is how I have survived and remained giving, even though I dealt with thousands of human tragedies in my years of nursing. I have consciously chosen to work from the heart each and every day.

Every morning after putting in a grueling twelve-hour weekend night, which is mainly what I worked most of my clinical years, I went home tired in my body and mind, but stronger and fulfilled in my heart. I will stop at that, as you can interpret and find the growth on your own.

The mental, emotional, and physical drain of this work will be tremendous. It also can be elusive. For some reason, people tell me, and I discovered the same, that they feel the drain the greatest when they take a break for a few hours, or after the death has occurred. I know I can remember only one minute of the day after my father died, which was upon waking up to the realization that he no longer breathes on the surface of this Earth, but I cannot recall one minute of the next twenty-four hours. This I would guess has much to do with how task-oriented the job is, combined with the mental and emotional gravity of being in the presence of a dying loved one. It requires so much mental, emotional, and physical energy, on top of our already full lives, that we just keep going, and it hits us when we stop.

Whether you're feeling it or not, the stress is there and building inside of you and needs to be released in as healthy a way as possible. I say that because we often give ourselves "consolation prizes." This is not my term, I have heard it over the years and I have been guilty of it myself. Two of my favorite consolation prizes are chocolate and Coke in a glass bottle. It is the overuse of a rationalization to do something that we know is not right or good for us that we all must pay daily attention to. Our use of a rationalization is another one of our many defense mechanisms that protects us from too much self-honesty. An example of giving yourself a dangerous "consolation prize" via a rationalization would be, "My husband is dying. It is painful to every aspect of my being, so I am going to start smoking again." Attempt to be aware of this and know I pass no judgment, but I do wish you health in your stress reduction. Continue to do whatever it is in life you do for yourself, and consider adding one or two of these suggestions if you realize you are not doing any of them: Start walking or jogging daily, go to the gym, go see a movie once a week or monthly, have lunch out with a friend, attend support meetings or counseling, or eat more fruits and vegetables and less junk, sweets, or fast foods.

Another extremely important thing, which so many of us neglect, is to keep well hydrated. Remember liquids that contain caffeine, alcohol, or high levels of sugar actually cause your body to urinate fluids out. Sugar is the worst culprit of the three; it has the potential to dehydrate at a cellular level first, not as a later consequence of dehydration. Increased water intake gives a greater and more consistent energy level, while dehydration negatively affects problem solving, coordination, and attention. So it is a win-win situation to drink more water, as the old teaching about drinking eight glasses a day has a great deal of wisdom to it. There are very few disease processes that require limited water intake. In rare occasions, dehydration can actually cause a compensation of increased heart rate and vascular constriction that can cause high blood pressure. So maintaining a proper hydration balance, even if one has hypertension, is crucial. Aside from the main disease processes requiring fluid restrictions of hypertension and heart failure, renal failure, advanced liver disease, and acute head injury, everything in the body works better with proper hydration. As proof that as society at large we are under hydrated, it is estimated that we could decrease visits to the emergency departments by 20 percent if we would remain properly hydrated.

Even trauma is included in those statistics, both in preventing and in the body's ability to handle major trauma. My friends and family tease me frequently because I push hydration, I only mind their teasing when I am grumpy from dehydration and/or hypoglycemia.

Hypoglycemia means a blood glucose (sugar) level below normal range, which is 70-100. When we drop below 70 bad things start to happen; if too low, dropping below 50-60, real trouble starts, including confusion, frustration, anger, decreasing or loss of consciousness, seizures, and even brain cells starting to die if it gets too low. The absolute worst thing we do during times of crisis is not eat. "I'm too upset" or "I'm too emotional to eat" is a truly dangerous rationalization to make at such times. Blood glucose levels below seventy help nothing in our lives, body, or our thought process during normal times, much less during crises. When we allow our blood glucose levels to drop too low, our emotions become much more sensitive, and it becomes tougher to remain in rational thought. Please, meet your nutritional basics during times of crisis; it is deserved self-care that can only help the situation.

Please also learn to talk about what it is like for you to be going through this. Whether it is with a support group, counselor, friend, or health care professional, talking will help. No matter who we are, what our training is, or how tough we think we are, the tragedies we see, the dying and the death do sink inside us and affect us. I feel that one of the greatest professional injustices I see in society is the misconception that frontline caregivers can handle everything they see, hear, smell, touch, and even sometimes taste. I am referring to every member of law enforcement, 911 call takers and dispatch, firefighters, social workers, teachers, EMS technicians, nurses, nurse's aides, doctors, counselors, and emergency department registration and department clerks. Many of these same fields have high rates of addiction, divorce, and suicide. Unjustly from the time of entry into these fields, they are taught to swallow and bury everything because they are not supposed to be human. It is as if there is an unspoken rule that if that is your title, you can handle the tragedies that will unfold before you. We are human beings before we are any of these roles, limited to human ability and capability. It is an unfair, unrealistic expectation, to think an assigned title negates the barrage of human tragedy that passes before us. I can promise these tragedies all go in and get stored somewhere in our beings. Whether stored in the mind and we display an overprotective calloused or indifferent attitude or addiction to mask the assault, or in the stomach and intestines displayed as ulcers or intestinal disease, or in the heart with cardiac or hypertension issues, it goes in and it affects us. No matter who you are or what you do, please let some of the pain and stress of these situations out to someone.

Whether you are a healthcare worker or not, if you are someone who for one reason or another keeps your feelings in, be it because you feel you should not or cannot express them, the region where you live discourages it, or your family background does not encourage it, please try to share some of what has gone in. At the local country store or breakfast gathering with your other farmer buddies for coffee, try "You know, my wife having cancer is tough," and leave it at that for starters. One spoken line may open up a conversion they also need to have from stored unreleased past experiences. It is a start, and chances are you will find out you're not alone. You may find your buddies start talking about their family members who are dying or have died with cancer. No one is above humanness, and as soon as you think you are, that's double trouble, and a guaranteed setup for self-destruction.

My own personal story with how I know it goes in, gets stored, and comes out somehow was a shocking out-of-nowhere surprise to me. In the late eighties, I did a six-month nursing contract in a large burn unit. A few years after that at another large teaching hospital, I would float to their burn unit regularly also. Every day we bring each burn patient into the "tank room" for debridement (removal of dead tissue). This is a large table where we give them a shower with a showerhead on hoses to bathe the person and remove what dead tissue we can. Pain medications are given beforehand, and some units also give the person nitrous oxide during the debridement. Then they are brought back to the room and all burns are redressed. My compassion is of course first and mostly for the burn victim going though this daily, but stop for a minute and think about the nurses, aides, and techs performing this procedure; to visually see this and cause this discomfort over and over requires both processing and some development of our own thick skin.

It was years later and I was cruising along thinking I had handled these ten or so years in teaching hospitals without internal damage. But then one day I was at a red light with someone in the car with me and a fire truck needed to get through an intersection. It started using that really loud, deep horn they can add in on top of the siren that was already wailing. As you know, if you have ever been right at the intersection when a fire truck used that guttural horn, it is extremely deep in tone and loud. As the truck was halfway through the intersection, this person said to me with annoyed impatience, "Is all that really necessary?" I first dropped my jaw, surprised at the callousness of the statement, as the person in the car with me was a nurse also. Then in a split second, before saying "Yes, it is!" I started having flashbacks of burned humans after burned humans, naked on that table being debrided, or arriving at the emergency department severely burned only moments before arrival. Then I actually could see the moment each was burned, trapped, screaming, fear and pain encompassing them as their body began to burn. I saw it all in seconds. Then, what actually came out of my mouth, maybe only five to seven seconds after their statement, was, "Hell, yes it's necessary! Every second it takes that truck to get through this light might be another second someone is burning alive," and I burst into tears for I saw the face of someone burning as I said it. I made it through the green light, pulled over, and let out years of tears from all the tragedy, stab wounds, gunshot holes, child abuse, suicide attempts, suicides accomplished, rapes, assaults, car accidents, first diagnoses of cancer found on emergecy department X-rays, and all the times I worked with and informed family members that their loved one had died; I could have listed twenty more. I didn't try to stop it, I let it out, and a few minutes later my tears calmed on their own. It lasted for a few more years, if I was at an intersection and a fire truck hit that deep horn, the siren alone wouldn't trigger it, but if I heard that deep horn I would cry again. I trusted my spirit was doing what it needed, and I never tried to hold back the tears. It stopped after a few years and hasn't happened again. I actively let those tears release as much as I could of what was inside of me, not just the burns. The fact that it took years told me I had seen too much.

An even greater request I have of you is to not isolate yourself from the support of others if the cause of dying or death is AIDS. AIDS has been a world issue now for well over thirty-five years. Almost every family in the world has had at least one death from AIDS. There should no longer be a stigma or a need to hide your head or dying family member in shame and isolation because of this disease, as was the case in the eighties and nineties. As I write this, the world is in its thirteenth month of the coronavirus pandemic. Worldwide there have been 112 million cases, with over 2.5 million deaths, and that number is still climbing daily.

Guilt can be a major addition to stress, so let's look at it again for a moment. I have had numerous calls the past six or seven months from family members telling me that they feel guilty about giving the coronavirus to someone who has died, or they tell me of a family member in crisis over feeling that responsibility. I always encourage people to seek a qualified counselor if the distress is affecting their being or life on any level higher than their normal responses to stress.

This pandemic is going to have lasting effects on so many levels to both individuals and society, beside the shocking number of deaths and debilitation it has and will continue to cause. Mass vaccination is starting, but too many more will needlessly die. The guilt in the people who initially downplayed its potential for political or monetary reasons is already starting to climb. I am so grateful to the people who are now speaking up via the media to admit they were naysayers initially but are now very sick or have experienced a sick family member, and are trying to tell people they were wrong and to take it very seriously. Thank you for your courage to say you were wrong in an attempt to help others. This chapter is about the emotional stress on caregivers, and every person who worked to prevent the spread of this virus is a caregiver. You are caring by giving your actions and energy to attempt to stop its spread. The anger being expressed from those who understood the magnitude towards those who did not is overwhelming. Picking and choosing elements of science is a double standard that is sad and painful to so many that have and continue to work hard, spending their life to help humanity through the sciences. A few months back I was in the next aisle in a grocery store checkout line, talking to a woman about seeing two people with their masks not covering their nose. She was visiting family from the East Coast, where she worked in COVID-19 research. She went into a monologue that summed it up, and I felt she had the right to: "My colleagues all over the world are putting in ten- to sixteen-hour days to find a vaccine to stop this relatively easy-to-not-spread killer. This did not have to happen like this, and the disrespect to science is so hypocritical. They want to follow the science to start and drive their car. They will follow the science to take a pill and keep their blood pressure down, so they don't die from a stroke. They will follow the science to heat up their coffee in a microwave, or to take antibiotics if they get pneumonia. They will even follow the science to take a pill if they want an erection, but they won't follow the science if it's going to cost them a dollar and cause them inconvenience! If this world had cooperated, we could have shut this virus down in months; all we had to do was not give it more hosts to kill and spread to."

I had never heard the duality of it all summed up so well. I had nothing to say, except to thank her for her time, knowledge, and efforts to help find a vaccine. I often think of the people around the world who had to dig graves by hand to bury their own loved ones or their neighbors. To the caregivers: from those who happily wore masks for self and others, to the millions of hands-on health care workers who risked, and lost, their lives every day to get us through this pandemic, I so very deeply thank you for the courageous giving of your time, knowledge, skills, and life.

Whether your guilt has to do with such feelings of cause and self-blame, feelings of inadequacy around the care given, the choice to not care for the dying in the home (which is not for everyone or every situation), for taking time for yourself, or because you have to continue to work, it is all unnecessary. Granted, easier said than accomplished. We have been trained from the time we could hear to feel guilt for what we have or have not done.

Again, I highly encourage you to realize that at any given moment in your life, you did the best you could at that moment. Hindsight is always sharp and clear, but we usually don't have that clear perspective when we are in the middle of the situation. When you look at a set of blueprints for a house, you can see all the rooms, but standing in the middle of a house, you cannot. Be gentle with the humanness of your being. You didn't give your husband cancer because there are additives in almost every food in the supermarket today. You didn't give your wife cancer because you worried about the home's financial situation. Your son didn't die in a car accident because you loaned him the car. Nor did he get AIDS because you didn't take him fishing more or make him go hunting with you. Guilt also is unnecessary concerning when or where someone dies. If your aunt with Alzheimer's screams every day to get out of the assisted living facility, don't feel guilty if that could not or should not happen for any number of legitimate reasons. Or, don't feel guilty if you broke away from your father dying to take a break, and he died while you were away. Each of these has been admitted to me in the past.

There will be times you feel helpless, and at times you will be. Don't beat yourself up over what is more powerful than you. Fear of hurting or doing the wrong thing can also paralyze one to do nothing. Trust yourself and your judgment; if you are still unsure, ask a professional or a resource within your health care team. Try very hard to be at peace with what today is, and what yesterday already was. The Earth is also too big of a ball for us to stop it from spinning.

The last tip I want to give is not to be overprotective to the point you will not allow others to give the care. I have known people who will go twenty-four hours, seven days a week, rather than give up the control for three hours to go to lunch and a movie with a friend. Yes, you are right; the other caregivers will not do things just as you have, but that is OK. Remember you will tear yourself down and give less than optimal care if you do not allow yourself breaks, even small ones. A few nights before my father died, I left his care to one of my siblings. I know they highly encouraged him to drink fluids, for his urine output had been minimal for days, but increased after they left for several hours that night. All is OK, they did what they needed to do, and my father was in a fine place of peace; I'd bet he drank for them and not for himself. That was the man he was: of few words, but wise or funny if he spoke, and he always put his family first. All is well if you return home and things are not as you left them; go get some you time anyway. I know I needed to sit in that cafe booth that night, have a hearty meal, and write for those few hours.

The reason this book is dedicated to "you, both the dying and the caregiver," is that you are both. The levels of difficulty for both of these roles will vary and shift at times. At times the dying will be at peace, yet at other times restless or frightened, and at times the caregiver will be at peace, and yet at other times knocked over.

Although Elisabeth Kübler-Ross's five stages of grief are key factors here, she states there is no set order or set rules to these stages. This is true for the emotional, mental, and physical stressors on the people assisting in the care of the dying and a person fast approaching their death. As with this rest of this book, this is a take-it-or-leave-it chapter. Each of us is very much an individual. What works for one may not work for another. Likewise, what is a stressor for one person may not be a stressor for someone else. Find in this chapter what will work for you and leave the rest.

Above all, if you are giving any level of love and care to someone whom you are close to, take care of yourself first. It is care of the self, not selfish behavior, and well deserved. At times, the mother lion must feed first.

CHAPTER 9

WHEN THE MIND DIES BEFORE THE BODY

"It is not the load that breaks you down. It's the way you carry it."
−Lena Horne, 1917-2010

"None of us want to be reminded that dementia is random, relentless, and frighteningly common."
−Laurie Graham, b. 1947

Back in the mid-nineties, I attended a talk on relationships given by one of the few married Buddhist Monks in the world, though I am sorry I don't remember his name. It was an amazing talk of his own personal experiences doing the hard, painful work of continuing to walk through marriage's tough moments with the belief you will make it through−and better yet, grow from the experience. He spoke of the tools to accomplish this−the vow of "till death do us part"−and reminded us of the many rewards that come with sacrifices and flexibility for our partners. He addressed the statistics of divorce rates and related an unstated percentage of that number to giving up and to our own inflexibility. He hit us with painful realities yet lifted us up to want to meet these challenges on a new level. There were about two hundred people in the room. As I looked around, I mainly saw what appeared to me to be self-questioning and self-judgment on the faces in the room. Most of the group I would say was over 45 and, according to his statistic, most people in the room were divorced. It appeared many were questioning his words in relation to their own lives. I was not using the great self-defense mechanism of projection, for I admit I was questioning my exit from past uncomfortable relationships that may have lost me an opportunity for growth. I was pulled back out of my own short attention span, and my mind's near-constant curse and blessing of humanistic evaluation, by him opening up the floor to questions. I was grateful someone asked a question because I was deciding, and gaining the courage, to ask my own concerning what I had noticed. I went ahead and spoke up in order to hear the wisdom in his answer, and I hoped it would comfort what I was feeling from myself and those around me. I asked, "Due to the fact that you mentioned the high rate of divorce, and therefore this room is filled with the people that make up those numbers, what would you share with us to help us not feel like failures or quitters, for not staying in relationships until 'death do us part'?" His answer was just as realistic and giving as his talk, and I watched the group relax and peace move back into their faces and posture as he answered, "There are many types of death before and besides the last breath of the body. If abuse is occurring, there is already death of the trust and respect of the abuser and death of the spirit of the victim. Infidelity and substance abuse create the same early death of the couple. If one must leave an unhealthy relationship to prevent further death of their being, they still fulfilled and honored their vow."

Though his answer touched upon the death of a relationship before dying, there are also other types of dying that occur before the body's physical death. My father's over eight-year battle with Alzheimer's, an all-too-common form of dementia, is a perfect example of the mind dying before the body, and always reminds me of that talk twenty-five years ago. Let me clarify, this is a metaphoric correlation, not a direct one;

one should not leave a relationship because their partner gets dementia. Quite the opposite, seeing that person to the end of dementia is what partnership is all about. I am only referencing the story because the mind can die well before the body. My father's sharp mind clearly died well before his body.

Dementia is only one form of death of the brain before the body; brain death can also occur from trauma, major stroke, or cancer. My father's mind definitely experienced a long, slow death over a number of years. My mother cared for him in their home for more than seven and a half years before placing him in a care facility for Alzheimer's patients. My father's struggle with Alzheimer's was fairly typical. Short-term memory and task-function loss at first slowly became greater and greater. In just a few years from onset, he was unable to dial a phone number, read, or find the right words. This advanced to an inability to find almost any word to communicate accurately, or to follow simple instructions for a simple task. "Dad, will you put this bowl on the table?" would result in him standing in the living room holding the bowl until you found him, or he might even place the bowl in the tub in the bathroom. This, from the man that knew the government and leaders of most countries around the world and could remember the cards played in a one-deck game of blackjack. He was the district manager for a pharmaceutical company and knew the first and last name of almost every internal medicine, family practice, and urology doctor in the southern half of Louisiana, Mississippi, parts of Alabama and a tiny corner of southeast Texas. He was frustrated and started to tell me so about four or five years into his eight-year run with the disease. In the end, his ability to coordinate food from plate to mouth had been decreasing rapidly for months, but he could still chew and swallow without too much difficulty.

About three weeks before my father died, he started to refuse almost all fluids and food. He would take only sips, mainly to wet his throat. He would periodically take a few tiny spoonfuls of yogurt, mandarin oranges, or something soft. But after two, or at most three, little bites he would say, "That's all," or move the glass away from his mouth. He said "thirsty" or "water" a few times after we brought him home, but he did not ask for food once that I know of. I would offer him both often. It was clear to us he could swallow but realized this was his only way out of his predicament. Towards the last week, he would not say anything to me except, "Is everything OK?" to which I would reassure him that it was. But he no longer said "That's all" if I offered him a second or third sip before moving the glass away; he would only turn his head to the right and tighten his lips, since I was standing on his left. He was clearly telling me "That's all" without words. I wouldn't push him; he had Alzheimer's for over eight years, not I.

Over the years, he said to various family members, "I am tired of this," "I want to quit," and he even told me when we were alone, "If it wasn't a sin, and what it would do to your mother, I would kill myself." Once home, he seemed to become very much at peace with himself, his choice, and his environment, rather than the restless man he was while in the care facility. Although at times he did become restless, sitting up, pulling at sheets, or when he had the strength the first few days home to wander about the house looking for my mother if she had gone to run an errand. But once we brought him home, he seemed at peace. He followed all my gentle requests, even showering when I asked him to while he still had the strength. Showers had become a problem at the facility due to frustration with the aides helping him. He had always been a measured, task-accomplishing man, he rushed nothing, except on the tennis court and having six kids in ten years. Nutritionists would have loved the slow pace he consumed his meals. I would bet they tried to speed up his showers, though I could be wrong.

One of my sisters told me she had gone to visit him a week or so before he decided to stop eating and drinking. The facility where he had been for only six months was for people with dementia, so it was secure. They went for a walk in the back outdoor area, which was surrounded by a tall wooden privacy fence. She clearly remembers him stopping every few yards and turning to assess the tall wooden fence, stating it was so obvious he was assessing an escape. He could not accomplish an actual physical escape, but he figured out his "escape" a few days later. It was my father who had taught me in high school, "Absolutely nothing in the body can heal or survive for long, without a periodic positive protein balance." He knew what he was doing.

With the rate at which dementia is increasing around the world, asking yourself some hard important questions will pay off down the road. Discussions with those close to you will also help; as well, they need to know your wishes. If the brain dies before the body, when is it time to let the body catch up? This is another question you will have to answer on your own. So at what point does it not make a difference what the annual laboratory work shows? This is a question I asked my mom about six years into Dad's Alzheimer's. His deterioration at this point was advanced—minimal communication, no longer understanding jokes or humor, and was sadly having increasing periods of agitation and anger. I lived halfway across the country during the years of my dad's decline, but I called her several times a week to give general support. On this particular call, she informed me Dad had his annual checkup the next day. I'd had their medical power of attorney for over fifteen years at that point, and she often asked me questions, so I felt safe in asking her why she was taking him for his annual appointment. She stated, "He might have rapidly advancing Alzheimer's, but I'm not going to neglect him.

Why do you think I shouldn't take him?" We had a discussion about the difference between neglect and allowing the body to catch up with the mind. She asked a few more questions and let me know she was going to keep his appointment and take him. I let her know I completely understood. A few months later, after further rapid decline of his dementia, she told me she now fully understood what I was saying, and that she wouldn't schedule further routine exams.

The brain's inability to perform necessary functions of survival is one of nature's ways of allowing the body to catch up to the brain's death. A basic example of this in nature is a coyote losing speed and night vision due to age; it will be a less effective hunter, and thus potentially die of starvation. I realize coyotes are also pack-hunting animals and would thus partially help feed the older and slower, and that we are not coyotes, but an illustrative example nonetheless. In humans, for the most part, we care for those who cannot care for themselves.

There are various schools of thought on this tender subject. Ask, "Will this choice improve quality of life or prolong this situation and delay the inevitable?" Answering this question for yourself is one thing, but if you are answering for another, then attempt to not answer for your own needs and fears, but for their situation and realities.

These are tough decisions for many; for others, they are not as hard. An even tougher and rawer part of these choices will lead to various family opinions and disagreements on what the answer should be. It has the potential to pull families apart, not closer together, especially if the critical decisions are at the present moment in an ICU waiting room. It's another good reason to plan and have open talks ahead of the need, to attempt to prevent your offspring from conflict at an already emotionally difficult time. I will discuss this more in Chapter Eleven, "Making Choices: Is It Suicide, Assisted Suicide, Murder, or Natural Death?" Again, making choices for the patient, not yourself, will greatly help decrease family strife as well. My observation of the two blatant driving forces of family conflict comes from too many family disputes in hospital waiting rooms and at the bedside: It is either ego when another family member has the authority over choices or an unwillingness to accept inevitable death for their own reasons.

This family strife reared its head when my mother was diagnosed with aortic stenosis a few years before she died. Aortic stenosis is the hardening for the aortic valve in the heart. My mother's early aortic stenosis had begun over thirty years earlier, because it was the first stenosis I had heard while practicing listening to heart sounds while I was in nursing school.

She did not care to do anything about it when I told her I had heard something abnormal; I even told her it sounded like a bad valve. Fast forward about thirty years and a new doctor takes a listen to her, and off the big ball of modern medicine goes rolling. She didn't want anything done thirty years later either, but allowed a few more tests and a cardiology appointment, but ultimately chose to have nothing done again.

Five of her six children accepted her decision, but one did not. This sibling pushed the hell out my mother to have the valve replaced, and eventually my mom asked me to talk to this sibling. My mother was 88 at the time, with failing health in a few directions. She most likely would not have handled the procedure and post-op rehab well, and she refused to go to physical therapy most days for even health maintenance. Her age was not the main factor; it was her inactivity. Later you will read of a man I knew who had his aortic valve replaced at age 90 and did fantastic. I confess, he was one of the few people in my life that my medical opinion concerning choice blurted out without thinking when he asked me if I thought he should have the procedure done. I am human, but you will hear later why it slipped out so fast.

Another time when choices need to be made around the mind dying before the body is one of the saddest and hardest times of death for all involved. "Brain dead" or "brain death" is when the brain completely dies before the body. It is most often caused suddenly by a traumatic accident or stroke that bleeds into the brain, and it is so traumatic for the family. The person will already be on a ventilator when this diagnosis is made and shared with the family. Because voluntary respirations stop with total brain death, without a ventilator, death would already have occurred. Patients are intubated after trauma or a severe stroke for several reasons, and the legal diagnosis of brain death requires some time; that is how this situation occurs. The tragic brain death of a healthy person is how organs are found and "harvested" for transplant every day. Families have the choice to allow this gift to others or not, and this too can sadly divide families periodically.

Due to age and age-related behaviors, most organs for transplant are harvested from younger people, who have been the victims of a trauma. If a person is in a car crash, say swerving to miss a deer on a back road at four in the morning with no one to activate the EMS system, and the brain dies in the accident, the body will also die quickly. But if this same crash occurs in town and a paramedic arrives on the scene quickly, and intubates and "breathes" for the victim who has no other fatal trauma, then a brain-dead situation will be presented to the family at the hospital.

Family members and loved ones often find the term "harvesting" upsetting, but the analogy of harvesting crops that will feed numerous people applies. Major organs for transplantation must be taken from a body with a functioning blood pressure and well-oxygenated organs. Otherwise those organs would die after transplantation into the recipient. The young person who died alone at four in the morning in the country-road accident cannot donate major organs, for those organs have also died. In order for organ donation to be possible, it is the job of the nurse in the emergency room or intensive care unit to keep the rest of the body "alive" until it is time to take, or "harvest," the organs. People who will receive the organs must be "matched" for the right blood and tissue type. The various teams will take the organs to different parts of the country rather quickly, and these are often transported by small private jets. At the same time one hospital harvests the organ, potential patients who have the same tissue type are being worked up in another emergency room to prepare to go into surgery to receive the organ. So many things must happen at once and relatively quickly; the legal paperwork and signatures from the family must be in order, to name just one. Once all is in place, the family gets time with their loved one to say goodbye. The donor is taken to the operating room, with the ventilator continuing to breathe for the person, and blood pressure is maintained. An organ must continue to receive blood and oxygen until the moment it is removed and prepared for transportation. This next step is done rather quickly, through with sterile technique, just like any surgery. First the kidneys, pancreas, and liver are removed, then the heart, and finally the ventilator is turned off and the lungs are removed.

Sadly, one person has died, but several other people, if numerous factors go well, may continue for more years of life.

The recipient of an organ transplant deserves mention as well, since they have a potential to not live through receiving an organ transplant at the time of surgery or the next few years after. Liver, pancreas, kidney, heart, and lung transplants are all major procedures with significant mortality rates even while the patient waits for a compatible donor. Mortality may occur as well as during the surgery or in the first year after the transplant due to the body rejecting the transplanted organ, and most transplanted organs live only five to ten years after the transplant, thus requiring another transplant to live further down the road. Every year the survival rates of recipients increases; these specialized teams are fantastic at what they do.

There may or may not be decisions for the family to make once they arrive at the hospital. Due to other severe injuries to the body, in the case of trauma, the body will often die even with resuscitation efforts. It is the same situation with stroke patients, if the pressure in the brain becomes too great. If the vital signs do stabilize, then you may have to make a decision to remove the ventilator to allow the body to die also. Depending on the situation, institution, and attending doctor in charge, you may not be asked to make the decision at that time.

To help you understand and be able to make an informed decision, let's clarify the difference between brain death and a coma. A coma is an unconscious or semiconscious state where the brain still has at least partial function. With brain death, the brain has lost all vital function. There are no cures and no potential reversal for brain death. A neurosurgeon cannot help or reverse massive brain cell death; even if the brain has been bled into, evacuating that accumulated blood from the brain will not change the outcome because the brain cells have already died. When the brain dies quickly, the choices are not easier but are often clearer than in slower brain death, such as my father's Alzheimer's. The time to stop or slow treatment with dementia and Alzheimer's will most likely be many shades of gray and not well defined. So learning to think about and have discussions now before the onset of these issues, with yourself or others, and creating a medical power of attorney, is so important. Talk about your personal standards of quality-of-life markers with these important, trusted people in your life, so you can know and respect each other's wishes. In only partial humor, one of my markers might be if I have Alzheimer's and you ask me if I want a piece of chocolate, and I say "no." That "might" turns into a definite marker if you give it to me anyway, and I tell you it tastes like liver and spit it out. If this happens, please stop taking me for my annual check-ups and laboratory tests.

Making choices around the need for resuscitation measures when the brain has died before the body is still a deep, heart-wrenching position to be in. Whether brain function is minimal from years of Alzheimer's, or there is no brain function due to brain death, the person's quality of life will not improve. I can tell you from personal experience that quality-of- life review helped me completely accept my father's choice to stop eating and drinking, and even further to not once say, "Come on, Dad, just one more bite." As I write this, I can still see him turn his head quickly to his right and close his lips tighter to communicate his choice to not have a second sip if he had accepted my offer for water. I'm grateful he and I had so many discussions about his choices before he ever had dementia; it helped me know what he wanted when he could no longer verbalize his thoughts. But even if we had not had the hard talks on and off over the years to learn what he did want (or did not want), all I had to do was "read" him for his needs, not my own, and then respect them.

CHAPTER 10

TRAUMATIC AND SUDDEN DEATH

IN SECONDS

The phone rings
You answer with a welcoming voice
But everything changes in the first sentence

You don't remember much
Half went to dark
Half went away

It was months before your voice returned
A year before you felt
Two before you forgot for a day

Although a part of you died too
You survived
Please live on for them

I want to start off with a beautiful story of the exact opposite of what this chapter is about because it is a fantastic lesson on how to prepare our youth for inevitable death. Age- appropriately answering all their questions is always the best practice. I once heard a great piece of child-readiness advice: "If they can think of the question, they can handle the age- appropriate answer."

I think my grandfather used such a wonderful tactic to help me prepare for the reality of his inevitable death. I share it with you as a balance of the exact opposite of the shock and non-preparation we get with sudden death. My grandfather did a great job of preparing me for his death. He lived to be 99, but he started to prepare me for his death early in my life. I would not be surprised if his talking to me in such an open, reality-based, softly descriptive, and preparatory manner had influenced my open acceptance of death from such a young age. I would say to him when I was a kid, some twenty years before he died, "Daddy Whit, how are you doing?" He would reply, "I've got one foot in the grave." Years later, "Daddy Whit, how are you doing?" "I've got one leg in the grave." Years later, he would reply to the same question, "I'm sitting on the side with both legs dangling." He was about 95 the last time I asked him, "Daddy Whit, how are you doing?" He replied, "I'm all the way in and just getting ready to lie down. Will you throw some dirt on me soon?" I had been a nurse for years at that point, and it dawned on me what a beautiful gift he had given me by saying that over the years. I remember our exchange to that last question of his. He had not only taught me to prepare for and accept his death; he had also taught me to talk openly about death. I said, "Daddy Whit, don't you want us to put you in a coffin first?" He replied, "I don't need one, but they make you do that now, don't they?" My grandfather, Luther Whit Yandle, 1891-1990.

No amount of "preparation" can prepare someone for the equivalent of being hit by a train, but if I lighten your shock even the slightest speck, maybe that train will only have forty- nine railcars behind it, rather than fifty. The biggest contrast between a slow chronic death and sudden death is the shock and lack of pre-grief, or time for the family to process the expected death of their loved one. It can be correlated to the difference between days to prepare for a hurricane and a millisecond to survive a tornado that forms directly over you.

One gives you time to brace yourself; the other thrashes and crushes your entire being.

Arriving at an emergency department where all you know is that your loved one is there after an accident is a horrible and helpless situation to be in. What will make it worse is the wait and the number of times you may hear, "We don't know at this point" and "We will have to wait." That is truly the honest answer to most major traumas. But I can share some tools, insight, and experiences for you to be more informed and aware of what is happening.

Removing emotions from the situation is impossible; I couldn't completely do that and would not want to, but attempting to stay in and work from the rational part of your brain will help you to make choices. This awareness will also help you to help others. In my years I have seen more traumatic or sudden deaths than any person should have to see. I refused to become calloused to the magnitude of its wide-reaching destruction beyond the life it takes.

Whether the victim dies or lives requiring major rehab, its traumatic effects will wave across families in every aspect of their lives. Over the years I grew to correct young interns, who found themselves bored in a rare slack moment, and only innocently wanting a hands-on learning experience would state, "We need a good trauma." I would quickly remind them there is no such thing as "good trauma," and that it often destroys or end lives, financially and structurally ruins families, and too often leaves someone with anything from paralysis to lasting decreased brain function. I would also remind them that without wishing a major car crash on anyone, the human tragedy will occur too soon anyway. I always welcomed those rare moments of breath and camaraderie; they meant the community was at a somewhat higher level of peace for a brief moment.

I use both terms to distinguish between something happening to the body (traumatic), such as a fall or crash, as opposed to something happening due to an imbalance on inside the body, such as a heart attack (sudden). As emergency nurses we see too many of both and use the simple acronym AEIOU-TIPSC to remember all of the big general causes of anything from a loss of consciousness to death. There are many variations of this acronym, and overlap and variations in what each letter stands for in different regions of the country, but most are pronounced "AEIOU-Tipsy"

AEIOU-TIPS-C:

- Alcohol, acidosis, ammonia (liver issues), arrhythmia (heart)

- Epilepsy, electrolytes, encephalopathy (or other brain issues)

- Infection, insulin

- Oxygen, overdose, opioids

- Uremia, or other metabolic changes, meaning the body's chemical homeostasis is out of balance

- Trauma, temperature

- Ingestion

- Poisoning, psychosis

- Space-occupying lesions, meaning a tumor or blockage anywhere

- Cardiac

Sudden death is not bound by age. I have seen people die as young as 18 with unexpected heart disease, and I have seen pulmonary embolism or strokes in as young as the late twenties. We all have greater probabilities of living long lives, but life is not bound by age alone; a little luck and preventative actions on your part play a role, too. Prophylaxis is not just having your teeth cleaned twice a year; it is a way of life to stay alive in this day and time, especially if the subject is moving in a vehicle with other drivers present.

I have always felt that communication with the family is a key part of the role of all nurses. If you are the trauma nurse, or you are the secondary nurse in the trauma room, try to keep that family posted. I know trying to get out to that family when the department is wide-open busy is not so easy to do, and at times you cannot if the department's acuity is critical, but when you can, do. To those waiting in the waiting room, it is heart-pounding and scary to sit there and not know, and the clock feels as if it is moving backwards, not forward.

The harshest reality I can prepare you for is also sharing the healthcare team's helplessness, too. The fate of the victim's outcome, whether they live or die, is not always up to the speed and competency of the EMS, emergency, OR, and trauma department staff.

Even if we do everything correctly and quickly, the outcome is a matter of physics and severity of trauma at the moment of impact from a car crash, or perhaps from the severity of bleeding into the brain from a stroke. An example is a car crash victim with multiple injuries that are not repairable before massive hemorrhage causing the patient to bleed faster than we can literally squeeze in units of blood, occurs before a trauma surgeon can repair the problem. Through two large IVs, and a quickly placed central IV line inserted into the largest returning blood vessel to the heart, we can put three units of blood in someone in minutes. So unfortunately, all too often the most I can do as a nurse is work with the parent's spouse, parent's, or children to get them through being hit by this shocking, life-changing, instantly appearing head-on train known as an unexpected death.

Even after all these years of walking into that smaller private waiting room where we often move the families of more critical patients to give them more privacy, it has never gotten easier for me to share shocking and painful information. But using that "cushion time," as I have always called it, is so important and has been the most helpful approach for many families. For both nurses and doctors, it is not easy to tell the parents whose teenager walked out of the house two hours ago they are now intubated, not breathing on their own, and have a severe brain injury. A percentage of nurses take the approach that it is the doctor's role to do this initial difficult communication, but in a very busy hospital and emergency department, the family may easily wait thirty minutes or longer for the doctor to come talk with them.

Please refuse to allow a family to wait in total fear and wonder. I have been doing this type of painful communication for years; in all those years, I never met a single doctor that was not more than happy to let me take on this role. Most even thanked me for handling it, so they did not have to, or when they could not break away from other critical situations. Yes, they too would go talk with the families once they had time. Just don't overstep information, and if you do not know, say so, but try to find out that answer for them: "I don't know the answer to that, but I will try to find out." Ninety seconds of fast and direct information to a family is better than another thirty to sixty minutes of filling in the blanks with their fear-driven emotions. Never stop putting yourself in the family's place, and never stop treating them like you would want to be treated.

If an unexpected major medical situation hits our world, it knocks us sideways no matter what. But here are a few gems that might help, whether you are the family or the neighbor driving a family member to the hospital. The first thing I suggest is something I have been teased about for years by my fellow nurses, but I promise it will make a world of difference. Encourage yourself and others to consume a drink that contains simple sugar; of course this is less for diabetics. I have given out truly hundreds of gallons of ginger ale in my career; I promise it helps everything. Soda, juice, or anything—just not diet. Crisis, fear, frantic action, and extreme worry can very quickly deplete the body of its simple blood glucose reserves. Many people think I am nuts for encouraging someone whose 65-year-old partner was brought to the cardiac catheter suite because they are having a massive heart attack to drink a glass of ginger ale and eat a few saltine crackers. However, it makes a noticeable difference and, as their sugar level rises and they finish the glass, I'll watch their tremors from shock and fear stop and the color return to their face. That person will exhibit a better understanding of what I am telling them about what we know happened and what we are doing for their partner. People who have consumed a soda, juice, or snack not only do not ask me questions that I have already answered but will ask appropriate questions. In general, their ability to give and receive information is much clearer with their blood sugar level greater than 70, as opposed to the lower lever they likely arrived at the hospital with. If I am talking to a family member on the phone and I have just notified them of a critical situation, I will even recommend they have a glass of something before they get in the car. It is dangerous enough you will be driving with a higher level of distraction and worry; hypoglycemia will only make everything worse. As well, I remind the driver to attempt to remain focused on the driving, as if that is their only task at hand, and not to talk or text on the phone to inform others. Yes, people do sometimes get in crashes on the way to the hospital; unfortunately, most have admitted to me it was their fault.

On the rare occasions when the drink was not consumed, it was rare that I did not observe one or more of the following: continued non-productive frantic behavior, repetitive questions, failure to understand a percentage of what was being explained, aggression toward the staff or other family members, or even uncontrolled worry in the parent at the bedside that directly increases the fear in small children who are also victims of trauma.

Providing this small gesture of a simple sugar to drink is not silly or inappropriate, but rather a tool that helps every aspect of this difficult nightmare of a situation. If you are called to the hospital regarding a loved one, and it is a major situation, please attempt to find someone to drive you there.

At the hospital, communication between you and the medical staff is crucial. This communication can be difficult for a number of reasons: lack of access to the staff, confusion over what you are being told, or a situation when there is nothing concrete to communicate– only "wait and see" knowledge. It is highly possible that you may have to wait some time until someone can inform you of what has happened and what is going on. If you haven't already called someone to come and be with you, now is a good time. If more than thirty minutes pass without someone coming to talk with you, it is time to ask, "I can see you all are very busy, but do you think someone can get away and talk with me soon?" Often when a trauma has occurred, it involves more than one person, and an entire team may be unable to get to you.

Though it is healthy to hope for the best, it is important to prepare for the worst in these situations, especially as more time passes. If you have been informed that CPR is in progress, every minute it continues, the greater the chance that the person will not live. Remember, brain damage is greater and greater with each passing minute of CPR. Once the team does enter the room to inform you, focus all you can on what they are saying until they are finished. If you do not understand what you have been told, ask them to explain it another way. Ask as many questions as you need to, but know that many will give an honest "We will have to wait and see" answer. That answer is the truth in those situations until sometimes days have passed if the person lives and is in an intensive care unit, or an autopsy is performed. Your health care team does not like not being able to answer your questions either.

The changes the body goes through after a major trauma are complex and very stressful to the body. Just because a person lives through the emergency department and initial surgery, they are far from being safe from death. The next few paragraphs are somewhat graphic, but remember this book is to prepare you to actually deal with dying and death when it is occurring. If death has already occurred, you will most likely be offered an opportunity to see the body. If you are informed, "You may not want to see them now," you may want to listen to that advice. There may be a situation when you are told, "You cannot see the body." Attempt to accept this and trust the staff. Another option provided may also be, "You may not want to see the body, but if you do, let me prepare you for what you will see." At that point it will be up to you to decide. If you are allowed to see the body of any post-trauma victim, be as prepared as you can be for a visual shock. Whether you are about to see your loved one alive or their body after death a nurse should always prepare you for what you will see before entering the room. I will start with what you may not notice: If your loved one has not been moved out of the trauma room, the room and floor will be a mess, possibly with blood on the floor, bed, and instruments. Hopefully much of that will have been cleaned up, but on a high-volume night, it can never be guaranteed. But the body of your loved one is what you need to be prepared for. There may be blood or vomit in the hair or on the body. No matter how much a nurse tries to prepare the body for you, it is very hard to get dried blood and vomit from hair without repetitive water rinses or cutting the hair. There will still be tubes in the body; this is because most coroners request all tubes be left in. That means you will most likely see one large tube from the mouth, another small tube from the nose or mouth, and IV lines that have been cut and tied or clamped and disconnected, and the urinary bag attached to the catheter may or may not still hang on the side of the bed.

On rare occasions, the family may need to identify the body for a positive name-to-body match. This is not always as clear-cut as one may think. I remember hearing about a case where two girls' identities had been mixed by no error of the health care staff, due to extreme swelling. One girl's death had occurred just after the accident; the other was in a coma for weeks before the families discovered it was not their daughter. This same thing happened in another case, but it was discovered right away when the parents walked into the intensive care unit. The misidentification had occurred prior to their arrival at the hospital. One family had gone through the shock of death notification, and then the joy of discovering the young man was alive. The other family painfully went through the opposite. This can and does occur for a few reasons. Females carry their identification in a purse which, for example, can end up far from its owner after a car accident, whereas men mostly keep their wallet in their pocket. Visual misidentification by a family can occur due to the extreme swelling that can accompany traumatic injuries, the disfigurement caused by the accident, or because the friends just look so much alike before the traumatic changes of the accident. You may be asked to identify the body either in the emergency department or, if the body has already been transported, in the morgue. The emergency department seems to be slightly easier for the family. It is a faster process, more people are around, and it doesn't require a long, painful, shocking, and scary walk down to the basement of a hospital or county morgue. Often in a morgue you will view the body through a window with an indirect low-intensity light. An even more shocking and painful reality is the identification may have to be made through body piercing, tattoos, or scars if facial features are gone.

If a major trauma has occurred and the victim survived past the emergency department and initial surgery, the first few days are still highly critical with a still high risk of death. This is an incredibly important time to use the tools provided to you in this book. Communicating and developing a good working relationship with the staff is imperative. The other tools we have discussed are to ask questions, drink fluids, eat, get away, and sleep without guilt. Be aware that the post-trauma body may still go through some major changes in the first few days and weeks. The greatest one you will notice is called "third spacing"; the body will become very swollen with water, so swollen you may not recognize the person. When I worked in intensive care, often the family would show me a picture of the patient before the accident, and often I could not make any correlation between the two. Even skin color cannot always help. Blood loss makes the skin so much lighter in color or tone that a patient's color appears so much lighter. When the skin is stretched with liters and liters of fluid moving into the tissue, it becomes lighter in tone due to the extreme stretching of the skin to accommodate that much fluid. If the family had to travel for a day or two to reach the hospital, allowing time for the body to swell from third spacing, it is not uncommon for the family to walk into the ICU room and say that is not their family member. But except for a very few rare cases of misidentification, it is their loved one; it is just the extreme swelling that occurs post major trauma.

This too was a difficult chapter to write, for I have spent years softening and attempting to protect people from this visual shock, yet here I hand it to you so raw. I deeply hope you will never have to experience any of this nightmare, and the inevitable, unavoidable death of friends and family will not be from trauma or in youthful years. I wish and hope that you will have time to process and experience pre-grief work with all deaths in your life. Preparing for our death and the death of others is something we should be doing a little at a time even before a terminal diagnosis or shocking phone call from an emergency department. For life is not bound by age, but rather by luck. For every day a capillary in our brain, the smallest of our blood vessels, decides not to weaken and bleed is a lucky day. Every day our body can attack abnormal cell growth, so cancer doesn't start enlarging, it is a lucky day. Every day we make it past every green light without someone flying through their red one is yet another lucky day. Do not fear these events with unnecessary anxiety, but do take actions to attempt to prevent them. I encourage you to drive a lot more safely, for it shows you care about yourself and the people around you. But please do not allow fear of near guaranteed future periodic tragic realities to take minutes from your life; rather joyfully wallow in this periodically muddy and amazingly long, yet short adventure known as your life even more because of its fragility.

Early death has no gifts, but the awareness and painful reality of sudden death can actually give us a gift, if we choose to receive it. The gift is gratefulness for life and letting go of its often-unnecessary struggles. It is painfully sad that it can take a diagnosis of cancer for us to stop and see this gift, or to stop being critical of those around us and release control, anger, and argument. Sadly, traumatic and sudden death removes that awakened richness a cancer diagnosis potentially ignites, so before that happens, accept the gift now.

Years ago, I heard a great bit of wisdom from a grounded friend of mine that shows another reason to embrace life and let go of the unnecessary. Take just one aspect of what is required for life to exist on Earth and it may help you embrace this day a little more. Just look at the perfect distance the Earth is from the sun and the perfect thickness of the ozone layer; alter these facts just a little in either direction and we would freeze or burn. Stretch, look up more often, raise your arms above your head, and bask in being alive today. We know that the Earth is made of the material of past exploded stars, and you are made of the elements of the Earth; thus, you are made of stardust. Embrace that you are alive and embrace your day, for you are made of the stars.

CHAPTER 11

MY FATHER JUST DIED

MY PARENTS MY VIEW AS GO I

As our parents their parents without choice planted without
choice tended or not
As they as you as I felt joy felt pain felt yes felt no
As I as they as you felt pushed felt pulled got hugged got hollered
As you as I as they had more had less once again had no say
As they as you as I had to start had to stop poor plan no plan
As I as they as you so sure so sure later realizing poor choices
As you as I as they did many wrong did many right learn some
repeat many
As they as you as I have been dealt ridicule and love
As I as they as you need want break build give forgive with hopes
to be forgiven
As you as I as they did better did worse
As they as you as I failed and succeeded
As I as they as you hopefully our best always with yet failures too
My parents my view as go I
(I wrote this poem in 1994. A time that seemed to me to be the peak
of adult children blaming their parent's for a greater percentage of
blame then sometimes deserved.)

I just reread the first page of this original chapter for the first time in twelve years or so and I had a great cry. I've softened since I first wrote this book fourteen years ago; I think time and a few more mistakes in life helped me with that. But I admit I was surprised by how clinical I could be about my own father's death. Below you will read only a slightly softer version, but I promise I'll keep it close to the original so this paragraph makes sense. This is also because this book is about cutting to the chase of what you need to know about dying before death and our healthcare system in relation to the same. It was good to cry again; death for the most part creates lots of tears when it involves those we love, and the magnitude of grief definitely directly correlates to how much we love that person. Laughter followed as I thought for a moment that I should include a chapter about Easter baskets and puppies, just to give us a break from the heaviness of the subject. Nope, no puppies; back to the heavy.

I will continue to use my parents and experiences as it is the closest reality of mine that I can give you. By sharing their experiences, it removes the slight distance of the clinical stories I share and creates an equal correlation to the loved ones you have and by whose deaths you will be affected. It is my way of making sure you know I am not just a third party in scrubs, but I was in my jeans and untucked, too-long, too-large, button-down shirt. My lips also trembled, and tears poured down my face, too, as my parents were taking their last few breaths before leaving me forever.

Please do not think I have become calloused to dying and death. Quite the opposite—I promised myself in 1983, when I started nursing school, not to ever become calloused to the tragedies of what I would experience in the wide scale of humanness that will pass before me. Nor would I deny myself the human emotional response to what was unfolding before my spirit, either. I could not have that emotional response at the moment of tragedy, because nursing is very task oriented and there is no time at that moment to allow our harsh emotions to obstruct professional and rational thought and task. I mainly worked very high-volume departments, with well over two hundred patients per day. Even if we just had an unrestrained child die from a car crash, I had to head right into another room and care for someone having trouble breathing or active chest pain that needed to be in the cardiac catheter laboratory ten minutes ago.

But I would process the healthy normal human emotions on my drive home, or a little more on and off the next few days. If our emotions are one of the main ways we experience and explore this expedition called life, why would I want to lose such a huge portion of life's experience by denying myself the percentage of emotions that are not the happy or joyful ones? To only welcome or allow the fun and easy emotions I feel would be cheating myself. It is better if we do not always act on these emotions and remain in our rational thought process rather than our emotional thought process to decide and act. Yet, I still want to experience the opportunity to grow from the painful emotions as well as the ones of joy. Anger is the most perfect powerful example. Anger is a natural emotion, but what you choose to do with anger should only come from having processed it in our rational mind. How many fewer instances of child abuse, shootings, stabbings, and domestic violence abuse would I have seen had anger remained in a rational controlled place?

This book may not have been written had I not cared to feel the pain of so many deaths. I may have moved these painful feelings and tragedies into a rational place to share with you, but cold and calloused I am not. Trusting, yes, and now I again tearfully share with you my father's moment of death.

My father died in his own bed, two weeks to the day from when we brought him home. He was basically unconscious his last two days. As I described earlier, his breathing was just slightly labored those last few days, and a little more the last twenty-four hours. He mostly did what is known as Cheyne-Stokes breathing, which is a shallow-rapid pattern followed by pauses in breath of ten to sixty or more seconds. For the last nine hours, his breathing was a little more rapid without pauses. His body was trying to compensate for the buildup of acid that had occurred inside his body from the dehydration, malnourishment, and poor respiratory effort. This happens when the respiratory system is trying—but is not able to—balance the acid within the body by rapidly exhaling carbon dioxide. So I knew the end was near. My family had spent the day on and off spending time with him, but they happened to all be in the living room at this time, because I had just given him some personal care. My mother kept asking me for "a report on Bill," and by watching other signs I could tell her when he was getting closer to actual death. The pulse in his wrist was gone, but the one in his neck was still there but weak; this told me his blood pressure was very low. His pupils were no longer reactive. His color was just beginning to change in his lips, and his skin was becoming colder by the minutes. I went into the living room to inform them, and my mother asked again for "a report on Bill." "I don't think it will be more than thirty minutes," I said, "an hour at the most." My family was too frozen to move or speak, so I went back into my dad's room and saw his color was very bluish-white, and he was lightly gasping for breath rather than the rapid breathing. I went back out and told them, "We don't have to wait that long." Mom, three of his four daughters, two grandchildren, and I surrounded him and sat on his bed, and touched or held him. He gave a few more minutes of breaths and stopped.

The rest of my father's body just died.

Except for me, everyone stayed with him until the funeral home took his body about an hour and a half later. I stepped out to call and deal with the authorities, the funeral home, and Life Legacy, the research foundation to which we donated his body. I had a letter from his doctor stating that my father had been a patient of hers since 1999, that he had recently been brought home for end-of-life care, and that she would gladly sign the death certificate. If hospice is not used, which we did not, it greatly helps the authorities feel comfortable about agreeing there was no foul play. After the investigating officer read this letter, their normal slight suspicion that there might have been there about his cause of death was gone. The officer was very polite and professional; he made a call, explained the situation, and the on- call county official then released the body to the funeral home. I talk a lot about having the paperwork in order; it pays off. Because we did not involve a hospice, the letter from my father's doctor covered and alleviated potential questions or complications that could have arisen. My father had not had pain or anxiousness, so narcotics or sedatives had not been used. My mother and one of my sisters had remained at the bedside; both were tearful, but also shaky and pale. I brought them both a glass of iced soda and gave them no choice but to drink it. They did, their color returned and their shakiness went away. When the funeral home arrived, I was outside to greet them. My mother had told me she did not want to see them remove his body from the house. I met them outside to handle any paperwork and to go back inside and give my family the choice to go to another room or to stay. Some went with my mom to a back room, and some stayed.

Two things happened that I would not have thought about when I walked back into the room with the funeral home to remove his body. They were not little things to my sisters, though; I could see that. Although completely covered, he had on socks, soft, well-made, disposable-plastic, fluid-catching underwear—a diaper, I should say—and a nice pajama top. As I walked into the room with the funeral home director and his assistant behind me with their stretcher in tow, one of my sisters said, "Aren't you going to put some pants on him?" I said, "No, but I am going to keep him wrapped up nice and warm in both his top and bottom sheet." That did the trick for her, she was OK with that. It also made it much easier to move his body onto the stretcher. I could tell the funeral home people appreciated that move, too, with two daughters and a granddaughter watching. I helped the two of them lift his light body over for increased ease and gentleness. The next difficult moment for the family standing in the room was whether or not to cover his face. I was learning now, too. In the hospital setting, when family is present, we uncover the face, but during transport the face is usually covered. The funeral home director handled it great; he arranged the stretcher cover so that right when he rolled out the door onto the driveway he reached up and covered Dad's face. Wrapping my dad's body in the sheets on the bed was a spur-of-the-moment thought, but looking back it was a sweet one in other ways also. It made moving his body a more gentle and smooth process. It also helped my sisters feel as if he were covered and "warm." It also solved the problem of the sheets "that Dad died on," as they were now gone, and so was my father.

I had been his primary caregiver for only two weeks, but that day, the next day, and the next two nights, I felt and slept like I was old Jell-O. My father died a natural death. He chose to stop eating and drinking, and weeks later his life and over eight years with Alzheimer's ended. He died at home, surrounded by family, with his body, hair, and mouth clean. He died in his own bed, not on a hard plastic hospital or hospice mattress. Of further gentleness, he died without being stripped naked, given chest compressions, having drugs injected, or having electrical shocks sent though his body. I am proud of my father's courage to walk past his limited remaining shell, and equally as proud of my mother and my family for granting him that peaceful end of life and death.

Yet again, tears and shoulders shudder that I care not to stop until they choose. The monster known as Grief has come back to play with me fourteen years later. Welcome, my friend, for your power to shake our core is equal to our love for those who have died.

CHAPTER 12

MAKING CHOICES: IS IT SUICIDE, ASSISTED SUICIDE, MURDER, MANSLAUGHTER, OR NATURAL DEATH?

"The best way to find yourself is to lose yourself in the service of others."
–Mahatma Gandhi, 1869 – Assassinated, 1948

"I see that the path of progress has never taken a straight line, but has always been a zigzag course amid the conflicting forces of right and wrong, truth and error, justice and injustice, cruelty and mercy."
–Kelly Miller, 1863-1939

We make choices throughout our lives, often with fears, doubt, awkwardness, and guilt. These factors rarely have a greater influence on us than in the area of dying and death. The choices and decisions we make are both for ourselves and others, and I can promise that making choices concerning your own demise and death are so much easier than the extreme burden of having to make them for others. I can also promise the choices you make for yourself will affect others, for they most likely will be seeing your wishes and choices through for you at the end of your life. This burden of decision can be enormously eased by becoming informed and by talking with the person and knowing what they want before their almost inevitable demise, unless sudden death occurs first. You are taking a huge first step by reading this book and becoming informed on choice, and by creating the legal paperwork of taking care of this unpleasant, uncomfortable, but necessary task.

There are dictionary definitions for suicide, assisted suicide, manslaughter, and murder, but not for natural death. I did find the dictionary used the term "natural death" as an explanation and example of "natural." There are also clear-cut legal definitions of the terms, but neither the courts nor the dictionary have determined the absolute definition of "natural death" that I could discover.

Let's begin by looking at these definitions Dictionary.com:

Suicide: The act or an instance of intentionally killing oneself.

Assisted suicide: Suicide accomplished with the aid of another person.

Murder: The unlawful killing of one human by another, with premeditated malice.

Manslaughter: The unlawful killing of a human being without malice or expresses no implied intent to cause harm.

Natural: Conforming to the usual or ordinary course of nature: a natural death.

Again, let's use my own experience with my father as an example, during the last days of his care. I don't know if my father's active choice to decrease his intake of minimal fluids and food was because he was tired of not having a mind or life, or because Alzheimer's had taken away his drive to consume foods or even feel hungry. He certainly would not, or could not, tell me his reasons, even though I asked him a few times the first few days. Whichever it was, the key was that he was not taking the food or water himself. His water intake seemed to be for the purpose of wetting his mouth and throat only. I say this because the first week he was only taking one or two sips. Then he would put the glass back down or hand it back. At that point, he could still roll onto his side or sit on the bedside without help and reach for his glass and sip; I made sure it was always present and full. Consuming yogurt or Jell-O was even worse, and while he liked mandarin oranges, he would sometimes slightly cough or choke. I would say the coughing was due to both the Alzheimer's, which had inhibited his ability to swallow, and the progressive dehydration that was also making swallowing difficult.

One of my sisters had a great idea; she suggested we sit him at the table and see what he would do if given the opportunity to feed himself. We did that with a bowl of yogurt and another of mandarin oranges. He had about six difficult-to-coordinate partial spoons of the oranges. Then, without saying a word, he slowly, gently, and quietly moved the yogurt bowl to the side and looked up at me, expressionless. The next day I did it with Jell-O; he did about the same. I had been spoon-feeding him also. I would ask him first if he would like to eat, but I would not say "one more" when he told me "enough" or "last one," which he could still do the first few days. My sister thought of the "sitting him at the table" as a litmus test to see if he wanted to keep eating at all. Remember, because of his Alzheimer's, he was almost completely unable to verbally communicate. I also had to be careful because sometimes he would say "yes" when he meant "no" and vice versa. I think this because I would ask, "Dad, do you need to go to the bathroom?" or "Dad, do you want to go sit in the living room with me?" and he would answer, "Yes." I usually would hold both his hands and walk backwards while leading or guiding him. Although he had said "yes," he would drop my hands and walk back to bed if we were getting close to the bathroom or living room. So I would assume that really was not what he had wanted to do in the first place. I am sharing all this to let you know what an unclear or fuzzy line even supposedly simple tasks and choices can be. The definitions may seem clear-cut and black and white, but real life is instead complex, fuzzy shades of gray most of the time. I hope this chapter will help you form your own answers and bring up some new questions.

If you have religious beliefs, they may influence your views about the subject of this chapter. However, I strongly encourage you not to allow your religious beliefs to completely discard this chapter or book. I am not going to consider religious views in writing this chapter, out of respect for the fact that each reader will have different beliefs. I have had too many people over the years express their fears, doubt, and guilt over this subject not to include this highly controversial chapter. I say this because one common view about death is that God gave us the abilities of modern medicine, so we are not going against God by using them.

However, there are just as many people who believe we are going against God by not accepting the natural death of someone and trying to keep them alive when God is trying to take them. Views vary from religion to religion, and from person to person within one religion, and many do allow religious views to influence their death. That, I respect. I also caution all of you to respect the views of others, and I would note that just because someone's views do not align with your own, does not mean their views are wrong. I feel respect is indeed a highly appropriate common icing that should spread wide and far across this subject.

To reference a rule of thumb that I personally have used to help me decide if death is natural, one way is to look at nature and human death before modern medicine. How did we as humans die before medicine started to attempt to postpone death? How do non- domesticated animals die in nature? I used to say humans and our domestic and farm animals are the only living thing on this Earth that are sustained by another living being when they cannot feed and hydrate themselves, but this changed once I saw a YouTube video of a monkey in India pulling another monkey, which had been electrocuted in a train station, out of the water to resuscitate it by roughing it up, and it would not stop. It was so moving; this monkey looked quite dead, and the resuscitating monkey did not stop its efforts for some time before the monkey revived. Also on YouTube, I once saw a dog keep trying to splash water on a fish dying on land. But aside from these rare exceptional cases, if a wolf is old or breaks its leg, it will die because it cannot hunt or transport itself to water. Its death will be fairly fast, even if not taken by other predators. It will become partially malnourished, but mainly it will die of dehydration. It will not be a long, drawn-out process because dehydration occurs much more quickly outdoors. In the past some Native Americans, once they were elderly and felt they were ready to die, would find a place that was meaningful to them, create a sacred circle, and sit in that circle until death. Some would do this alone, but many had the support of family and spiritual leaders, with ceremonies. Whether dying or not, dehydration occurs rapidly outside, and even faster with wind added to the mix, whereas dehydration in a closed-up, modern-day home, with insulation, can take much longer. The Native American way and these amazing people of various cultural beliefs have much to teach us about life, community, and respect for the fragile environment that sustains our very life.

Having found some clear definitions for suicide, assisted suicide, manslaughter, and murder, now let us compare these with the definition of "natural" that uses "a natural death" as its example. First, suicide is defined as intentionally killing oneself. Is allowing a natural death "killing oneself?" If someone has heart disease and knows the heart condition is fatal without medicine, is it suicide if they choose to stop taking the medicine? Without the intervention of the human-made/synthetic chemicals, the heart would naturally decrease or stop having functional beats. If a person with cancer has had chemotherapy for a year and is tired of the nausea, the pain, and the wasting of body and says "no more" to the chemo, is that suicide or natural death?

Our culture is very uncomfortable with suicide. It forces us to create a sense of guilt and even embarrassment, whether it is from a mental health condition, terminal illness, general chronic illness, dementia, or the natural expected decline in geriatric years. According to both the Center for Disease Control and Prevention and the National Institute of Mental Health, many people headed towards a suicide attempt will give indicators, such as increased substance use, aggressive behavior, withdrawal, dramatic mood swings, impulsive or reckless behavior, collecting and saving pills or buying a weapon, giving away possessions, tying up loose ends, organizing papers, paying off debt, and saying goodbyes. Please reach out for help if you or someone one you know is showing suicidal statements or indicators.

Unfortunately, someone's suicide is not always preventable, and it is extremely rarely the fault of others. The family members and friends of a suicide victim were not the ones experiencing the mental and emotional pain of that person's mental illness, their physical pain of terminal disease, or their limited life function, nor the one experiencing the fear of a near and inevitable death.

Unfortunately, the rate of suicide in adolescents and the middle age have sadly rapidly risen over the past twenty years. The painful and yet understandable short-sighted blinders of adolescence, acute episodes of mental illness, and overwhelming despair deny those in crisis the vision to see a better tomorrow. Attempted and accomplished suicides are all too commonly seen in hospital emergency departments. This book is meant to deal with imminent death, and if someone is having suicidal intentions and has formed a plan, if not detected soon enough, imminent death may be the outcome. There are so many wonderful organizations out there attempting to prevent suicide; the National Suicide Prevention Hotline at 1-800-273-8255, and NAMI, the National Alliance on Mental Illness, do fantastic preventive work through sharing their stories and through prevention talks in schools and other groups. If you call

NAMI, 800-950-6264, they will help you find or arrange such a talk. There is a texting hotline that the younger generations seem more comfortable using, and replies are from humans not computers: The Crisis Hotline at 741741. NAMI also puts on talks for family members of those with mental illness to help family and friends support those with mental illness on a higher level. One of the main goals of NAMI is also to alleviate the stigma of mental illness, which is important in this era, since it touches every family in the world in one way or another. NAMI was the first recipient of support from The Yandle, John D., Sheehan, and Daigle Foundation, also known as "The Human Bonding Foundation," to which 20 percent of all gross sale proceeds of this book will be donated.

My personal question: Why is autism one of only a few neurological and mental health conditions diagnosed on a spectrum? If we remove our self-protective filters and get painfully honest with ourselves, we all may fall onto the spectrum of one or two diagnosable neurological issues or mental health conditions. Let me attempt to clarify: Autism is a neurological condition and not a mental health condition; however, there seems to be overlapping information and confusion because it is also often listed as a mental health condition, and I have also seen it listed as a developmental disability. One could also have a neurological condition that causes symptoms of a mental health condition, such as Lewy body dementia, also known as Lewy body disorders, which also include Parkinson's disease dementia, depression, anxiety, hallucinations, and paranoid thoughts, to name a few. I recently read its severity also can be placed on a spectrum. With Lewy body disease, protein deposits cluster and build throughout the brain, so a neurological issue presents itself partially as a mental health condition. Robin Williams' autopsy revealed extensive Lewy body formation. What is important here is whether brought on by a diagnosable neurological condition, mental health condition, or just the normal imperfections creating strengths and weaknesses known as the human condition, all minds will have limits and imperfections.

I am going to use autism as my personal example of how our minds can place us all on a spectrum in one category or another, but I could give more than one example of a spectrum I could land on. Accepting that the human mind is not a perfectly formed computer program is one of the first steps to working with the powerful mind's guaranteed imperfections. Improving and working to strengthen those normal imperfections makes each of us beautifully unique with amazing special talents, weaknesses, and strengths.

Sometimes I feel I am undiagnosed but on the spectrum of autism, and I am not ashamed to admit it. I think it is part of the reason I have trouble not keeping some of my thoughts to myself within today's standards of decorum. I admit that I also had to learn, and still am, how to hold greater eye contact. I watched a beautiful series recently about people with autism attempting to find love and to learn the basics of a healthy loving partnership, and to value the thoughts and needs of your date or partner. Thirty minutes into the first episode, I had to stop and be honest with myself about my weakness according to social standards in my relationships, and some of the mistakes I made in the past that damaged relationships.

These wonderful, amazing people, who answer questions with remarkable honesty, helped me be honest with myself first. I did not, and cannot now, deny I have many of the same challenges they face. This series can help every one of us learn to do a little better job of stepping out of ourselves in all relationships.

Since this chapter includes suicide, and suicide and all mental health conditions are on the rise in our society, I feel putting the cards on the table face up is important to help decrease the stigma of mental health conditions and help decrease our climbing rates of suicide. I also know the issue of suicide from the inside, as in the seventh grade I tried to kill myself. I am to this day so grateful I failed; life is hard, yes, but also truly an amazing gift, experience, and exploration. I grew up with extreme learning disabilities and migraine headaches, and both were only getting worse. They culminated in the seventh grade, when I was pushed to the edge by a teacher who openly picked on me in class. The night before, my mother, whom I had informed of the ongoing issues I was having with this particular teacher, attended a parent-teacher conference and informed this teacher that although I could read just fine to myself, reading out loud was a great struggle and embarrassing challenge for me. The next day in class this teacher said out loud to me, "Vincent, why didn't you tell me you couldn't read?" My heart and spirit sunk to the lowest level of my present 57 years of life, and I collapsed inside of myself. I was already at the bottom of my class and had already basically missed the first seven years of school. Just after dark that night, I took every pill I could find in the house, including the roach tablets under the kitchen and bathroom sinks. One of my sisters found me, and I woke up the next day in the ICU. I am so grateful I did not succeed, and that I learned from that desperate act to remove my layers of pain, insecurity, and feeling of educational hopelessness. At the age of 12, I realized nothing and no one is worth cutting short this painful yet amazing gift of my short life. I had no trouble accepting and working with my weakness and strength-filled mind after that.

In addition, about twenty-five years ago, I had another milestone in accepting and working with my limited human mind. A buddy of mine was having a situational crisis, which means an internal or external event causing a crisis in life, function, or thought. We were talking and I recommended finding a counselor right away, and I shared with him that I had sought out counseling for situational crises in the past a few times. When I am upside down in life or situation, or have dug myself into a hole and I am foolishly still digging, a trained, unbiased third party opinion is a wise tool for the professional human to seek. This person was up for the idea and asked me if I would help find a counselor and go along, and they admitted they had never done such a thing before.

I made some calls, and the next morning I was sitting in a waiting room and my friend was in a first counseling session. To pass the time, I walked over to a display that had a pamphlet for each of the top maybe ten or more mental health conditions of the time, such as bipolar/manic depressive disorder, depression, obsessive compulsive disorder/OCD, schizophrenia, narcissism disorder, compulsive behavior, alcoholism/addiction, sexual addiction, borderline personality disorder, and a few others. I took them back to my chair and noticed on the back of each pamphlet was a ten- or twelve-question test to help you evaluate if you may have the disorder. I thought, "Take the tests and be honest; you have an hour to look into yourself, just like your friend is doing." I didn't reach the five or six yes answers required to lean towards a diagnosis of the disorder, but I did have a respectable number of yes answers. I took the pamphlets to work with me and asked a bunch of people I work with to take the test and just tell me if they had more yes answers than they thought they would.

Predictably enough, except for the one person I would say leaned heavily towards narcissism, every single person jokingly or seriously admitted they were surprised how many yes answers they also had. About six months later, one thanked me for showing them the pamphlet and admitted they too had sought counseling.

This milestone, as I call it, was humbling and yet brought me great peace, comfort, and acceptance, not only in myself but in all the humans walking their paths next to me or crossing mine. It was also at this time that I realized all mental health conditions should be on a spectrum. This awareness and acceptance of humanness also placed my judgment of others on an even lower level than I already worked to keep it. For some reason it also helps me want to look out a little harder for my own hypocrisies and double standards, that all humans have just by the nature of our inconsistent and self-protective minds. Just as with my suicide attempt that turned my life around, this awareness and honest confession made my life easier, not scarier.

Assisted suicide is defined as suicide accomplished with the aid of another person. This is another area where fear and guilt can get in the way of the care being provided. I quickly discovered the most difficult part of making decisions is family unity on the plan, and whether or not they feel as if they are "assisting." I have a sibling who even brought up the subject of a feeding tube for my father, for fear we may be "starving him of nutritional sustenance." This sibling's concern was, "Are we denying him sustenance when his body can still process it?" It was a legitimate question. My answer was that his body cannot process it; he cannot swallow, and he is choosing not to. The reply was, "But what if we got it past the obstruction, meaning his throat" (I remembered thinking to myself but not saying, "But his mind is not an obstacle; it appears to making a clear choice") "with a feeding tube, would not his intestines still absorb sustenance?" This sibling said, "When someone has an airway obstruction and cannot breathe, you give them a tracheotomy, right?" I replied, "Are we talking about a 19-yearold or an 80-year-old who has an eight-year history of Alzheimer's, who can no longer communicate, and who chose on his own to stop eating and drinking weeks ago?"

The discussion did not really go much further. I also referred them to Mom, since she was his primary medical power of attorney.

Murder is the unlawful killing of one human by another with premeditated malice. A look at the definition of malice will make this even clearer.

Malice: A desire to harm another or to see others suffer extreme ill will. The intent, without just cause or reason, to commit a wrongful act that will result in harm to another.

So, according to these definitions, if an act is to be deemed murder, it must have the elements of being committed with a desire to harm, see another suffer, or have ill will for the other with intent. **That is the exact opposite of everything in this book**. I hope it is also the opposite of any intent in the action we do to help another die a peaceful and as pain-free a death as possible. To get slightly more technical, we could discuss the topic of manslaughter, which is "The killing of a human being without malice or expresses no implied intent to cause harm." For example, an intoxicated driver who kills someone they do not know, hate, or have a motive to kill has committed manslaughter, not murder.

The main reason for bringing up this last subject of murder and manslaughter is I have been asked so many questions concerning over supplying pain medication to their loved ones. "But what if he/she stops breathing from the pain medicine?" I have been told by cancer patients that they "only thought the pain was bad" until it moved into their bones, and then they "knew it was bad," or "it made the other cancer pain feel like a tickle." Pain medicines can cause the breathing rate or effort to decrease. However, decreasing pain medicines will cause increased pain, and if patients have been on opioid pain meds for a period of time, withdrawing the meds would most likely cause narcotic withdrawals. There are no easy answers here, but guilt and fear are obviously a reality, or so many would not have discussed this with me. My advice has always been the same chant you are hearing throughout this book, to answer these questions for the patient, not for ourselves.

If you cannot alleviate yourself of such an internal conflict and burden, ask yourself this question: Will I feel worse letting them live in pain or die without pain? Appropriately treating pain by following prescribed dosing is doing the right thing. Before you answer the question, "Live with pain or die without pain?" please remember the medicines are not given to decrease the breathing; the medicines are given to decrease the pain. Ask yourself another question when you think your loved one is in pain by the grimace on their face, or because their pulse rate is high, or because they are moaning or crying out. If the person still had the strength, ability, or level of consciousness, would they reach over to the bedside and take some more pain medication? Please try not to allow fear or guilt to stop you from giving the pain management the dying person needs, deserves, and has been prescribed. Just do not give a greater amount or more frequently than prescribed.

All of these choices are hard enough for people to make even if they feel confident they are doing the right thing. What can make it even tougher is whether or not other family members agree with each other about how the end-of-life questions and issues are handled. If everyone is on the same page, it makes it so much easier because the burden is not on one person. However, when the family does not agree, it adds more pain and stress to an already very difficult time. Two things must be respected here. The first is that family opinions will rarely line up and be in total alliance. The second should supersede the first, and that is the patient's wishes. I knew that no matter what my sibling thought about a feeding tube for my father, it wasn't going to happen, because my mother was still alive to say "No," and she had the final word. Even if she had not been there, I knew I had been given my father's medical power of attorney before he was diagnosed with Alzheimer's, and I had asked him his wishes. I had been explicit about potential situations that could occur, and he told me he did not want oxygen and feeding tubes when he was end stage and near death. He, like most people, said "no" to every intervention I asked him about, except medications for comfort. My father protected and cared for me his whole life, and I was going to show him the same level of protection when it was my turn to care for him.

Another thought and feeling that a different sibling shared with me during my father's last days was, "If it had just been me, I would not have had the courage and strength to not have placed him on oxygen and give him the feeding tube." I reminded that sibling we are honoring Dad's wishes that were stated seven years before he ever had Alzheimer's. Her reply: "I am just telling you, Vincent, if it were just me, I would not have been able to stay strong and hold out. I would have placed him on oxygen and a feeding tube, placed him in a hospital, and visited him every day." It had been thirteen days since we brought my father home. I respected the honesty and trust in me that this sibling expressed. My mother and three of my five siblings told me that it was hard that his death was so slow. My reply to them was, "Even with oxygen and a feeding tube, this stage most likely will still happen just weeks or months from now, and if we had employed oxygen, nutrition, and hydration, this stage would have been painfully far longer than this." That "painfully" I just wrote would have been much longer for all involved, but much more actual physical pain for my father first and foremost. When I pointed out to my sibling that even with turning him every two hours or so, my dad's bedsore had opened slightly after just thirteen days, and that it would get nothing but worse with each day, especially without protein to help it attempt to rebuild tissue to heal. This sibling again said, "I am just telling you I would not have been able to last this long, and I would have placed him on oxygen and a feeding tube. I would have not been ready to let go of him; he was my buddy." I appreciated the self-honesty.

This is why I reiterate over and over to pick someone who will follow your wishes to be your medical power of attorney, and stand up to those who for whatever reason want to ignore your wishes for their own reasons and emotions. As you can see, this sibling even stated it was for their own reasons. I feel they believed what they were feeling was love. But it is a clear example of a decision made for one's own fear and needs rather than concern for the patient's well-being, wishes, and comfort before imminent, inevitable death. I have seen family members often willing to prolong a loved one's pain and discomfort rather than deal with their own fears and discomforts of watching the end process of dying, as well as trying to avoid their fear of the pain of grief.

I am grateful when those family members aren't the ones steering the ship. I will never forget a very elderly woman I cared for during one of my handful of years gaining experience in the intensive care unit back in the early nineties. This woman was very elderly, in her mid- nineties, and was sent to the emergency department by the nursing home staff since she did not have a DNR, and she started to show the normal signs of approaching death. She had been in a nursing home for many years without proper therapies, such as physical therapy to keep her moving or to prevent contractures, which at its worse extent is the tightening up and contracting of joints until the person lives in a fetal position on their side, and joints can no longer be extended. She was so contracted that her knees were permanently near her chest and could not be straightened. This woman had no ability to verbalize except moaning. She would moan and grimace when moved for elimination cleaning or every few hours, as should always be done for anyone in bed; when we moved her to be stuck her for labs, to restart an IV, and even her daily bath caused her to moan. Her medical power of attorney was her only son. Although he would only visit her on Sundays for minutes, he kept telling us to do "Do everything." It was about halfway through her second month that the staff, including physicians and hospital administration, started to attempt to get the son to allow us to move her into hospice care. He was not going to allow it and kept threatening to file suit if she did not receive "the best of care," and he kept saying, "Do everything." She was intubated and placed on a ventilator shortly after arrival from the nursing home, and he pushed for tube feedings and began to verbally escalate if anyone attempted to talk to him about her realistic condition. She spent over three months in that ICU before dying; we gave her the best care possible, called her by her first name, and combed her hair often because it was the only time she appeared at peace from the time she arrived in the unit. She did not die alone; we were really great about this in that ICU. But she did die with much worse bedsores than she ever had to have, even with turning her every two hours, because her nutrition status was never going to promote healing with how many factors were working against her. She died after having multiple unpleasant procedures carried out daily, intubated, on a ventilator, and, yes, we did do a round of CPR and compressions on her frail little chest. All because we had to. To this day, I have never seen or participated in such disrespect for a body trying to die.

It is so important to not delay openly discussing with your family what your wishes are, and to have that paperwork drawn up by an attorney, or someone certified or knowledgeable to do so. Each state, even county to county, can have different policies and procedures for protecting your rights for "out-of-hospital do not treat or resuscitate" orders. Learn to talk openly about your end-of-life wishes, and the wishes of those close to you, since one day you may be making decisions for them. Attempt to learn to say the words "dying" and "death" with openness and comfort. Even if you are married, make sure you pick a backup or two for your medical power of attorney, and make sure it is someone who will respect, follow, and protect your wishes. There is always the chance your spouse will die first. The second half of the statement is the key: Pick someone who will "follow and protect" your wishes, not just "respect" them. If you are not married, the authority will most likely be your parents, children, or siblings. I now know that I am unsure whether or not I could trust two of my siblings to follow my wishes.

When the family does not agree, decisions will first go to the spouse, then to the person assigned to be the medical power of attorney, then to closest family members. It is a pyramid of authority that may change from state to state. It is hoped that no one will start contesting this authority in the courts to gain control of your decisions once you can no longer state them. Accusations of incompetence or motivations for selfish gain or foul play will be thrown on those with the medical authority by those that want it. All of this is so unneeded and stressful when death is imminent and inevitable anyway. The pain of death without legal and family strife is a heavy burden on its own. Courts, accusations, issues of control, and power struggles at this trying time again can show that decisions are being made for other individuals, not for the dying person.

Let me also be realistic about how difficult this can be in reality, as opposed to the ease of just writing these words in a book. My two siblings who wanted a feeding tube and oxygen for my father had created a further stress issue beyond several verbal questionings, and this was something that my mother had to pay for in a way. Thank goodness my mother was still alive and could "put her foot down," as she said, and ended the conversations relatively quickly. But still this would have been an unnecessary strain on her. Her husband of fifty-six years was dying in their home, and she had to have that stress added in, not to mention the second-guessing it caused her. She asked me a few times after their statements if she was doing the right thing. I would only ask her back if she was respecting Dad's wishes, and that would reassure her for a period. She realized she was doing the right thing for her husband and got comfortable again. Had she not been alive, having the medical power of attorney would have placed the decision on me, and I would have stood my ground. If the courts had been involved, that would have been tougher. My heart is with you, and I wish peace, strength, and wisdom to be with you if you are faced with this level of conflict or challenges by a family member, forcing these types of decisions at an already horrible time.

To protect yourself and others at this time of your life, in most states there are four different legal issues you need to understand: An out-of-hospital DNR for the EMS system, medical power of attorney, do not treat, and do not resuscitate (DNR). Although there is a difference between a do not treat and a do not resuscitate, they may at times be one document. It is very important to understand that various states, and even counties/parishes, may have different types of out-of-hospital DNR regulations and documents. Consulting an attorney in the past was one of the only ways to get these documents created, but this is no longer so. Most hospitals now provided this service, and there are businesses that do nothing but create legal documents for end-of-life issues. These services are not as expensive as attorneys, but are usually just as safe and well-versed in the salient law of their state. In choosing your medical power of attorney, it is important to consider first who will respect and stand up for your wishes. Other considerations include someone knowledgeable in medicine, who has strong communication skills, and is available.

The difference between do not resuscitate and do not treat is that in a do not resuscitate, if your heart, breathing, or blood pressure are no longer supporting life, then no or limited procedures will be done. A do not treat defines levels of treatment for various levels of limited function or diseases. This can be as direct as not giving antibiotics if someone develops pneumonia or a urinary tract infection, or as minimal as not having a PSA level checked to screen for prostate cancer in a 96-year-old man with lung cancer. We have all known elderly people who at some point stopped going to doctors. This is a choice that should be respected. Just because we are not ready to accept their mortality does not mean they have not accepted their own mortality and feel their lives have been full—or painful—yet complete.

Although paperwork may be in place or ideas shared, it is a human inalienable right to be able to change our minds, both as the dying and the caregiver. Not all situations or feelings can be predicted. Attempt not to feel bad or guilty if your own views change or if you have to alter the plan of care for someone for whom you are responsible. If possible, yes, stick as closely to that person's wishes as possible. But if the plan must be changed, be gentle with yourself and others if you or they don't completely follow through with the wishes of the dying. What makes it easy for me to say and feel this is that I don't think my father would have wanted me to beat myself up had I placed him back in a hospital. Though clear answers are rare in these situations, be gentle with yourself and others, as that gentleness is most likely what the dying person would want.

Again, try very hard to start talking about dying and death with your family, friends, and loved ones. No, it will not be easy at first—none of this is—but start and continue, and it will cease to be a fearful and hush-hush subject. We as a society seem to have a false belief that if we do not talk about death, it won't happen. It is going to happen; you just have to decide if you want some say-so in how it happens.

CHAPTER 13

MODERN HEALTHCARE'S SUPPORT AND FEAR OF NATURAL DEATH

"A problem cannot be solved at the same level which it was created."
—Albert Einstein, 1879-1955

WHEN

When will right prevail
Not self
But right

When will choice
Be for the good
Not the gain

When will more
Be seen as less
Will less be seen as enough

When will I
Become us
Before us is no more

In all the hospitals across this country where I have worked, I have encountered many beliefs in reference to allowing a natural death. I have asked a great many of my colleagues about their beliefs concerning death and dying, and more specifically on the actions that are carried out during near imminent death. For the most part it is easy to summarize: "When I hit my late sixties, I want to have 'do not resuscitate' tattooed on my chest." I've met a handful of colleagues with other varying perspectives, but truly the tattoo statement echoes from the majority. In the late eighties I did some overtime in a Catholic Hospital that wouldn't allow a natural death, no matter the circumstances. But even the Catholic Church has started to accept both natural death and cremation. The most prevalent belief is that more people should be allowed to die without medical interventions during the final stage of life. This means do not intubate, do not give chest compressions, do not shock, and do not give cardiac drugs if death is imminent with a DNR. A few believe we should do some interventions, to see if there is a response or improvement from the intervention. The rarest, and rapidly fading, belief is that it should not be up to the medical field to decide and that we should do all we can with all that is available. But the one most common statement made by so many health care professionals, unsolicited, when unnecessary or futile interventions are in progress is, "Don't let them do this to me if I am ever in this condition!" Actually, it has been practically a chant that I have heard over and over.

So why does the healthcare field do the things they do at the point of imminent death?

Because we must! We fear the family, or just one family member, who does not accept the inevitable death of their terminal or elderly family member. This, ultimately, means we fear the legal system. To be even more specific, we fear the attorney who will bring a lawsuit against a doctor or hospital for not "doing everything possible to save Grandma" in her time of natural death, in an attempt to "save her life." These litigations, along with the huge percentage related to gravity being a constant, have been a huge contributing factor to the total costs of health care to all. These civil suits are also a contributing factor to unnecessary pain and suffering caused to those of us trying to die a fast and peaceful death, but the healthcare field must legally protect itself from these unwarranted huge costs.

The sad truth is that a great many medical lawsuits involve "to code or not to code" situations. This is why having the proper legal paperwork is so important. For the most part, the medical team does not desire to do these procedures and disrespectful actions to a person whose death is imminent and unavoidable. But rather, the medical field requires legal protection, so they are forced to take these actions when natural death is imminent. The good news is that changes are slowly occurring. Until the late 1990s, the EMS system would "code" obviously dead people in the home to legally protect themselves, and to supposedly make the situation easier for the family by "doing something" and removing the body from the home. Many counties and states now protect the EMS system and allow them to contact the coroner or medical control to have the person pronounced dead. Many have gone even further, appropriately allowing the paramedic to make the decision to not start CPR or to stop, and they deserve that authority, not only because they see a shockingly huge number of deaths, but also their training, knowledge, and experience could easily prevent a family from days of drawn-out ICU false hope, as well as save the family huge unnecessary expenses. The body can then go directly to the funeral home, not have resuscitative measures performed, and not be taken to the hospital or county morgue. This also prevents the family from receiving a larger bill from the EMS system or any billing from the hospital. Another welcomed change in the past thirty-five years so that hospitals no longer run all codes for that archaic golden rule of twenty minutes if the resuscitation efforts are having no effect, as was the case when I was a rookie in 1985.

In rewriting the above paragraph, I just traveled back to my first three years at Charity. I will trust you with the core of my being right now. I do this to validate my healthcare sisters and brothers, who I know for a fact also have too much stored inside of them from far more than futile coding of the elderly. It was extremely hard to repetitively be a part of that physically disrespectful and highly futile abuse of a very elderly person who deserved a calm peaceful death, with zero chance of remaining alive. I was very young and very clinical and did not see or feel how hard it was at the time. But like all the terrible things we frontline hands-on workers see, touch, hear, small, and sometimes taste, it goes in and gets stored somewhere in our mind and spirit.

Furthered research has allowed us to stop if the heart is showing no response to the resuscitation efforts, depending on the situation. Due to increased awareness and teaching, more and more families are saying "no" to unnecessary efforts. Also, most hospitals have policies to ask patients or family members during the admission process about "living wills" or "advanced directives," so wishes in proper legal form can already be known and added in the chart, and thus respected.

Unfortunately, too many of us, doctors and nurses included, are still uncomfortable talking about, or even using the words, "dying" and "death." The word has even left our vocabulary for those not in the healthcare field: "Passed" has replaced "died." I've noticed friends of mine that have worked in the healthcare field say, "My Dad died last year," whereas all others will say, "My Dad passed last year." Children have a hard time grasping the permanence of death due to many influences, including these euphemisms. Another influence on our youth are their video games. No one ever really dies in their video games; a new game brings back those they killed, including their own character. I have known parents who partially joke they are scared to teach their kids to drive if they have been playing

Grand Theft Auto. They fear their young kids can't separate reality from video games and will actually act on their "game thinking," that it would be cool to drive on the sidewalk, hit a person, or earn points for hitting another car.

We in the healthcare field take oaths at our graduations to be "patient advocates" and to first and foremost "do no harm." Accepting inevitable death and providing for as pain-free and dignified a death as possible is how we accomplish one aspect of that oath. When we allow the opposite of this comfort and dignity to occur unchecked, unchanged, and unchallenged, then we are doing harm and we are not being the advocate for patients who are unable to speak for themselves. Think about the gentleman in the first chapter who wanted to go home and die, but his family told him he was staying and was going to get better. I almost got in trouble for trying to be his advocate.

I can promise you the great majority of individuals who make up the modern healthcare system want you to have a peaceful, painless, and respectful death. Doctors do sometimes make decisions to allow uninterrupted natural deaths that do not meet the standard of strict legal protection for themselves and the hospital. I have known numerous wonderful caring doctors who have the same feelings once death is unavoidable. At the same time, some doctors will make very conservative decisions to be legally protected at the time of obvious irreversible death. Appropriate paperwork and the right legal guardian, or next of kin, is the only near-total assurance that the healthcare team can allow this peaceful, respectable, natural death to occur.

A concerning subject I have heard spoken too often in sarcastic humor from the general community, but never the healthcare field, is that of lost income if inevitable death were more widely accepted and more natural deaths occurred, especially at home. A frequent question I hear when giving talks to small non-healthcare groups is "Could the medical field not want to let go of the profit involved in these procedures and admissions?" Whether the administration of the hospital is looking at the hospital's profit and loss and salaries, or the individual doctor is looking at billing for procedures and visits, we are indeed talking significant financial numbers. I initially wrote "financial loss," then changed it to "financial numbers," because I am not so sure there would be a loss for two reasons. As I stated earlier, if we accepted death once inevitable, then there would be more available time and money for prevention, early detection, and faster intervention once an issue was discovered.

Furthermore, is it a "loss" if more people are allowed to die with greater dignity and respect, in their own beds, over health care profit?

Addressing this issue is admitting there is an elephant in the room. Not addressing it is accepting the status quo of modern medicine and equals telling the public, "Let's not talk about that right now." Because I do talk with the non-health care population so frequently, I hear this subject all too often. These people want to talk about it; they already know some hospital system CEOs make over $10 million annually, and that several top administrators under them make $2-5 million annually. They already know hospital reimbursements come from a huge percentage of insurance and Medicare/Medicaid; they know the system is tilted off kilter and that every one of us pays for that through taxes, insurance premiums, and self-pay. I can't believe how often I hear these numbers stated. I did not put this elephant in the room, but I am just not going to look the other way, so let's talk about the elephant. As balanced as I am to both praise and to point out areas we all can improve, how do I defend such CEO numbers and public awareness? The opposite side of overpay is society's begrudging of the salaries paid to physicians, and those salaries are in some areas a part of the problem, but not in others. I really feel for the doctors; they tell me they too hear it, but it is usually in the form of a quick sarcastic comment from a patient in reference to billing numbers—the standard line of, "Well, I guess they needed my help building that new back deck," in reference to the cost of having a heart catheter, double root canal, or surgery on a dog performed. Dentists and veterinary doctors deserve to be included here, and they often have it worse. I really feel for our doctors of dentistry and veterinary medicine; it is as if society feels they do not deserve even a reasonable profit for all their many years spent learning to safely care for their patients or your pets, or respecting their equally high cost of operation.

The one place the general public feels needs to be beefed up is hiring more nurses, and I agree. One person at a talk I gave years ago had already done the math: "If a CEO gave back a chunk of their salary to hire more nursing staff, maybe I wouldn't have peed on myself because no one showed up after I hit the call bell several times." He went on to say something else I agree with: "More of both nurses and nurse aides, too, could be hired with the ridiculous salaries CEOs are paid; the aides are an equal part of the team, and I did not need a nurse to be pulled away from someone doing worse than I. A nurse's aide would have helped me just fine." This person was mad, I mean really mad, and of course I validated him. I hear the same complaints from nursing staff, too: "I don't need more money; I need more help." This is the most common nursing statement I hear when they are discussing CEO salaries. I have heard that statement from nurses too frequently for thirty-five years.

I have never been one for blaming another without attempting to accept my portion of responsibility for the problem also and then moving to solutions. I say "attempting" because my human ego is often my own worst enemy and is highly capable of overusing my defense mechanisms. This can prevent me from seeing the amount that I have contributed to a problem in my life, the environment, society, or economics. We have become a society of blame over solution-based discussion, which makes it too convenient not to accept our share of responsibility for any given problem. Yet we must be realistic; very few complex social problems have only one answer. The many sides and issues of complex problems such as our healthcare industry will have many correct answers from all directions. There is no question that compromise from each of those directions is always a part of a balanced and sustainable answer to almost any issue. Therefore, as scary as it is to write, both we as the health care consumer and those seeking huge profits must accept our parts in resolving the high cost of the health care crisis.

We all know we all pay for frivolous lawsuits against the healthcare field. If I fall one day during an admission to a hospital or assisted living facility, I am asking my family to please not bring a civil suit against the facility because gravity is a powerful constant. Whether I was confused with the side rails up or fully oriented with the side rails down, and even if I die due to the fall, please do not file a suit. I do not want to be a part of this bigger-picture problem. It is not only the defending and payout of these civil actions that run up our health care tab. Those civil actions create a huge down-the-road cost to all of us, because it creates a massive amount of "preventative medicine" expense. I place "preventative medicine" in quotes because it's not the good type of preventative medicine that prevents an illness in a person. Rather, it is "preventative" as in preventing liability exposure to civil suits. I can promise you a percentage of the tests and procedures that are done are for the purpose of not only diagnosing, but also to hopefully protect the doctor and hospital if a civil case is started. Back in the 90's I had a one-frame joke on the outside of my work locker that was a man sitting on a doctor's exam table; in the sketch he is holding out his finger and the doctor is looking at it closely, and the doctor was saying, "It looks like a papercut, but let's run lots of test to be sure." Sadly, that joke is not only making fun of the healthcare field, it is also taking a jab at unnecessary liability exposure costs to protect the physician.

It is not only the lawsuits that contribute to your high costs of health care. We know so much about wellness and nutrition, but too many of us choose to ignore what we have learned, and the healthcare field constantly attempts to teach us. I will again include myself and admit my hypocrisy. We know for a fact that processed sugar and animal fats both are highly unhealthy for us. I have decreased my intake of them both, but I can not seem to stop completely. It is extremely well researched and documented that both animal fat and processed sugar work on the same pathways in our brains as addictive drugs. Rats in the laboratory even show the same behaviors over fat and sugar that rats show when they are addicted to opioids. Our choices to ignore so many well-known facts of wellness greatly increase the time and financial drain of our healthcare system. These blatantly dismissive behaviors are literally killing us, and diabetes and cardiac issues remain way too high. But I can't seem to walk away completely, and it is one of the stronger self-disappointments. As hard as it is to hear, we all can add to the problem or the solution. Exercise is not different; it offers only personal benefits and decreased cost to all of us. Then when we do have a diagnosis presented to us, we often want a pill to fix it, rather than the lifestyle change to resolve this issue at its origin with much fewer side effects to the patient and expense to us all.

The statin drugs, which decrease our cholesterol levels, are the perfect example. A few years ago, my cholesterol came back a speck high on my annual exam. My doctor wanted to place me on one of the statins and was surprised when I said no thank you, and that I wanted to fix the issue at the core of the problem, which was my behavior, not taking a pill. Not only did I not want the potential side effect of the drug, but I did not want to unnecessarily have my insurance company, which ultimately translates to you, the premium and tax payer, to have a further financial drain. By changing the root of the problem, my behavior, rather than adopting a surface-only Band-Aid fix, I created a wider win-win for the bigger picture.

If my father had not come home to die and had spent those last two weeks in a hospital, what would the costs have been to both you, the payer of insurance premiums, and to my mother? It is hard to give an exact number, as it depends on the level of procedures we would have allowed had we been there twenty-four hours a day to say yes or no to an option. But in two weeks of even floor care—not ICU—the bill easily could have ranged from high, to very high, to painfully high, or much higher if we had not known to keep him out of the ICU. Few insurance policies or Medicare or Medicaid reimbursements would have covered 100 percent of the bills—that's "bills," plural, because you and I both know the radiology department and the radiologist, the pathology department for every lab drawn and the pathologist, and any consulting physician or service also may have billed. But because we kept my dad home, the healthcare field received zero from my father's death. We did not even call in hospice because I was his hands-on caregiver.

I do want to give credit here to the many physicians, nurses, and administrators who are such strong advocates for respectful and natural death. I often refer to the modern healthcare system as a large rolling ball with its own strong, forceful momentum. Yet there are other forces behind that large ball. You the patient, health care providers, healthcare institutions, the government, the legal system, and insurance companies all play a role in this huge moving mass. I have known many wonderful health care providers who wish nothing more than for modern medical care to reach the people worldwide without discrimination on race, gender, religion, or the ability to make a dollar. They too are tapping and pushing on that powerful rolling ball of medicine to try to slow its speed and force towards realistic health care for all. But so are the people and institutions who are out for money, including the pharmaceutical companies. Whether near death or not, we all must work to help the system control the skyrocketing costs of our health care.

Profits must be made by our modern healthcare system and providers, or our institutions and individual caregivers will disappear. To deny profit is unrealistic and would be the inevitable death of any system or business and would not be realistic in our system of capitalism. I absolutely do not want to make a political statement of any sort, but could we at least learn from other health care systems around the world? If 60 to 70 percent of health care dollars are spent on the last six months of life, then this book is the place to address the subject. How can that money be diverted and put to better use, rather than being spent to prolong imminent death? This is a huge question with many multifaceted answers; if all parties have contributed to the problem, then all parties can help in turning it around. One suggestion for consideration is prioritizing preventative surgeries and early diagnostic testing, instead of X number of dollars going to admitting terminal or advanced dementia patients to intensive care units. Instead of spending X amount on chemo and radiation therapies once they show no signs of helping, those dollars could be spent on precancerous screening for breast, uterine, cervical, lung, testicular, and prostate cancer to allow for greater treatment success rates because the cancers are detected and treated sooner. Or divert that money for more safety research and driving-impaired prevention education, so we have fewer brain- dead teenagers from which to harvest the organs. We have already greatly reduced teen deaths through spending money on prevention; why stop now? Part of those same saved dollars could go to education to prevent the tobacco, food, and alcohol abuse that creates the need for the lung, heart, or liver transplant in the first place. How many years will it take, just as it took so many years to get a warning label on tobacco products, before sugar is treated and labeled as the pretty, tasty, yet poisonous substance we know it is?

The toughest and most sensitive area to mention are the beautiful innocent prenatal infants and babies born with major neurological and organ malfunction. Here my only thoughts are in prevention. We could start by spending the money for more and earlier ultrasounds and amniocentesis, to provide parents with earlier knowledge of these potential major complications. I wish parents and guardians all the strength and courage they need to make these tough choices. As well, my hat is off to the neonatal ICU nurses who work with this situation day in and day out; they are the bravest of the brave. They make emergency and adult intensive care nursing look like a cake walk. I wish more nurses would speak up about what they see and deal with in their fields, as their views are invaluable in redirecting our healthcare field. I always say, "Families go home, doctors write the orders then walk away, and the nurses and nurse aides stay and do the work, cause the unfortunate pain that goes with hospitalization, talk to the patients and family members for long hours, and answer most of the questions."

I want to thank the literally hundreds of patients and family members over the past thirty-five years, while in hospital or after discharged, who said to me something along the lines of, "The doctors were great, but it was the nurses and nurse aides who really did the hard daily work, talked with and reassured me, and got me through my illness; thank you for what you do." You are very welcome; it was my, and is all of nursing's, pleasure and deepest reward.

Ultimately, it is important to remember that we are all tapping and pushing on that great rolling ball of modern medicine and are contributing to how the dollars are spent. We as the patient or family member who makes the decisions move that ball more slowly or quickly by our choices to do, or not do, and also by your expectations of the healthcare system. So many, from funeral homes, to family members, to ourselves, try to put a monetary value falsely correlating to our level of love in relation to our loved one's death. Funeral homes are masters at correlating money spent to our level of love for the person who has died. We also feel the same way about procedures in the hospital. Tracing back to the issue of guilt, even with death imminent, family members have told me time and time again, "I would feel horrible if I didn't have you all do everything possible."

I deeply hope this gives you the knowledge to empower you, not just for end-of-life choices but for all of your health care choices. Even this painful morally and ethically charged chapter of how your decisions affect our financial healthcare tab should empower you to ask questions and take back a little more control of your own health care choices. The non-acceptance of near death of a family member can financially ruin a family and potentially harm a nation's ability to continue to provide already highly expensive health care to the living. I recently heard of a family without insurance that had an older member die of COVID-19-related complications. This person was in the hospital for only forty-eight hours, and only twenty-four of those hours were in the ICU. They received an initial bill of approximately $100 thousand dollars.

This subject is precariously perched with many factors pulling, and pushing, the purse strings. I say "pushing" because we as the sometimes-unrealistic health care consumer, or as originator of so many lawsuits, as people who fail to take care of ourselves with all the factual knowledge we too often ignore, must accept our contributions to high health care costs as well. Every last one of us, from CEOs to me with my love of small Coca-Colas in glass bottles—in every direction, we are all responsible for the cause and effect to our troubled healthcare systems.

CHAPTER 14

GENERAL COMFORT, SAFETY, AND PAIN

"It is said that time heals all wounds. I don't agree. The wounds remain. Time—the mind, protecting its sanity—covers them with scar tissue and the pain lessens, but it is never gone."
—Rose Elizabeth Fitzgerald Kennedy, 1890-1995

Much of the following information is from my clinical experience through talking with patients and from administering pain medication thousands of times. I was taught in nursing school that part of the definition of being a professional is constant review of what you are doing and constant evaluation of its effectiveness. Pain control has always been a very important issue to me. My father, who was a district manager for a pharmaceutical company, gave me a button in 1986 that is the international sign for "no pain." It has the bold word "pain" in black on it with the red circle around and through it. I wore that button every shift—and I mean every shift—for twenty of my twenty-one years in bedside nursing. It is amazing the number of compliments and comments this button elicited from patients and family members. It also conveyed to people that I did care about their comfort and would actively work to decrease and, in some cases, hopefully alleviate their pain.

Unfortunately, I have also been the cause of their pain; IVs, tubes, and catheter placements unfortunately cause pain. Much of what happens in a hospital cannot be controlled. At times we can't control how long patients wait to be seen or go to a test, or whether or not a chemotherapy round works to reduce a cancer growth. We can, however, actively attempt to decrease or alleviate pain.

There are several sources for the information in this chapter. While much of it is common medical knowledge about pain medication, a great deal of the information is from what patients and their family members have told me about their experiences. Some of the information is from my clinical observation of the effectiveness, or ineffectiveness, of different medications and from observed and informed side effects of the drugs. If after taking a certain medication patients repeatedly told me they were nauseated, or I repeatedly held a bucket and placed a cool cloth on patients' necks while they vomited from this medication, I reached certain conclusions. These direct observations are another basis for the information found here. Please note, I am only sharing general information; I am not suggesting what medicines you should take or how to take a certain medicine, as that is the role of the physician, physician's assistant, or nurse practitioner. No two people are exactly the same, and what works for one may not work for another. I encourage you, with knowledge and guidance from the healthcare field, to be your own judge and research technician and the pilot of your own medications and health care.

One of the reasons I have spent my years of nursing in teaching hospitals is that information is constantly changing. I absolutely love learning about the human body, and despite what we may know one day, we learn the next that research has discovered something else about that drug, procedure, etc. Research and development never stops because medical knowledge is constantly evolving; most medical books have some obsolete information in them within a year or two of publication. This book is not an exception. It is one of the reasons that when one works in the healthcare field, especially a teaching hospital, "I know that!" should not be in one's vocabulary. The reason is that how something is done one day most likely will eventually change, hence the term "practicing medicine." This leads me to another old saying I have always appreciated, "Constant change is here to stay."

Throughout all the years that I worked in level-one emergency departments, I never forgot that a medical school student, who could have been four years old when I started nursing, may have just read the latest article and have important updated knowledge to share with me. I always loved working in the hospitals where it was a two-way street, and nurses and doctors taught each other. I love learning about the human body, and I want to keep learning what is new—and so should your health care provider. Always ask questions if you have them, such as these: Is there a different medication we should consider? Is there another medication that will cause fewer side effects? Is there another way this medication can be administered? Does it come in a patch for continuous release? And so on. The goal is to provide greater and more effective comfort and pain relief for each individual.

A perfect example of changes in treatment is the pain medication known as Demerol. Until around the turn of this century, Demerol was the most frequently used hospital pain medication, but it caused horrible nausea and vomiting. Unless someone was allergic to it, Demerol was essentially the only IV pain medication I gave for fifteen years. Now, many hospitals do not even stock it. It was shown to have dangerous and uncomfortable side effects, to be less effective, and not last as long as other pain medicines. In my clinical observation, it also caused as much or more nausea and vomiting than morphine. The shift led to morphine, fentanyl, and Dilaudid being prescribed more. Each medication very much has its place and can be very effective. This is also true for the pain medicines in pill form such as Vicodin for low-level pain and Percocet, Oxycontin, and Dilaudid for greater levels of pain.

Before diving into pain medications, it is important to understand the difference between pain that is bad and pain that is good. The separation of these two is paramount for pain management, getting off of pain meds after surgery quickly, and the speed of rehabilitation progress after surgery or injury. Yes, pain can be good. It reminds us we are alive, and it reminds us we have been injured to humble us and to prevent injury or illness in the future. Even emotional and mental pain means we love or have felt loved; it means we have feelings and emotions to explore life and self, and it means we are breathing and not dead. Pain is only a nerve transmission; it is literally only chemicals moving in and out of the micron space between millions of nerve cells in a line between what hurts and your brain.

Pain is only a message that is sent from somewhere in your body up to your mind, unless it is an actual reflex. Reflexes don't actually go all the way to your brain; they only go to your spine, then shoot back to the extremity that withdraws from the hot burner in a fraction of a second. But your interpretation of pain really is only all inside your head. Now, I have fractured bones three times in my life, and I know pain can hurt really badly; I am not calloused to severe pain. When experiencing pain, I ask myself whether it is good or bad pain. Bad pain is not to be ignored, and can come from physical, mental, or emotional trauma; this pain also occurs when your body is trying to tell you there is something out of balance or an injury issue that needs advanced attention. Bad pain should hurt; it is that pain that hopefully motivates you to seek help. Good pain, on the other hand, means the issue has been fixed, is healing, or you are preventing illness before it occurs.

A frequently occurring trauma that is a great example of good vs. bad pain is someone falling and having a hip fracture occur. Not always, but frequently, that means a break in the neck of the femur bone just before it goes into the socket/joint of the pelvic bone where it sits and rotates as we walk or stand. One has severe pain because the outside of bone is wrapped in nerves, and broken bone edges are either pinching those nerves, if it is a small fracture, or have torn them and are poking those nerves and other tissue structures, if a major fracture has occurred. This is bad pain, and one must seek attention right away; this pain is the body saying, "Something is very wrong and must be fixed." Hip fractures can bleed so much so quickly that death can occur. Into a complicated surgery you go; they cut through layers of skin and muscle, they touch and move tendons and ligaments that really don't like to be touched, much less moved, and they literally saw off the femur bone below the break.

They ream out the bone to make room for the prosthetic upper structure of the bone, then they cement and screw it into place in the bone, and they work the ball top back into the joint, then they start backing out stitching layers as they close you back up. Yes, you are also going to have serious pain when you wake up, but that is good pain. You are alive. You have lived through a major bone being broken that is capable of bleeding out your blood volume into your leg and hip, and you have lived through a rough surgery, but you have been repaired.

The new structure may feel like you are going to fall apart, but it is so much tougher than you think. Yes, if it is right for you to accept the pain medication, please do, and I validate the magnitude of even the good pain.

But in a few hours when the staff comes to first sit you on the side of the bed and dangle your legs, push through that fear of pain; don't say "No! Wait!" over and over and become paralyzed. Tell yourself, "Yes, I can; this is good pain," and do not listen to that good pain parading as bad pain telling you "No." Stand when they think you are ready and tell you to do so. If you tell yourself this and follow the professional direction, your good pain will leave you more quickly because you will heal more quickly. I believe you when you say it feels like you are damaging all of the doctor's skilled work. However, the great majority of post-hip replacements do not damage anything after surgery due to the physical rehabilitation work, and you are not damaging anything. Ask your doctor questions to help you stay on schedule: "At the end of the second week or rehab, what would you like to see me be able to do?" I have had several people that I taught this way of looking at pain tell me later they felt safer not using as much and getting completely off all pain medication more quickly, because they knew it was good pain. They began to see pain as only a message on a nerve path as opposed to something in their mind they thought would destroy them. I have also heard they feel they rehabbed the injury faster without the fear of good pain or internal damage to slow their progress.

An example of good pain that prevents future and greater pain, expense, and health issues is having your teeth cleaned or a cavity filled. Yes, it can hurt, yes, they are poking and picking at your teeth and gums with sharp things, and yes blood may appear in your spit or the suction line, but they are trained professionals helping you keep your teeth. Something amazing my dentist taught me was that he could actually drill out part of my tooth without first injecting a local anesthetic, also known as numbing medicine, such as lidocaine or Marcaine. To help me understand further, he reminded me that my teeth do not have nerves in the actual tooth material, as long as he did not have to go all the way to the root nerve, and that it would not hurt to drill without a numbing injection first. My dentist was right and has since done several small drillings over the past fourteen years without local anesthetic, and I was not in pain in the least. If I had not trusted, I would have had four or five times where I had to experience the pain of a needle being inserted, and the momentary burn of the medicine going into the gum before it started to numb a second later, for no reason whatsoever. There are times to listen to your pain and the fears that instinctually surround it, and times to conquer the fears and pain.

Because I like balance, I'll trust you with a great answer given to me that negates a percentage of the pep talk I just gave you. John, whom you will meet further in Chapter 15 "Promoting life ...," was in his mid-nineties, and in the hospital just a few days after a small spinal compression fracture that was stable, meaning no risk of spinal damage with movement. It is day three and he is still hitting his PCA button heavily. PCA stands for patient-controlled analgesia, and it is the best and worst thing to come along since sliced bread. You push a button and it delivers IV pain medication at a rate no greater than the maximum dose the patient can have. This device is great in several ways; streets should be named after the inventor(s). To start, it can be programmed to give a set amount automatically at set intervals, such as X mg every Y minutes. The next great feature is that you can control it, which means you don't have to wait for a nurse to have time to go get your medication when it is scheduled again. This gives you the freedom and flexibility to give yourself a small dose periodically as needed. Instead of X-Y mg of every two hours, one can give themselves, at the push of a button, 0.X mg every Y minutes. These more frequent smaller doses prevent huge peaks and valleys in pain. This takes away those two hours or more of steady rises in pain until the nurse is allowed to give you your next dose, as the doctor wrote the order. The downside of having the PCA pump in hand is over sedation, less motivation, an unrealistic expectation of no pain through a rehabilitation period, and the high potential for abuse that can continue for the pleasures of euphoria rather than any real remaining levels of pain. We know for a fact people abuse this device for a few reasons. The first is that nurses get direct observation of pain's signs and symptoms correlated to what we are being told by the patient. But the other way we know is at the end of every shift, the ongoing nurse and the off-going nurse check the PCA pump together. One of the things the pump tells us is how many times the patient pushed the button. Sometimes the shift-change check shows that number is in the thousands when at most the bump was set to deliver in that 12 hours was 36 doses, or one every 20 minutes. Yet it is three days post-surgery, and they are walking to get juice and crackers from the snack room every hour, and therefore the patient's actions do not correlate to the extreme attempts to self dose for actual pain. A PCA is a beautiful thing, but it is a good idea to get off of it and encourage other people to get off of it as soon as decreasing pain levels and healing allow.

So John asked me on day three, "How come this time it is harder for me to get up and go? Aside from my age, I am not getting up and pushing myself like I normally can." I answered by validating him with age and injury, and I told him that crushed bones do indeed cause severe pain. Then I gave him the same pain talk I had before when he was in the hospital, and that I just gave you above, ending with, "If you want to get up and go, then push the pain medication button in your hand less!" He has been looking at me the whole time, and as I finished my ten-minute, as usual way-too-wordy answer, he raised his eyebrows at me, and with three days of PCA pump comfort in his eyes and voice said, "Well, that's all well and good, but they aren't your neurons; they're mine."

First let us look at fentanyl, because it is a major player in both acute and consistent baseline pain control. Fentanyl comes in both injectable and patch form. The injectable form works well for short-term relief of pain, as in during a short procedure. Fentanyl has a short "half-life," which is the term used to describe how long it takes for half of the drug to be gone, or metabolized, from your body. However, the fentanyl patch is very much a key player in the role of pain relief in chronic long-term terminal pain management. Unfortunately, it is highly abused by many for recreational reasons, and because the patch continues to release medication constantly, it is the cause of numerous recreational overdose deaths. Fentanyl patches work as a constant-release pain-control tool. When a pill is taken or an injection is given, either into the vein by the IV line, or into the muscle (known as IM for intramuscular), it will have a peak effect then a decline in its pain control as the drug is metabolized and excreted from the body. However, when a fentanyl patch is applied, it takes several hours to begin to work, but then its pain control effect remains constant for a few days until the patch starts to run low on medication to release. These patches come in different strengths as pain levels increase from spreading cancer, increasing chronic pain, or resistance to lower doses building requiring higher doses for the same effect. When a fentanyl patch is used to give a baseline control for chronic pain, other medications can then be used for what is called "breakthrough" pain.

Breakthrough pain is just that—pain that breaks through the primary pain medicine's ability to control it. For example, if Percocet is being used to control pain and for the most part is working, but maybe once or twice a day the pain will "break through" Percocet's limitations to control pain, then in addition another medication may be added to get the pain back under control, then not used again until the pain increases and breaks through again. When pills and patches are no longer doing the job on their own, it may be time to step up to intramuscular/IM injections or IV administration. Although these are procedures and support that hospice can provide, many try to remain on oral administration with increasing dosage, and changing to liquid form almost always occurs with time as the person becomes too weak or coordinated to swallow a pill. Most hospices have what is known as "standing orders" for pain medicines, which allows the nurse to change medications without having the patient seen by a doctor in the office or hospital setting. This will save unnecessary and uncomfortable transport for the dying person. Sometimes but rarely, depending on numerous factors, families will be taught to give these injections, but hospice is often available to give these injections around the clock on the rare occasions IM is used. Your willingness and confidence that you can give the injection is a key factor in being given the freedom and flexibility to do so yourself. When end of life is the issue, a general rule of thumb is that it is better to add pain medicines to the plan rather than stop one and start another, unless of course one is stopping the medicine because of unwanted side effects.

The three most common IM/IV pain medicines are fentanyl, morphine, and Dilaudid. It is generally understood that morphine and fentanyl are the first choice, for they are not as strong and are less addictive than Dilaudid. However, in my clinical experience, I have found that morphine can cause headaches, increased confusion in the elderly, and noticeably more nausea and vomiting. Further, it can sometimes be not as effective and does not last as long as the very small, slightly more frequent doses of Dilaudid. All three medicines will have a decreased chance of nausea and vomiting if given lower recommended doses and very slowly by the IV route.

There is nothing wrong with asking nurses to give medicine very slowly. Even when I found myself very busy during a hectic shift, once hooking the syringe to the IV tubing I would slow down enough to give the medicine gradually. I always found this slow administration an excellent chance to talk with and teach the patient and family about why and what they were waiting for, discuss what we have found, check in with them if the disease had been a long, chronic illness, and see if they have any questions. This time was so worth the effort. Not only was the medicine delivered with minimal side effects, but also much valuable knowledge and information was shared. I also learned from these interactions more about the person sick before me, and often had a few minutes to do some more teaching. One of my mantras I created in the emergency department, sadly due to seeing the negative consequence of the opposite, was "It is better to do something slower and right than fast and wrong." Not only is giving medications slowly the right thing to do for your patient, but it also takes less time to give a medication slowly than to give it quickly then have to correct a problem, such as nausea or vomiting, that may have been prevented in the first place. Prevention is a valuable time, money, and pain saver.

My mother's death had an unfortunate situation that many can learn from. I want you to know I also did my research right after my mother died a few years ago, and again over the past twenty-four hours, to make sure I'm in check and balance here. This is another great opportunity for both the healthcare field and the layperson. It is both an opportunity for some in the healthcare field to double check both their communication skills, and assess their level of flexibility for individual patient needs. Unfortunately, this occurred in a large metropolitan area, and that does make a difference in how the masses are treated. If a regional healthcare system is taxed with a greater patient-to-provider ratio, we unfortunately are moved through a little more rapidly with a little more cookie-cutter care. That may be a contributing factor for what I am about to share, but it is by no means an excuse. Don't get me wrong, sticking to textbook care is wise in many ways—it's following the research. The only problem with unwavering textbook care is that not all human beings can be put in the exact same textbook. The proof is again the term "practicing medicine," as treating human beings is not an exact science. Unfortunately, sticking to that research for doctors also protects them from the liability exposure of losing a lawsuit if civil action is brought against them, but it removes some of their comfort in individualizing care too far from the center. But this situation did not have to occur as it did, and I tried painfully hard to prevent it.

Dr. Elisabeth Kübler-Ross was a Swiss-American psychiatrist and pioneer in near- death studies, and she is also the author of the 1969 international bestseller *On Death and Dying*. In this groundbreaking book, she introduced her now famous, and accurate, five stages of death and dying: denial, anger, bargaining, depression, and acceptance. In 1972, she spoke to the U.S. Senate Special Committee on her specialty subject of aging and the right to die with dignity, and on one's rights to make their own decisions concerning their end of life. In 1974, a handful of medical professionals opened the first hospice in Branford, Connecticut. The double-edged sword for hospice occurred in 1982, when Congress passed the first law to allow Medicare to reimburse for hospice. It was excellent that it became available to so many, but "ouch" that now good old profit became involved in an institution started almost a thousand years ago in the eleventh century. Hospice was not started for profit; it was started out of need, dignity, and respect. Hospices are fantastic! They are the best thing to help get unavoidable death out of hospitals, and back into the patients' own home, to die with that dignity we all seek our entire lives, and that we hope we obtain with our death.

It is a very special and giving person who chooses to go into palliative care, as the end-of-life specialty is now called. Because expected death in the next six months is often a hospice admission criterion, these people are choosing to walk into a field for which, on average, every patient you meet most likely will die in the next six months. This indeed takes a special type of giving and courage. Yet hospice is now no different from the rest of the healthcare field, filled with all types of people; profit is paramount to keep their doors open, to keep people employed, and above all to continue the beautiful care the hospice tradition has provided to so many for so long. But it also must be managed and guided by the recipient of its services. I will warn you, I failed to protect my mother.

I also want you to know, before unfolding the next part, that many people do just fine with morphine, but my mother had received it years before with a hip fracture and we knew for a fact she did not do well with morphine. It caused her such problems with vomiting and confusion during that admission that I added it to her allergy list.

I shared with you about the morning of my mother's last fall in the chapter "Procedures that attempt to postpone death." Now let us jump ahead. Twenty-four hours had passed since she fell and completely fractured the upper portion of her left humerus bone in her upper arm. Due to the extremely low calcium density of her bones, they were like cork, and would not hold a pin or screw for an orthopedic repair. She was already enrolled in, but had not had to use, hospice care for her aortic stenosis, had increasing shortness of breath, was showing increasing signs of dementia, and had clearly expressed she did not want oxygen or surgery at her 90 years of age, "period," as she would sometimes say. She had told me numerous times she missed Dad, who had died ten years earlier, and did not want life-prolonging procedures. The emergency doctor had no issue with my request for her to receive Dilaudid– not morphine– before she was transported back to her assisted living facility. The doctor at the facility had no issues with me requesting Dilaudid and was fine with my recommendation for smaller doses a little more frequently to prevent the side effects I shared with you earlier of nausea and vomiting, headaches, and confusion.

Then, during day two, any movement caused her extreme pain; remember she had a complete fracture with jagged edges on both sides of the bone, and the bottom half of the fractured bone was pointing up and angled out slightly towards her outer arm. Her arm was immobilized in two directions, known as a sling and swathe, but still every roll to clean her, bathe her, or put her on and off the bedpan caused her extreme pain. I attempted to keep all turning, etc., to the first hour after she received a dose of Dilaudid. As she had requested and I promised her, I was her primary caregiver from the moment I arrived the morning before when the fracture occurred.

It had now been over twenty-four hours since her fall with no issues with the pain medication, but the hospice nurse, to whom I had given a first-edition copy of this book, wanted to change her from Dilaudid to morphine, "Because it is our standard." I of course politely attempt to redirect this action using all the reasons why, clinical experience, no bad side effects on the Dilaudid, complete fracture with extreme pain on movement, and that I am the author of the book on death and dying. But she was very persistent and continued to return to, "It is our standard." So I requested to talk with the on-call doctor. I spoke with this doctor on the phone, introduced myself, spoke in the same advanced medical terminology I would use with a doctor I am working next to in the ED or ICU, and the story again was the same as above: "It is our standard." Now I admit, I was getting frustrated on the inside. I am a human being with limits, just like you. She agreed to come evaluate my mother, and I was grateful for an opportunity to discuss this with her in person. I will warn you to be prepared for how this story unfolds.

This doctor arrived quickly, in under an hour, and I introduced myself and also handed over a copy of my book while we exchanged some professional background courtesy. If she had doubts of my background before on the phone, she now knew she was not talking to a layperson by any means. I always like to ask doctors where they did their residency. It is amazing how often I run into doctors I have worked with during their residency across this country, airports, hospitals, even a car crash once on the side of the road where I had stopped to help and so had a pediatrician I worked with as a resident in the late eighties. My favorite reunion was maybe seven years ago when I ran into a doctor I worked with when he was a surgery resident back in the mid-eighties. I was in pre-op as my mother was going in for the hip repair I mentioned. When he realized it was me, he literally picked me up and spun me around right there in pre-op. He introduced me to the nurses and mom's anesthesiologist, who was standing there, and the charge nurse admitted she had picked up the phone to call hospital police before she realized he was giving me a huge hug, and we were not attacking each other. One of my sisters was standing there also, and she too thought he had attacked me; that's how excited he was to see me.

That is how well I get along with and work with doctors. When a resident gives a report to their attending physician they give the patient's history, medications, allergies, the history of the current illness or trauma, their findings on their assessment, what they think the problem could be, the differential diagnosis, which basically means "Let's not miss anything so what else could it be," and the recommended diagnostic studies and treatment for now until more is known from the studies. I had given this type of report to attendings and residents for twenty-one years to get the care rolling for people before a doctor had time to see them. I had given this hospice doctor that type of report on the phone, and again when the doctor, the nurse, one of my sisters, and I sat down to discuss this situation after the doctor had first physically assessed my mother upon entering the room. I included morphine as an allergy in this report. She asked me what the allergic reaction was. After I informed her, she told me, "Because it does not involve hives or shortness of breath, the nausea, vomiting, headaches, and confusion were side effects, not an allergic reaction." If you live that high in the textbook, technically she was correct. I'll let you be the judge of that.

I got nowhere with her either after the four of us had talked for a good fifteen to twenty minutes; she simply, maintained, "I want to switch your mother to morphine because it is our standard, and I would like to place her on oxygen, because her oxygen saturation (which is the percentage of oxygen in one's blood) is a little low." Well, of course it was low; her left upper arm was the size of a large grapefruit filled with a respectable percentage of her tiny little body's blood that normally would be carrying oxygen throughout her body, and she was on regular doses of opioid pain medicine. The worst part of that oxygen recommendation was that I had just informed them several times that my mother's wishes were not to receive oxygen at any point at the end of her life, as well as reiterating the nausea, vomiting, headaches, and slight confusion she'd had with morphine years ago when she broke her hip. Remember, she knew it took my father two weeks to die with scant fluid intake; she'd had experience before her own eyes, and she had placed herself on hospice a few weeks earlier. This doctor and nurse hounded me for maybe five minutes to allow oxygen and completely ignored the many reasons presented to her in medical terminology to please not change my mom to morphine. I accomplished no oxygen but failed on the morphine prevention, and the doctor changed my mother to morphine. She did agree to allow regular doses of Zofran to hopefully keep her from experiencing nausea or vomiting. They left, after aggressively and clearly attempting to make me feel negligent, tilting into abusive and cruel, by simply respecting and staunchly attempting to protect my mother's wishes and refusing to allow oxygen. My mother was peacefully sleeping through all of this.

I was in professional shock at one: Hospice wanted to completely ignore my mother's last wishes not to be placed on oxygen, and two: My dying mother had her pain meds changed to meet their textbook needs, not her clinical needs, which had already been proven for a day and half to be working without nausea, vomiting, headaches, or confusion. For my mother's sake, I had hoped to be wrong and that the morphine would work fine without complications.

At this point I had not left her since I arrived with the EMS the previous morning. I slept on the couch in her room, but I had stepped out several times to get meals at a restaurant when my sisters were there to give me a break. Of course Mom had been sleeping on and off for a day and half by ten, groggy when awake but not confused, no complaints of pain other than her arm but only with movement, and actively telling me she really didn't want to drink because being on and off the bedpan caused her arm to move and extreme pain occurred.

When no one was in the room, she had also asked me if she would die faster if she drank less. I had answered her honestly.

A few hours later, she received her first dose of morphine. About an hour after that she started complaining of a headache and asked me the first question that didn't make sense to me since I was a teenager. She also just didn't look or sound like my mom. I called the hospice to ask for her to be changed back to Dilaudid. A different nurse called me back, and I gave her a full introduction and report on the changes, and I was told, "Yes, I received a report on your mother, and let's try a little longer; sometimes these side effects work themselves out." Never in twenty-one years of clinical nursing had I seen a side effect to an opioid not just get worse if not discontinued; I had received another pacifying, dismissive answer. I again failed with the nurse and asked to talk with a doctor. She was now complaining of increasing pain and a need to urinate, but she knew that would increase her pain and asked for another dose before being moved onto the bedpan. It is getting late on a weekend night, and I allowed another dose of morphine. She urinated and then settled, but woke up restless a few hours later. She was harder to calm and appeared uncomfortable in her skin. I tried warm rags, cold rags, and sips of juice to try to give her some simple energy; she slept on and off but was restless even while sleeping. Just after midnight, she woke up, told me she loved me, vomited, and then died a few minutes later. When the hospice nurse arrived to handle the post-mortem paperwork, I let her know I was upset my mother had vomited before she died.

Not knowing I have seen a thousand people die, she told me, "That's normal." I was still holding my mother's cold hand, smoothing her hair with my other hand, and I said nothing further.

Let me start by telling you we will never know if her restlessness and vomiting was from the morphine or the normal decreased blood flow to the brain that can occur with the decreasing oxygen level in the blood, further compounded by the decreased blood pressure perfusing less blood into her brain. But I do know for a fact that my mother never showed one sign of confusion, headache, or nausea and vomiting while on low-dose Dilaudid during her entire hip fraction admission or the day and a half before being switched to morphine. I wasn't upset that my mother died, for she was a tiny woman, a great percentage of her blood volume had bled out into her arm from the fracture, and she was very welcoming of dying at this point. I was upset that the hospice had met their needs over my mother's, that she most likely would not have experienced those side effects had she remained on Dilaudid, and that I had been told vomiting was "normal" before death as a pat answer to someone who had seen the last breath of far more people than any one person should ever have to see.

Before rewriting this chapter, I called a handful of my professional buddies and did some online searching. Vomiting before death can happen, of course, but it is rare, and more often than not it is seen in cancer patients. My mother did not have cancer. Her restlessness, headache, confusion, and vomiting most likely did not need to happen. I will never know for sure, and I must accept my own advice that all is OK with the dying. She most likely would not remember those last few minutes if I could ask her. It is also the great reminder of what I always tell people to empower them about controlling their own health care: that except for a few rare occasions, such as head injury, intoxication, or acute psychiatric episodes, you can always tell the healthcare field, "No thank you," and you can always make reasonable requests, but you can never make them do anything. I wonder what Dr. Elisabeth Kübler-Ross, 1926–2004, would have thought?

Unfortunately, death being another part of life is just like life, in the respect that nothing comes without a price or trade off. Ultimately, not giving pain medication out of fear comes down to causing a return of increased pain or worse. What could be worse is potentially placing the person into narcotic withdrawal, just like heroin withdrawal, at such a time as near-death. It is not that the person has become an "addict"; it is that the body has become dependent on the drug. Many families have asked me about long-term use of narcotics and whether the user will become an "addict" or "a junkie." Pain is the reason the medicines are being given, and their intended purpose is the alleviation of that pain. Narcotic withdrawal has been described to me as the body "crawling and screaming from the inside out." This is not a sensation I would want to add to the terminal person's already-existing aches, pains, and fears. Caregivers often have fear and guilt over "giving too much pain medication" when attempting to keep someone comfortable, even when death is imminent, and persistent pain has been an issue. If you only give what is prescribed, you are not giving too much, you are giving what is ordered.

Ask yourself the following questions when faced with uncertainty about pain medication amounts and frequency:

- Have more or stronger pain medicines been required as the cancer or disease process advanced to maintain comfort?
- Do I think the disease process continues to grow even though the person is now very weak and has a decreased level of awareness? In other words, does bone cancer keep growing, and thus continue the need to increase someone's pain medication, even if they are less and less alert?
- Would I expect that, if they were able to talk to me, they would tell me their pain has returned or continues to increase? Or if awake and able, would they reach over and get more medication themselves?
- Do I want to send this person into narcotic withdrawal before their death?
- Would I want to continue to receive pain medicines by someone who loves me if I were in pain and unable to speak or give myself medicine?

If further reassurance is needed, remind yourself that decreased respirations are a side effect of the medicine that is being given for pain, not the desired effect or purpose of the medication. Attempt to give yourself permission to treat the pain without fear and guilt. I cannot stress to you enough not to allow fear and guilt to prevent you from giving holistic, complete, humanistic comfort as you can. Remember, we are talking about an inevitable death with or without pain medicine. Continuing the same pain medication plan that last worked is not speeding up death or assisted suicide; it is maintaining pain control.

Something I do when caring for someone dying in the home is start charting, just like I did in nursing, not for everything, but for pain stated or what I observe, and pain medications given, the amount, frequency, and response. I chart the time, and the reason I am giving the pain medication, such as it being the regularly scheduled time or the patient verbalizing a complaint of breakthrough pain, or if I see increasing restlessness once they are no longer verbalizing. I do not give more medicine or more frequently than prescribed. This way, if the police or hospice nurse needs to document anything after the death, all will be in order. If I documented half a milliliter (by the way, a milliliter/"ml" and a cubic centimeter/"cc" are equal) of morphine was given every four hours, and ten doses had been given over two days from a 30 milliliter bottle, then I will be able to show the hospice nurse or detective who arrives to the home after the death that 25 milliliters remain in the bottle. This also protects me legally and reassures my conscience that I did not go past the doctor's orders. This book is not about Kevorkian or assisted suicide actions; our body will die when ready, if allowed.

Some signs to look for in a person with a decreasing level of consciousness to help determine whether pain is increasing or the pain medicines are wearing off are increases in restlessness, heart rate, respiratory rate, or blood pressure, and sweating or pale skin. These signs could also be caused by other changes that are occurring in the body. However, for the sake of the person's comfort, I would not rule out that the cause could be either increased pain or potential narcotic withdrawal from lower pain medicine levels. The good news is as long as narcotics are not completely stopped, or decreased too much too quickly, withdrawal is rarely an issue.

One more highly predictable side effect of narcotic pain medicines, that is not often discussed or warned of, is constipation. Narcotics can and most likely will cause severe constipation. As long as someone is able to consume solid food, I recommend you give either two bowls of cereal or two muffins high in bran/fiber each day. If the person is no longer able to eat, then consider some prune juice if they are still able to swallow safely or add prune juice to other fluids. Remember that once solid foods are no longer consumed, the need for bowel movements will greatly decrease anyway. However, if solid foods are blended and given, then the need to have bowel movements will continue. The food is still considered a solid;

you just "chewed" it with the blender. Many doctors will place someone on a drug called Colace, which is a stool softener, to prevent constipation from pain medicines. This drug is so helpful but often not enough to prevent constipation if someone is on higher narcotic doses. It is also important to know that with most fiber supplements, you must also increase the amount of water you drink. Taking fiber without increasing the amount of water you drink can actually cause constipation.

Another important note about narcotics: Once the person taking them is no longer able to give themselves the medicine safely, remove the narcotics from the bedside. This has less to do with them taking the wrong drug or too much of it than it does with someone else stealing the medicine. That is a tough thing to say, but pain medications do walk, and the dying person needs them for pain far more than the recreational user needs them for pleasure.

I want to address one more class of prescription drugs and touch on the subject of alternative choices. The drugs used to treat nausea and vomiting are known as antiemetics. Emesis is the medical term for the substance known as vomit. At this time, the two most common drugs to treat nausea and vomiting are Phenergan and Zofran. Phenergan is usually the first choice, although thank goodness fast fading in the clinical setting. Until a few years after the turn of the century, Zofran was mainly used to treat the nausea and vomiting of cancer patients on chemotherapy. It is a very effective drug that does not have two of the major side effects of Phenergan: burning with injection and a drunk or hungover feeling lasting up to one day or more. Phenergan can be given by the four main routes of administration: IM, IV, in pill form, and as a rectal suppository. The most important and painful side effect of Phenergan is direct pain in the vein during the injection if given too quickly or not diluted. The muscle will burn for some time and then will be sore for several days if injected into the muscle/IM. I have found that Phenergan causes little or no discomfort if given in the farthest entry port into the tubing from the patient, and if the tubing is not pinched during the injection so the IV fluid continues to dilute, and if given over several minutes. Pinching the tubing during an injection should be done with very few medicines. If I were to pinch the tubing and carefully spend several minutes injecting that medicine, then releasing the pinch will allow the medicine to go in as an undiluted concentration of the medicine over a short period of time. Phenergan will also give you a very heavy drunk or hungover feeling for twelve to twenty-four hours, or even longer if the dose is large enough. I have often seen it also increase confusion in elderly people. Small doses often work with smaller or older people, and more can always be given if the first dose does not work. From my clinical experience, I am grateful to hear Zofran is being used more.

There are a number of alternative drugs that have been both shown to work for various complaints. Marijuana must be mentioned for its ability to stop or decrease nausea and vomiting, control pain, and increase appetite. Since I first published this book, the explosion of legalized marijuana, and its extract CBD, have swept the country to greatly increase its availability and decrease criminal penalties. Many people have informed me that marijuana was the only thing they found to stop the nausea of chemotherapy or other various medications that can cause nausea and vomiting.

Talk with your doctor before taking Benadryl, also known generically as diphenhydramine, but it has been known to help with abdominal cramping, nausea, vomiting, to help sleep, and with restlessness. The antihistamine effect also works as a smooth muscle relaxant and is capable of helping the intestines to slow and calm when irritated or inflamed. Diphenhydramine is often given in the hospital setting in what is known as a "GI cocktail," a bitter, slightly varying concoction depending on what part of the country you are in, to help numb and calm the gastro-intestinal tract. Nurses, please, always check to make sure you have a good blood return with your existing IV before giving Benadryl or Phenergan, they both can cause serious tissue damage if the IV is infiltrated and these drugs extravasate into the tissue.

Most people hate to have IVs started because of the pain or bad experiences, and I cannot blame them. I have allowed a handful of new nurses and nursing students to start IVs on me, if I saw they needed some redirection and confidence. IVs hurt, but I have a few tricks that might help. It is not always possible before having an IV started to get yourself well hydrated, for this is often the reason for starting an IV. However, if possible, get yourself well hydrated before the attempt. Another great trick is to elevate the heart much higher than the hand or arm. Try this easy experiment. Get into an upright sitting position and place your hand palm down in your lap. Notice that the veins are elevated above the level of the skin? Slowly raise your hand until they fall back even with the skin. This should occur when your hand rises just past the level of the heart. Try it again. Sitting way up in the bed and dropping the level of your hand or arm lower than your heart level will cause the veins to enlarge and make a bigger, easier target for starting an IV. If a person is unconscious or unresponsive, the hand can still be dropped off the side of the bed to help dilate the vein. This little trick is also helpful to understand "elevating" an orthopedic injury; it has to be higher than the heart level to really help reduce swelling of an injury.

Even if you know you are a hard person to start an IV on, or to obtain blood for routine laboratory tests, you may want to keep that to yourself. It can cause undue pressure on someone who is very capable of starting your IV on the first attempt. All health care professionals sometimes miss blood draws and IV starts. I once went a very long period without missing an IV start, and starting IVs is something I was very good at. Because I am not embarrassed to be human, I will share with you that I blew that long no-miss IV start streak when I missed a "pipe," as we call huge veins, of a vein in the forearm of a college baseball player. It was huge, more like a culvert under a roadway than a little old pipe.

Actually, I say I am not embarrassed to tell you, but I was embarrassed at the moment. He was cool with it, though; he even told me about his last major error during a big game. The acceptance of humanness is a beautiful, peace-creating gift to both self and others.

One last big trick that I have used with almost every IV start, time permitting, whether the person was anxious or not, is to help people truly deeply relax beforehand. No, major trauma patients don't get this talk; your arm just gets held tightly, and you might hear "Big stick" if you are conscious and not dangerously unstable. But this sweeter technique that I developed early on in my career works so incredibly well. It was half out of personal safety necessity and half because starting an IV on someone who flinches, or worse yet pulls away, is not easy and also potentially very dangerous because so many patients in inner-city teaching hospitals in the mid-1980s were sadly HIV-positive when I first started nursing. I'm going to share the technique with you so you can tell yourself and do this same exercise if you are about to be stuck for labs or an IV. Give it a try right now as you read the exercise.

I would start by raising the head of the bed higher to help the veins enlarge, as I tell you why I need to start an IV and ask permission. I'll have you uncross and relax your legs, then relax your hips, and now your spine. Now I would tell you, "Feel as if we have given you a drug that would paralyze your whole body; you can't move even if you want to." If I see you are remaining tense, I might rock your legs and arms a little and remind you that you have no ability to move, and you are completely relaxed, "heavy on the bed." I found that lightly rocking the legs and arms while stating these directions helped your legs to become like Jell-O. By lightly rocking your legs, you could feel the muscles relaxing, and I could feel the actual level of muscle relaxation accomplished. I'm also getting you used to touch as a stepping-stone to the arm work and needle stick you are about to receive. This is even more important if I have to start two IVs on you; for a higher-level illness or injury, people often tense up even more for the second stick because they were just caused pain with the first stick. As I continue setting up to start the "line," as we call it, I will reiterate everything I said to relax you in an even calmer, slower voice, now including, "I'm going to start working with your arm, placing a tourniquet, looking at your veins, and you are going to feel me touching and working with you, but remember your arm is completely paralyzed, so you can't move it." At that point I usually feel the full weight of their arm in my hands; if not I get to help them pretend it is paralyzed. As I clean off the site I'm about to enter, I keep saying, "Your arm is paralyzed, unable to move; you are going to feel a stick in a moment, but you can't move. Your whole body is heavy; you are so relaxed that you are not lying on the bed but instead the bed is holding you up. Feel the bed pushing upward to support your unable-to-move body." As I go to insert the catheter, I'll say it two more times as I am lining up to enter, feeling to make sure you are completely relaxed. "You are going to feel a stick, but you can't move because you are paralyzed." The last time I finish saying it, I insert the catheter. It is amazing how many people's arms remain completely relaxed, and I'm told as I tape in the IV, "That was the most comfortable IV start I have ever had." It really didn't take much more time than it does to walk into a room, state the what and why of starting an IV, set it up, and start it, maybe thirty seconds to a minute or two at most depending on the level of fear and the ability to fully relax. But those two minutes are so worth it. Yes, the department may be busy, but you are not the one getting stuck, and your patient being relaxed in the long run may save you time. I use this same technique on myself when getting blood work, or even in the dentist's chair. I hope you will talk yourself down to this level of relaxed comfort the next time you have a blood draw, dental work, or any medical procedure. If you are the one starting the IV, I promise you will not regret learning this technique. As you know from starting IVs on unconscious patients, it is so much easier to start a line on a 100 percent completely cooperative arm.

There are hands-on measures that can increase comfort that do not involve medications. These are little things that can make a big difference, that do require just a little time and effort. These little efforts will not only give the recipient increased comfort, but also give the caregiver increased reward and a feeling of doing a more holistic, humanistic job. As long as someone can still get out of bed and is steady, even if you assist a little, allow them to do so. Even though some of us may have secret desires to spend a day or two in bed, it is not a pleasant thing when it is a forced reality. Having someone safely stand at the bedside can help everything, from mood to muscles. It's a complete winner, and the same thing goes for sitting in a chair a few times a day. My father was restless, but going out to the living room, until the last few days when he could not walk, would settle him for a time, and he would look around with increasing alertness.

Even if you are in bed, raise your arms above your head as often as you think of it and look up frequently. Raising your arms above your head over and over, whether bedridden or not, has so many benefits, such as muscle movement, circulation, and mild cardio-pulmonary stimulation, and the frequent expansion of the ribcage and lungs is highly beneficial in strengthening pulmonary function and even a little prevention of bronchitis and pneumonia.

Since assisting people out of bed started for me over thirty-seven years ago in nursing school and working for the home health agency, I have been asking people and assisting them to stand up straight and to look upwards a little before we attempt to walk. Most of us become bent over with age or with sitting in bed too long due to illness or injury. Standing should always be done in stages, or your family member has a chance of ending up on the ground. The first pause is sitting on the bedside. The next pause is the most likely point to lose someone quickly to gravity. Before standing, tell them to tell you right away if they become dizzy, and tell them that they should just sit back down if the dizziness is really bad or has a fast onset, and tell them to keep the back of their legs still touching the bed or chair in case they need to sit back down quickly. If someone has been in bed for a period of time, or if someone is on cardiac or blood pressure medications, have them just stand there at least another thirty seconds or more. I also like to have them stand up a little straighter and to get them to turn their head upwards to look up.

The most important reason for these slow stages to accomplish standing is to prevent fainting, known as syncope. This can occur when not enough blood reaches the brain once the legs go far below the heart and the brain raises higher above the heart. Under-hydration is one of the main causes of this, but it also could be anything from just being in bed for too long to a cardiac issue or drug that prevents the heart rate from increasing in speed to compensate for that body's change in position. Whether near your death or not, understanding this basic body response is incredibly important throughout all of life, first to keep you as strong and as healthy as you can be every day, and second to keep you or the person you are caring for off the floor from nearly or completely fainting.

What repetitively happens inside your body when you stand is one of those human body miracles that occurs every time you move to a standing position from any other position throughout your day, and it should never be taken for granted, and should be understood by every human being to help them live safer, stronger, and yes even happier lives. Remember the three main major factors affecting your body's ability to circulate blood? They are the heart, the vessels, and the blood volume, which equals the pump, hoses, and fluid in the pumping system in an orchard. Let us not forget good old powerful, persistent gravity that is even working on the inside of your body, constantly wanting you to faint. When you stand, even from a sitting position, blood wants to settle out of your head to fill up the legs that just straightened out and need a little more blood, and your legs give gravity a place to steal blood from your brain and take it to. This blood wanting to drain from your brain is even greater if you are standing from a lying position, because now you have raised your head much higher than the level of your heart, as opposed to sitting, where your head is already above your heart. Every time a healthy and hydrated person stands, several checks and balances in the body occur really quickly to compensate for gravity wanting to pull the blood from their brain; with hydration, gravity loses and you don't faint. When this amazing action occurs quickly and has the proper hydration level to accomplish it, you feel nothing and go accomplish life without hitting the floor. How it works is simple: You stand, your body has various ways of knowing a potentially dangerous internal event is occurring; blood flow to the brain starts to decrease from gravity's pull, so your heart is told to speed up, and blood vessels may constrict to help increase the pressure also. Blood flow increases to the brain, the cells continue to receive oxygen, and all is well. So when you stand, bend over then right yourself, stretch, or get back up from a kneeling or squatting position and become dizzy, you most likely are dehydrated.

For this reason, people on cardiac or blood pressure medications are taught to not walk away from the bed or chair immediately after standing, and to keep the back of their legs touching the chair in case they do need to sit back down quickly. These medications can affect the heart and blood vessels' ability to perform the normal rapid compensation you just read. In the clinical setting we call this "orthostatic," when the body cannot compensate quickly enough, and we call the assessment for this "checking for orthostatics." You can easily do a modified study on your own, even from a sitting position. In the clinical setting we like to check them by having someone lie flat or near flat for a minute or two, and then we have them sit on the bedside for a brief moment and take their pulse and blood pressure; then we have them stand and wait a moment, then take the pulse and blood pressure again.

Textbooks have always stated to wait two to three minutes after each change to take the vital signs. I found early on by doing my own study, wherein I would take those vital signs of pulse and blood pressure at one, two, and three minutes, that one minute was optimal and gave me accurate results. The reason is that I found that healthy, well-hydrated people had accomplished the necessary compensation of increased heart rate and returned to a normal heart rate in one minute, whereas even dehydrated people had finished compensating and returned to normal numbers in three minutes. Only severely dehydrated people had not finished compensation at three minutes, and almost every one of those had complained of being very dizzy at one minute anyway. We consider someone to have "positive orthostatics" if during these checks they complain of dizziness, or they lose strength or balance and have to be returned to bed. But by the numbers one is considered orthostatic, and most likely dehydrated, if they have an increase in the pulse from lying to sitting or standing of ten points or greater, or if they have a ten-point or greater drop in their blood pressure. Even if you are trying this at home, a pulse alone will help you determine hydration status of someone who is ill or not feeling well. Even in your normal day, if you go to a standing position and you are dizzy, have a glass of water or three, unless you are fluid restricted due to preexisting conditions. Remember there are situations when hydration may not be the only problem and it is also a cardiac or vascular issue due to medications or an undiagnosed cardiac or other issue. If hydration doesn't resolve this problem, or it occurs more frequently, contact your doctor and look into it.

The other reason I like to have people look up once they stand is not only to prevent negatives such as falls, but to add in a great positive that enhances the spirit. Aging and too much time in bed cause our entire spine to curve forward. The bend in the bed when in the upright position, tilting our heads forward to look straight or down, the pillows pushing our head forward, and even sleeping in the fetal position all bend our spines over, forcing our heads to tilt farther and farther towards the ground. Many are completely looking down. I'll say "OK, let's slowly look up and around. You know where the ground is; you don't need to stare at it. Trust it's there; now, let's put your shoulders back from that bent-forward, shoulders-hunched position. OK, now lean back and straighten up slightly, starting at your hips, because they have been bent forward, too. Keep breathing." It is not uncommon at this point for them to become a little wobbly; you are returning their center of gravity to the normally healthy upright center, where it should be. Their inner ear balancing mechanisms have become used to maintaining balance in a bent-forward position from years of leaning farther forward with their head looking towards the ground, so that also needs a minute to calibrate. This more erect upright position can also cause a little unsteadiness because of the orthostatic issue I just taught you about. Their head is now higher, and the body lined up; gravity might pull a little blood volume down from the brain. At this point I'll remind them, "OK, keep your eyes open and your legs touching the bed; look up a little more to help your head straighten even farther, and it is good for your soul to look up. Now pretend there is a string attached to the top of your head and it is pulling you up towards the ceiling; let's get just a little taller." I am doing all the same actions right in front of them as I direct them. I need it, too; the stretch feels great, and it gives them a visual. Have them take a big breath, and ask them if that was easier and fuller in this new position. Most are even smiling, and or at least grinning, feeling more alive, stronger, and upright.

I love watching the transformation in people when I do this; even that last string-to-ceiling trick sometimes gives them another inch or more in height. I mean it—I truly love to see their eyes brighten, inches gained, and before I even say anything, many tell me they feel like dancing. You will have helped them not only to stand upright but also to feel alive; you will have helped lift not only their spine, neck, and head, but their spirit as well. That to me is the essence of nursing. Textbook knowledge and its application can keep people alive, but lifting one's spirit is the reason to live, and that is also a reason to accept your last breath if death is about to finally win.

You have also allowed for the three minutes for the orthostatic position change to compensate. I'll tell people at this moment to do this every time they stand, whether someone else is assisting you, or you have healed and strengthened from your injury or illness and you can safely do it on your own. The other really fun thing I will do is once they are fully upright, and the situation is appropriate, I will change my arm position and ask them if they "Would like to dance without actually moving our feet?" I have had the best answers and laughs at this moment. Elder women often say "sure" and immediately start to rock. Sadly, too often they will tell me, "I haven't danced since my husband died." Or in humor, I have been asked at that moment, "What are you doing after your shift?" I don't want to be accused of gender discrimination, so I'll ask the same dance question to some men, too. "How about we just call it standing up straight and not dancing" is their most frequent response. I once had a man say, "OK, but fast before my wife comes back." The funny thing about that was his wife had been dead for years, and we had already kept each other laughing for days. But he did actually start rocking with me. I like to do this up-righting and elongating over and over with people, as the benefits from just one up-righting are often so immediately visible. Encourage them to do it every time.

This small action is the third most commonly stated act of appreciation I have received over the years. Number one has always been for taking the extra minutes to teach patients, and their families, about their disease with a little more explanation and time about cause, effect, and complete care, as well as to encourage questions and not hope they don't have any. The second most common appreciation stated is, "I'm sorry I got mad at you for taking my blanket and socks off; I feel much better now," after helping people get rid of fever and "chills" of a high body temperature. Although teaching hospitals' emergency departments are very busy, I figure if I have to help someone stand safely, why not take the extra minute to do a shorter, modified version? In the long run these few minutes to upright someone a little further and straighter might end up saving time or further injury. Floors are hard; if you are ever about to faint anywhere for any reason, please remember it is always better to sit and/or lie down on a floor quickly as opposed to falling on one. I don't care if you are in a grocery store; it is better to feel embarrassed than to fracture your skull, neck, arm, wrist, or hip.

Speaking of hard floors, when a fall or fainting episode is in progress, safety must come first for both parties. If someone starts to fall and you know you are not going to be able to safely catch them, do not try. Only if you feel your size, strength, and wellness in relation to the falling person's size safely allows, then attempt to gently guide them to the floor, if you cannot safely prevent a fall. It is important to learn how to fall, one can read tips online or take an actual course that teaches the techniques by physically doing them. These classes also teach a few techniques to safely attempt to stand back up, since so many elderly people are unable to get back up after falling, even without injury. Too many injuries occur to the person trying to stop someone from falling rather than attempting to guide them to the ground safely. Instinct will force most of us to attempt to stop someone from falling, but care of the self must always come first. If you are unable to safely stop or guide a fall, move out of the way; there is no reason you both should get hurt. Call a neighbor or family member, or even some fire/EMS will help put someone back into bed. Remember, some police, fire, and EMS may have to start a protocol of care if you call them to help. On the other hand, some officials may just place the person back in bed. Having all the legal paperwork in order and in hand will persuade them to help without wanting to take someone to the hospital.

Once someone is unable to get out of bed, sometimes just placing several pillows on their sides will keep them from rolling or working their way out of bed. Hospice can provide a hospital bed, if needed or wanted. The reason I did not get one for my dad was that was one of the many questions I asked him long before he ever had Alzheimer's. He was so cool when I asked him if he wanted a hospital bed or to remain on his own. He asked me the pros and cons of both, and I ran off a list for him of the first handful that came to mind: "Well, number one is the comfort of being on your own bed over a plastic industrial mattress; you get to die in your own bed, your room doesn't start to look and feel like a hospital room, the hospital bed raises to make it easier to care for you for the caregivers and their backs, but you will be the one dying so please don't let that affect your decision. The bed will remain in the room until hospice picks it up and that could be hard on Mom to look at; at the same time the bed you died in would be gone, but again it's your death, not Mom's, so pick for yourself. You could fall out of both beds depending on multiple factors, such as side rails up or down, and hospice will bill for bed rental." He thought for literally what seemed like two minutes of silence before he said to keep him in his own bed. Falls from hospital beds with side rails up do happen and can be a double-edged sword. I can tell you from years of experience that sometimes a hospital bed just means someone is going to fall from that much higher, or get caught in the side rails trying to get out of bed while confused. Many confused or restless people have climbed over hospital bed rails.

It is very important to have a person turned every few hours to prevent bedsores and muscle soreness. The rule of thumb in nursing is to turn someone every two hours, but in the home setting that can get to be a bit much for both the person in the bed and the caregiver. But do know that the two-hour standard has been shown to help prevent bedsores. Bedsores are an actual breakdown of tissue that occurs relatively quickly due to decreased blood flow into an area under constant pressure. The sacral area of the lower back is the most common area for these wounds to occur, and they can actually open up, continue to enlarge, and become more painful and potentially infected. So many factors can compound the issue of bedsores in a person near death, from chemotherapy constantly killing new cell growth, (which is basically how chemotherapy works), and that completely prevents healing, to the low protein balance of someone respectfully no longer wanting to eat. Preventing a bedsore if possible is the key. You can also use pillows to prop someone onto their side, to get them off of this area frequently. I also like to place a pillow between their legs so the knees would not be putting pressure on each other. Once on their side, bringing the higher leg farther up also helps them remain turned onto the side.

My father only appeared to be in pain or discomfort when I turned him, and he would grimace or stiffen slightly until the last two days. But I knew that leaving him lying only on his back, or constantly on one side, would also become uncomfortable to him. I attempted to be as gentle as I could when moving him to his side or up in the bed. The grimacing of the dying when being turned is due to the soreness and tendon, ligament, and muscular structures inside the body breaking down from being bedridden for far too long. That grimace is one of the contributing factors to me wanting to write this book throughout my nursing career. Since my actions were the momentary cause of this grimacing in the person quickly approaching their death, I always felt as if it was their only way of saying, "Please stop; my body and spirit are done." Strangely enough, my father would also grimace in apparent pain when I would lightly rub lotion on his feet and legs. I would continue at the same rate and pressure and ask him, "There, Dad, does that feel better if I go a little softer?" He would relax his face, and I would continue—so strange. My guess is his Alzheimer's was telling him any stimulus, even pleasurable, was a discomfort. The simple act of rubbing a lotion on someone's feet, arms, or back can do wonders to provide some relief, distraction, and even a momentary pleasure to the dying. When he was unresponsive, I did not stop giving him these rubdowns, just in case he could feel it. Keep in mind that many lotions can have a drying effect on skin. Make sure it does say "moisturizing." The cocoa butter creams are great for dry, flaky skin, but use what does the trick for each individual.

Once someone can no longer get out of bed to the bath or shower, hygiene gets tougher, but sponge baths with a few washcloths and hot soapy water, if done once or twice a day, will help. Try not to be embarrassed about cleaning what I call the "pits and parts." It is very important to keep the armpits and groin area clean. Buying baby wipes in bulk has gotten so inexpensive that they can be used for an entire bed bath. Most drug stores carry what is known as a "no need to rinse" shampoo. It is a product that is rubbed into the hair and towel-dried out. I used it the two years I did ICU work and again with my dad; it works. Oral care must also continue. Once the person is unconscious, this will be tougher as well, but it can be done. I was using a toothbrush dipped over and over again into a glass of half water, half mouthwash. There are products on the market called mouth swabs that are foam tips on plastic sticks that work well. I could not find any in the drugstores, though, so I improvised with gauzes and a rubber band around a child's toothbrush.

Something else I did for my dad's general comfort was talk to him when awake or "Roughing him up," as I like to call cleaning and turning someone. Even when he was unconscious the last day, I kept talking to him, for it is well understood that hearing is usually the last of our senses to leave us. I talked to him in general and also to tell him what I was doing to him. The last few days he was awake I would tell him, "Everything is alright, Dad," or "Dad, everything is as it should be." To this, he would say, "Is it really?" The dying also deserve reassurance. My mom, siblings, and I, in various ways and various times, told him it was all right to die, or that there was no need to fight any longer. I would ask him the last few days periodically, "Dad, are you ready to move on?" He would slightly nod his head the first few times I asked him, before he could answer no longer.

CHAPTER 15

PROMOTING LIFE IN A BOOK OF DEATH, WITH A FEW PUPPIES AND EASTER BASKETS

"If you don't tell anyone I said it, I won't tell anyone you
laughed."
—Vincent Dodd, b. 1963

UNTIL

Life is too short to blink beyond periodic pause
We don't grasp that until our clock speeds up

Our clocks have accelerators but no brakes
Only a battery that lasts exactly one lifetime

Your battery can be recharged a few times
But never changed

Please keep going
Until you are good and ready to quit

"Never do for the patient what they can do for themselves" was literally one of the first foundations of nursing care that I was taught in the early weeks of nursing school. This was then followed up with, "Not only will your overly helpful actions not help the patient; they will actually hinder their healing and rehabilitation." A fantastic example of this is demonstrated in a changing trend in the treatment of certain types of orthopedic injuries that I witnessed throughout my clinical career. What the field of orthopedics research began to reveal was that although many injuries do require full immobilization and no weight bearing until healed, with some injuries, healing actually occurs faster by not immobilizing in a cast or splint. In certain situations, the body realizes it is injured and is not going to get much of a rest to heal, so it realizes it had better "heal thyself" quickly. Unless there is some rare reason your doctor wants you to stick to bedrest, increasing activity always promotes healing and maintains general health, strength, balance, and movement. In my nursing training, there were also examples that showed allowing people to do as much for themselves as they could also increases one's confidence and builds energy. The body is interesting that way; the more energy we use in a day though movement, the more energy it creates for us to feel and experience more and more energy. Sometimes the body is tired because it needs rest, but sometimes we are in a negative vicious cycle of "tired" because we are sedentary and making it worse by not moving our beings. The body will either produce more energy when we are active, or it will decrease its energy production when we are sedentary. Tiredness does not always mean rest is needed; it often means activity is needed.

In humor and seriousness, I used to "torture" my mother (as she would say) when I would refuse to do something for her. The classic memory I have was me spending time with her in the evening: taking her out to dinner, having great discussions and laughs, usually diving into the humanities, and returning to her assisted living facility to talk a little longer.

Typically as I was getting ready to leave, she would say, "Do me little favor and go move my clothes from the washer to the dryer." It always made me wonder, does she do laundry every night of her life, or only the nights she knows I am coming to visit? To which I would give her a hug and kiss good night and tell her, "No, do it yourself" and walk towards the door. Without ever realizing what she was actually saying about herself, by textbook definition anyway, she would reply, "You bastard," as she laughed her beautiful, mischievous laugh, knowing she had cussed for humorous shock effect. I would glance to see her big grin that went all the way into her eyes as I walked out the door, silently blaming my nursing school, and reassured myself with a slight twist on the original, "Never do for your mother what she can do for herself."

She knew my reasoning for not moving her clothes, and half of her—well, maybe only 35 percent—appreciated it. You see, my mother had a great example of the attitude for getting older and accepting aging, but she was not a shining role model for how to physically walk into the last years of aging. The proof was in the X-ray of her arm the morning she fell; her bones showed an extremely low calcium content. She had an accurate saying that I doubt was hers originally: "Growing old is not for wimps." But past that, she was a glowing example of how not to age. She found a reason to discard every physical therapist who ever tried to help build her strength, which every speck of research shows helps keep calcium in the bones and has a positive effect on every aspect of the mind, body, and spirit. Exercise and movement are a win-win situation, even if doing so only involves raising your arms above your head three hundred times a day with both your legs in traction, lying in a hospital bed.

She was so bad that if someone pulled out of a parking spot three spaces closer to the restaurant than the one I had just pulled into, she would point it out and want me to move to it. Of course, "You bastard" followed my answer.

Even though her second favorite response to me saying no to any of her requests she was completely capable of fulfilling herself was, "You are horrible," while again laughing, I knew I did not deserve these less-attractive titles she bestowed on me. By her getting up and moving those clothes to the dryer herself, she was maintaining some level of strength, slightly improving balance, exercising her cardio-pulmonary function a wee speck, keeping a flake of calcium in her bones, and reminding her approaching-90-year-old body and spirit that she was still not only alive, but also capable. Had I not "tortured" her, although we will never know, she may have fallen earlier in her final fall years and not had those few more years of laughs with her six kids, meals out as she so enjoyed, shared a mutual love with her cool little dog with a big personality "Buster," or gotten to call me all those endearing names before telling me to "Get out before you make me wet myself from laughing." Let me tell you, having a sense of humor, being in your late eighties, and having had six kids created a rough, constant challenge for her, as witnessed by her repetitive chant, "Stop making me laugh—oh goodness, I hope I can make it to the bathroom." Not intentionally, but I had figured out a way to get this non-exercising woman in her eighties to actually run sprints: by helping her laugh. Well, OK, not exactly sprints, but high-speed shuffles anyway. Ever the nurse, I saw her shuffled sprints to the bathroom across a restaurant as great urinary continence exercises and a bit of cardio. Yep, "I'm horrible." It was about the only exercise I could get her to do, so I kept torturing her with humor. Her assigned but endearing titles for me were well earned and worn with pride. No, I never gave her a laugh for the intention of a bathroom sprint, but it was her only regular exercise, induced by her sense of humor. She knew I felt this way, and she would make it back to the table and I would offer her water and say, "Here, Mom, you also are dehydrated, have some water." Again she would call me on it laughing and tell me, "You just want me to shuffle another lap to the bathroom." Really, at that point it was just for laughs, and the fact that like most of us, and the geriatric population as a whole, she did live under-hydrated.

Now let's contrast that memory with someone that I someday hope to emulate.

Particularly, I hope to emulate a huge portion of his will and drive to literally lean forward into aging, dying, and death with a beautifully high level of bravery and grounded wisdom, and above all to follow through in daily actions, not just intention. I met John a few weeks before his 90th birthday. I lived nearby and we became close friends. Over the next eight years, I became his private nurse and he somewhat became my second father. If there was a Council on Cool High-Five Do-It-Right Aging, John would have been their poster boy.

I have met many people who absolutely refuse to lumber, slumber, and passively accept their slide into their upper years and death. My first encounter with such a man who gave an above-average, high level of effort was during my four years of college. I frequently witnessed a very old, very tan, and very spry man jog through campus, often shirtless. He usually passed though in the late morning, 10 a.m. to 1 p.m., even on hot days. He was my first observation of leaning forward into aging in action. John, and this persistent and determined man from college, both remind me of the first half of one of the lines from the Dire Straits song "Money for Nothing," which says, "That's the way you do it!"

My mother and John were polar opposites in the self-care required to travel through your last years. These years are already hard enough on the body, mind, and emotions, so exercise and constant activity do lead to a higher level of ease. John was amazing at making sure he did his part daily to maintain that optimal level of function and gumption for his last years. I saw it in action a few weeks after meeting him and having hours of conversation. I pulled into his driveway one day while it was moderately raining, and I saw this "young" man, weeks away from his 90th birthday, halfway up a ladder in the rain. I jumped out of the car and bellowed a greeting, immediately soaking wet, and offered to help. Luckily, he stopped ascending and came down to let me go up and finish his task of unclogging a drain on the roof's gutter system. The next time he asked for my help was a few weeks later to change flood lights in the trees, also up the ladder. During the first few years of our friendship, I called him my "ten-foot friend," only silently in my head of course, because he would only allow me to help him if the task were higher than ten feet.

John applied in action what I had been taught the first semester of nursing school. In his case it would be changed slightly again to "Always do for yourself what you still can." He walked for miles every day in his rather hilly neighborhood. He did a little yard work here and there, into his mid-nineties. He would run a couple long outdoor extension cords into the woods and cut up medium-sized branches that had fallen, with a small, light electric chainsaw.

As I have always observed, most people fear gravity as they age and begin to slow down every aspect of their lives. We lean back in fear, not forward, and we stop picking our feet up, thinking we will find safety in shuffling, rather than keeping a sure step as we enter our last years. John refused to follow that self-restrictive path. He would fall, bandage, wait a few hours or until the next day, but he would get out there and finish cutting up that branch. Even after his two hip fractures and one compression fracture of his back in his mid-nineties, he never stopped leaning forward and trying.

Mom was so bad she once walked out of physical therapy in the middle of the session because she "did not want to do it" and she thought the therapist was "rude" for doing her job and pushing her. I remember that therapist; she was so nice, intelligent, patient, and encouraging. Unless this woman was PT Jekyll and Ms. Hyde, I think my mother should have stuck to the first excuse, that she "did not want to do it." The scary, funny thing is one of my sisters had dinner with her and two of Mom's regular dinner friends in the assisted living dining room the night she walked out of PT. She told me Mom was talking about walking out in the middle of the PT session, when the two other women lowered their forks in surprise and with joyful excitement to hear there was such an option. One said, "We can do that!?" then the other woman, "We can just leave?!" like school kids learning a new way to sneak out of PE. I think my sister said something to quell the uprising and steer the conversation away from not doing highly beneficial physical therapy. I helped her to complete a few more sessions before she stopped going all together during the last few months of her life by telling her this truth: "You know, Mom, some insurance companies may not reimburse for the session if you don't complete the hour, unless you're having a heart attack." I told her the same thing can hold true for signing yourself out of the hospital against medical advice. She teased me back, and jokingly stated her true wishes by following up with, "What are the typical signs of a heart attack?" I told her I was not telling her so as not to help enable her out of PT. She said, "I'll wing it," and her mischievous grin followed. I never pushed her again; as her medical power of attorney, I understood it was only my place to protect her wishes and their consequence, not to tell her they were wrong. Besides, I was 51, not her 90 years. I wasn't tired and hurting. I wasn't having shortness of breath when walking down the hall. I didn't have advancing aortic stenosis and steadily advancing dementia. It was not my place.

John was also proof it is never too late to start higher levels of self-care. He was a smoker and not a regular exerciser until age 50. Yet even more proof that it is never too late was his ability to rehab himself after two hip fractures and a compression spinal fracture in his mid-nineties. Yes, he had help from rehab professionals, but he also pushed himself daily. We all rehabilitate ourselves, or not, after trauma or illness; as well, we all maintain our health by the choice to do so. I share this because I care about you, and I don't want you to self-limit and think you are "too old to start now" or that you have preexisting conditions that stop you. The benefits that come immediately and tomorrow are endless from pushing yourself a little more daily.

Aortic stenosis at 90 years old did not stop John. One afternoon, I walked into John's den because his door was always unlocked. Whenever he heard the door open, even though he could not see who it was, he would always bellow twice, "Come in! Come in!" After this greeting, he would always ask about my well-being first and I asked him of his. But he always asked first. On this particular day, he replied, "My walk was harder today than usual." We ran through the obvious; he had really learned to pay greater attention to hydration levels since we met. He even learned to be aware of his early signs of dehydration. He also appreciated his higher and more consistent level of energy throughout the day when he maintained a higher hydration level. He complained of no other signs as I ran through the classics, no chest pain, shortness of breath, nausea, vomiting, unusual sweating, or radiating discomfort. He decided to hydrate up and try again.

The next day he told me he felt just not right again, but it happened sooner in the walk. He went to the cardiologist, and that evening John told me they wanted to replace the aortic valve in his heart due to stenosis. This is the same problem I told you my mom was diagnosed with. She chose to not go under the knife and left it alone. In her case, I understood and accepted, as she had several cards stacked against her. She was in poor shape to start with, a smoker, had other preexisting conditions, and she was honest that she would not have committed to real rehab efforts. John asked me my opinion. Rare for me, but I actually gave it to him. "John! To anyone else I would tell them it is not my place to share an opinion, and I would objectively list the pros and cons of having the valve replaced in relationship to their age, condition, underlying pre-existing conditions, and their driving spirit to follow through on the hard energy required rehab to someone's full potential." But since I knew John already scored in the 90th percentile for each of those considerations, my answer was, "Yes, have it done!" I again listed all the reasons I felt so safe in speaking up, including the downsides, so he still knew it was a higher risk at 90 and that it would still be a hard recovery. I also told him he would make it look easy. He asked, "Will you coach me and get me ready?" I accepted. We had about one week to get him ready for the big game.

First I taught him what I shared with you about pain. In his case, because there was not an initial traumatic injury, all of his pain was going to be good healing pain. I reiterated this and encouraged him to work to attempt to ignore and push past the pain as much as he could. We also talked of course about accepting pain medication at first. But then to prevent constipation, weakness, and potential imbalance and fall issues, we talked about how important it was to get off of those pain medications as soon as he could. Pain medications and rehabilitation have a balance to find. Too much pain will delay rehab if someone can't push past it. Yet too much pain medication for too long will also delay rehab, increase fall risk and other side effects, and may ultimately delay optimal healing to faster full recovery.

Next we started breathing exercises, and he did them throughout the days leading up to surgery. I taught him that at his age, the two critical points of recovery both relate to being on the ventilator for too long and getting his breathing up to full function immediately once the anesthesia starts to wear off. I told him this may happen before his eyes even open and he was still on the ventilator, or later after the ET tube into the lungs and ventilator had been removed, but no matter when, he would have a breathing job to start the moment he was aware of himself. I had John start raising his arms above his head every hour and to take deep breaths that he actively assisted with by raising and further expanding his shoulders, chest, and abdomen while inhaling. Every day we talked about this, because he needed it to be a muscle memory for him, meaning it would require little thought to accomplish. I needed him to start the second he became lucid enough to remember. I also taught him his hands most likely would be restrained if he obtained this lucid functional point while the ventilator is still attached and breathing for him. I also reminded him to wait to raise his hands until his eyes were open and the nurse was close to not upset all the tubing that would be tangled across everywhere. But, again, I reminded him to start raising his arms as soon as he could.

We covered nutrition, just the big basics really, for when the hospital trays were set in front of him. The protein is a must, as nothing can heal in the body without a positive protein balance. Even though I knew his family would be bringing him custom meals to supplement, I wanted him to be aware of the importance of every bite at this early stage. The carbohydrates were the next most important. He needed his body to use the protein for fast healing where the old valve was cut out and the new valve is sutured back in. When major healing needs to be accomplished, protein needs to be available for rebuilding of damaged or repaired tissue, while the body's energy should come from the carbohydrates. It gets in the way of fast healing when the body has to steal some of its energy from the protein that should go to rebuilding tissue. He tied it all together with half a multivitamin morning and afternoon; I would be bringing that to him. The reason I teach to divide multivitamins is vitamin C and the B vitamins are water soluble. This is why your urine is so yellow after you take a multivitamin; your body grabs what it needs and discards the rest through the kidneys, as opposed to vitamin A, D, E, and K, which are fat soluble, so your fat cells can store those for later use as needed.

I even had him prepare to stand up straight and look up the very first time the nurses helped him stand, and every time after that. John did everything I taught him, including when I helped him stand a few times in the ICU the next morning. At his request, the staff helped him into the chair a final time before bedtime the first night after the surgery. At 90 years of age, the day after having a new aortic valve placement, he was discharged out of the ICU to the telemetry floor, less than twenty-four hours after the surgery.

He did not stop there; he continued to push himself often during the day, and a few days later, he was discharged home. I had made arrangements to stay with him for a few days and nights, or three, just in case. No sooner had his family left after getting him home and settled did he tell me he wanted to try to go for a walk. We made it out the door and maybe 100 feet, up a slight incline, and he wanted to head back. He rested an hour and said, "Let's go again." He made it about 150 feet this time. One more time before sundown he said, "Let's go again," and he made it 200 feet. Within a few weeks, he was almost back to his several miles a day on a very hilly walk. John lived to 98 without another cardiac issue.

It was not just during illness or injury that John took great care of himself, as opposed to my mother, who was diagnosed with Type 2 diabetes, and did not need insulin, but did require dietary changes and an oral medication to control her blood sugar level. However, she could not stop eating York Peppermint Patties and desserts, whereas John worked hard to keep his weight below a certain number because he knew his 90-year-old heart did not need to work even a speck harder to oxygenate an extra pound. He also knew he felt better when he ate less throughout the day, as well as in general when he weighed less. He was a real person also, and normally had two or three flavors of Blue Bell ice cream in the freezer for controlled digging when the cravings hit.

John's awareness, in action not just theory, to continue to do for himself as much as he could was evident in his love to have a fire burning throughout the winter. From the time I met John, he welcomed me to, and I enjoyed, manually splitting his firewood with a splitting maul and wedge. I like to call that form of functional exercise "farmrobics." If I split wood any less than two or three afternoons a week for forty minutes or so, I could not keep up with how much he loved burning fires. But he had a condition for me. The area where I split the wood was about ten yards into a thicket of brush, and that path was maybe another forty yards to the door to his den. He would only allow me to split and stack the wood right there the first four years or so, for he wanted to haul it into the home himself. Then for a year or two he would only allow me to bring it into the garage to stack and dry, and again he would bring it into his den. I would say it was only the last three years he actually allowed me to bring it all the way into the den. He was so sharp, he noticed every year that I was making the pieces ever so slightly smaller.

As far as preparing for his death and last weeks, I was equally impressed. But before he got to that point, he did fall and fracture his hip twice, and had a fall with a spinal compression fracture, too. Each time knocked him farther over and made it that much harder to rehabilitate himself, but he pushed himself every time. He made it look easy by effort and internal drive, until his last fall at 97 years. Before I tell you the few neat things about his view on rapidly approaching death, let me tell you something that happened to him that we can all learn from.

John suffered from neuralgia for painfully too many years of his life. Neuralgia is an intermittent shooting pain that runs along nerve pathways, often in the head and face. His was much of his head, mainly the top-ish area. He was a stoic man and mostly tolerated the often-frequent shooting pains throughout his life. It was even hard to watch at times; I felt for him, and sometimes he would grimace every sixty to ninety seconds during a conversion when he was having bad spells. They did start to get stronger and more persistent the last five years or so of his life. He certainly did not want to live on narcotic pain medications, but with time we did figure out that 600mg of ibuprofen morning and evening did a great job of controlling the pain in both frequency and intensity. Granted, it is not a good idea to take ibuprofen daily for long periods of time, as it can affect numerous systems in the body. But here is where living in the textbook to practice medicine can cause some major problems. Had this next event not happened to John, and three or four critical days of rehab at the age of 97 had not been lost, I bet he would have accelerated in his rehabilitation higher, faster, and sooner, and experienced a more upright last few years. That was something I knew about John: if he could, he would.

After John's last fall before his death, he was admitted to a rehab unit on discharge from the hospital. I was not there for the transfer and admission or maybe I could have headed this problem off at that pass, and maybe I should reread my chapter on guilt. Because the textbooks state long-term ibuprofen use causes issues, the admitting doctor made a textbook move and took him off the ibuprofen two times a day and placed him on a strong drug called gabapentin. Gabapentin is used to treat seizures and chronic pain, especially if the origin of the pain is suspected to be neurological. The only problem is it can cause some major confusion, irritability, sluggishness, and balance issues in an older person. It did just that to John, and worse, because the neuralgia pain and frequency also increased. But the bigger worst part was that I could not get the doctors to take him off of it and place him back onto ibuprofen, because the textbooks state not to keep people on ibuprofen. Over the last few years, I had informed John several times of the long-term effects of its use, but his answer was, "I'm in my upper nineties; how long term do you think I will live?" and "I'd rather live a few less years with less pain than more years with more pain." After one day into this rehab admission, he was so not himself on this gabapentin that I begged doctors to call me back and talk with me to get him off of it. After three days of no luck getting him off this medication, John was beside himself, very grumpy, and weak, with confusion increasing, and showing no real effort to rehab. Who was this man?

Finally, on a Sunday evening, there was a doctor I had never seen sitting behind the counter writing in a chart at the station. I said hello and asked if she had a minute. She introduced herself and informed me she was covering for the weekend. I introduced myself, gave her a four-minute history of myself with my background, and then introduced John by giving her his history and present situation in medical terms. I told her our seven-year history at that point. Then I explained the reasons for my request to stop the gabapentin completely, and I literally got down on both knees, placed my hands together, and said, "Please, please take him off the gabapentin and put him back onto the ibuprofen, and I'll even wash your car." She laughed, told me to get up and that I didn't want to wash her car, because it was a mess, and that yes, she would stop the gabapentin immediately and place him back on the ibuprofen. After twenty-four hours, John came back to us—everything, from mood, to appetite, to his normal old fantastic desire to do the work to get stronger and home. But those days lost, yes on top of his age, greatly contributed to his inability to pop back up on the old John high-level push. I personally thank that doctor for working with me and having the courage to step out of the textbook.

Gabapentin is not the only drug that the elderly should be cautious with. Muscle relaxants can also cause some serious issues. The number of elderly people who are placed on muscle relaxants for back pain, including my mother, and who then have issues with drowsiness, coordination, and even falls is unbelievable. Muscle relaxants relax the entire body, not just the back. My mother summed it up well: "I now hurt more from lying in bed for too long I feel like I am unstable and I'm going to fall, and now other parts of my body are starting to hurt; everything feels like it needs to be tightened, and I feel like all my screws are loose." After she said that, she saw my eyes get big and my grin widened, and she laughed, realizing she had admitted to having not one "loose screw" but many.

All medications have their place and time, but as Ms. Murphy taught us while teaching us the special considerations of caring for the geriatric population, "This population is so much harder to fine-tune; all medications must be considered on a broader scale of cause and effect. Some medications have a much greater potential to cause more problems that it can solve in all populations, but that fact is multiplied in our geriatric population." I remember that day in class vividly. Ms. Murphy had dressed up in a classic vision of a woman with character in the more mature population. She came in shuffling, hunched over with a cane, purse over her arm, scarf dragging just like my mother's would years later. She bumped us, the purse dragged across our shoulders and scraped our ears, she dropped dirty scrunched-up tissues on the desk, and she stopped and stared and cracked us up with beautifully nosy questions.

Then she taught the class in her role until she got too hot and had to take off the first several layers. She then filled us with her "gems" on more levels than I knew needed to be considered in caring for the geriatric populations. Most of those gems involved the words "respect," "tolerance," "patience," and the awareness that we have absolutely no idea what that stage of life looks and feels like. So much wisdom and humor flowed from that woman. When she went silent, tilted her head forward, and stared, you had to quickly review, "Did I miss something funny, or did I do something wrong?"

On and off over the years, John and I had check-in conversations about what he wanted his death to look like. That's important because wishes may change. First he had asked me if I would see him though his last days. Then he wanted to make sure I knew when it was time, that I would make sure I kept him "clean and comfortable." In his typical short, dry humor but also being serious, he would always reiterate to me, "The comfortable is more important than the clean," with a sharp stare to make sure I knew how important the comfortable was. I bet he told me that six times in eight years, and always with the same repeat and emphasis. So, naturally, I asked him what "comfortable" looked like to him. He had read the first edition of this book and he knew the answer. "If you think I am in the last few hours or days, and I am in pain, don't wait too long between the pain medicine doses if you see me getting restless or the pain increasing." He told me he hated the restlessness of some nights due to the neuralgia, or the times he recently came up from anesthesia after surgery, and he feared feeling that and the caregiver not knowing. I told him I would not give him more medicine than prescribed, but I promised to not let it go past the shortest number of hours between doses. He was good with that deal.

Ultimately it was his neuralgia that got so bad, with near constant and increasing intensity, that brought John to his death. He had chosen to sign on with hospice a few months earlier; he was tired in both the big and little pictures. Remember it was eight years ago, at the age of 90, when he was discharged from the ICU in less than twenty-four hours after an aortic valve replacement. I doubt I would make it out of the ICU in that little time if I had that procedure now in my mid-fifties. Then he was the main driving force to rehab himself two more times completely after the valve replacement due to falls with fractures. It was that last fracture, and losing those critical first few rehab days, that knocked him so far off track that his true age and his powerful will to do for himself as much as possible finally met each other.

Add in his already highly realistic and healthy acceptance of inevitable death after his "long short life," as he described his lucky years of life, and he had reached his end.

This wonderful man who so wisely expended his energy has so much to offer us on how to live a great life. After you heard the double, "Come in! Come in!" after walking into his den, "How are you?" was always the next words he spoke, and he did want to know how you were truly doing. I always felt he had the energy and true heart to ask and care for others because he first understood the importance of healthy self-care. It is hard to genuinely and frequently extend yourself to others if healthy self-care does not come first. I am not talking periodic surface care, but good, persistent, consistent, daily self-care. He lived by his actions, right down to a salad with cottage cheese and peaches or pineapples for dinner most nights. But he wisely accepted all meal invitations from his family and friends.

For your own good, do not ask others to do what you are capable of doing for yourself, even when you reach your nineties. John's actions remind us to respect but not fear gravity, and to remain upright and lean forward into life, not backwards. Even after gravity has its many smaller wins, upright yourself and continue after each one. Guide your life by choice to remain active, not by granting yourself arbitrary age limitations. Then, and only then, accept your inevitable death, but not until you have repetitively given it your all. John personified my favorite chant: Keep going until you are good and ready to quit.

One more painfully funny Mom story to close out: A few years after my dad died, she had joined the singles club in the retirement development where she lived. She missed Dad; they had been together fifty-four years. She tried the singles thing, but it never panned out. One man on a singles website did send her a very special proud picture of himself, which ended her desire to date. It also made her miss my dad more—go, Dad! She called me to ask if I would accompany her to a singles banquet the group was putting on one evening. She told me it was their annual big deal banquet and it included dinner and dancing. It was also the farthest I ever saw my mom do a bathroom shuffle sprint. The ballroom was about 40 percent full, and she and I had our own big round table with maybe ten empty seats to ourselves. She even commented on the distance to the bathroom when we sat down. She was an extrovert and never had trouble making friends. People loved to talk to my mom. She had some unique views, and, to steal one of her terms, she could be "a pistol." On and off, ladies kept walking up to us and saying, "Hi, Carol, is this one of your children?" and greetings and brief niceties would be exchanged. Everyone was dressed up, with balloons on the tables; it was a sweet time. Yet another woman walked up; the introductions occurred, and this woman obviously knew Mom had daughters because she asked about one she had met. Then she asked Mom, "Do you have any other boys?" Mom lit up to have a "Tell me about your kids" question; her voice went up as she joyfully replied, "Oh, yes, Vincent, who is my youngest has a brother ten years older; he is my first born, the four girls are in the middle ...." Then she went on to elaborate, and elaborate she does! Without obviously knowing the term she is about to use has another meaning, she states, "And let me tell you they are like night and day in how different they are; my oldest son is just as conservative and *straight* as he can be, but with this one *anything goes.*" I know what she was trying to say, but I am comfortable enough with my sexuality so I don't feel a need to interrupt to correct her in that department, and I was too busy trying to keep a "straight" face and not crack up. Mom was still talking about my brother's and my differences, and this poor woman was no longer listening. She had tilted back a few inches and was staring at me. Most likely "anything goes" is still resonating in her head, for she was looking at me with wide eyes, dropped jaw, and speechless. All my poor mom was talking about was the difference in general humanistic tolerance and social views. I was about to lose it and crack up. Mom was still oblivious to how this woman had interpreted her use of "straight," and to add icing to the cake, I intentionally started to nod while looking up at this totally in-shock woman.

Mom finished her paragraph by respectfully giving us both praise for being good but very different sons. The woman righted herself, closed her mouth, and without hesitation gave the standard, "It was very nice to meet you" and turned quickly and walked away. Mom can see I was near tears in restrained humor, and beat me to telling her by asking, "What did I say that is so funny?" I wasn't paying attention to the fact that she had reached for her coffee and was sipping when I told her what she had said, and the woman's reaction while she talked on. While trying hard not to, she spit-laughed, though desperately trying to hold it back tightly pursed lips, a tiny spattering of coffee onto the table. Now I was laughing so hard I was crying and couldn't see, and she was laughing so hard her eyes were closed, her shoulders were hunched forward, and she barely got her coffee cup back to the saucer, when she said, "Oh, no, I'll never make it to the bathroom before I wet myself." She was still laughing so hard she could barely get up. I tried to help her, but my eyes were still watery, she had a long scarf around her neck and stuck to the chair, and off she went, and the scarf remained behind. It was the closest I'd ever seen my mother to near actually running, yet still shuffling. She took a long time to get back, telling me, "I didn't quite make it, but who cares; it was worth it. I was laughing to myself on and off in the bathroom while ladies came in and out." We laughed again over what those ladies must have thought when hearing a woman in hysterics in a closed bathroom stall, and she tried to apologize for the impression she accidently gave that woman. I didn't care and thanked her instead. She was right it; was highly worth it. She and I laughed a lot, but that one won

My mother was a creative and non-linear thinker, who could be a wonderful motherly pain at times, but I would not have traded her for anything. She loved to teach and promoted education, receiving her PhD at the age of 58. She was passionate about the prevention of child abuse, and her commitment grew even stronger during her last seventeen years of teaching emotionally disturbed adolescents in a state psychiatric hospital. She would have loved knowing she continued to teach and help others to learn, and laugh, by sharing her aging and death in this book.

CHAPTER 16

THE GRIEF MONSTER

DENIAL TO ACCEPTANCE

Quick look away
Something is ugly scary and messy

Quick turn and run
It will cause me pain sorrow and self-review

Turn away
Nothing to see and feel here

No I am ready
Let me experience all

It was handed to me
It must be a poorly wrapped something

Somewhere inside
I have the strength to bring it in

Somewhere inside
I have the will to look

Somewhere inside
I have

Slowly
I see that now

No matter how comfortable I become with the reality of death, it has never lightened the effect it has on the grief I feel. Death, and the acceptance of death, has a mixed relationship with the monster known as Grief. Death brings grief to us, and our acceptance of death helps begin the process of weakening the strength of grief. Yet death can be unrelated to grief if we felt no connection to that which has died, be it person, plant, animal, or relationship. Grief truly can be a monster—a painfully powerful monster so large, mean, and consuming that it overwhelms and engulfs us, chews us up, and leaves us feeling dead ourselves.

There are many types of death that led to grief, such as death of a relationship, or of a circumstance in life, such as leaving a job or community, or again the death of trust. Although my approach to death here has been clinical and informative, I never forget the pain and shock the loss of a loved one will have on us. This raw saturation of dying and death will hopefully open the layers we protect ourselves from our own mortality with. It is not only to help you take control of your continuous walk to your death, and the walk of those close to you; it is also to help you with acceptance.

Increasing acceptance, even a speck, will slightly lighten the shocking stench and force of a Monster named Grief appearing before you, whether the expected arrival of the monster or the shocking violent ripping that it inflicts with an unexpected sudden death. Even a slightly faster and greater acceptance of death after it has occurred will allow you to move into the more productive and even loving stages of grief. Otherwise we sit and spin too long, refusing to accept the sun has set. Denial is a natural part of handling the bulldozing shock of the emptiness and loneliness that death gouges out of us. But denial in another direction can be truly detrimental to healing after death. The truly detrimental denial comes when we attempt to deny ourselves the respectful pounding the monster of Grief has arrived to treat us to.

The only really wrong way to grieve is to not grieve—to not allow the pain and process, to drown it in intoxicants, or shove it down deeper and deeper, then attempt to cover it with layers of anything we think will keep us from feeling it. I met this really neat woman years ago who owned a business I periodically dropped into. A few years had passed between our last visit and me recently moving to the area, when I walked in and started up a conversation while I paid for my purchase. She informed me her husband of many years had died almost a year ago. I asked her how she was doing with that and how bad was the grief still. Her answer summed up the exact opposite of what I have discover about grief: "I can't get the grief to lighten up no matter what I do: alcohol, dinner with friends, I even took a cruise, but no matter how hard I try not to think about him, or how much I try to keep myself busy, I miss him and it keeps getting worse." Normally I am not a flippant, humorous person when listening and talking to someone in the throes of grief pain, but she told it to me with humor in both expression and inflection, and we have always joked heavily with each other. So I replied with an exaggerated tone and gesture, as well to respect that she had a business to run at the moment: "Well no wonder you're stuck in grief; you're doing it all wrong! You can't push a 2,000-pound monster away; you have to confuse it by embarrassing it with a hug. We little humans can't suppress a monster of Grief with even our overworked systems of denial.

Instead embrace the monster standing before you, because it wants to play and shake you with the painful loss of your lifelong love and companion. Attempt to never again suppress a painful thought of your husband's death and the pain, emptiness, and loneliness that it has inflicted on you. When you find yourself thinking of, or feeling the pain, stop for a minute and sit with it. Actually tell yourself, I am going to stop and think and feel of him and the pain. For if you find the courage to play back with the monster, it will get bored and start to think about turning and walking away to find another resistant victim to play with. But don't make the mistake some people make by confusing grief starting to weaken in strength and walk away with loving your husband less. The day you find a few hours have passed without the pain is not the day you stopped loving him; it is only the day the monster started to get bored. Don't ever expect the monster to forget you completely; it won't forget where you live, and it will come to rough you up periodically."

Another customer walked in the door. My friend thanked me and promised to change her ways, and I exited. I walked back in a few months later to the biggest hug and smile. "It worked! I stopped trying to deny the pain. I sat with it, and it has been so much easier. I am feeling myself again. I am feeling stronger; I accepted the pain and his death, and I feel it less and less—thank you!" I know it works for me, but I promise you the monster periodically returns. The unrestrained cry I had while reading the first few paragraphs of the chapter "My father just died" is pure proof. That was fourteen years after my father died, and even I was surprised how hard the grief monster shook the hell out of me for a few minutes, and I let it.

Whatever your belief, having a fear of death to the point of not being able to face it or insisting on prolonging it with interventions is like trying to argue or say no to nature, science, or God. No matter what your understanding or belief is, death is inevitable and unavoidable. My trusting you in sharing my life experiences from my heart, openly and with respect, is to attempt to help you through the inevitable death of others and yourself. Becoming comfortable with death is a process; be gentle as you learn to lighten the fear and burden of death and the core shakings of grief. For if love, respect, or appreciation is involved, lightening is all that can be obtained.

If death can be accepted and we can get more comfortable with the reality of all living things dying, then grief is purely grief. Admittedly, this is a strange little incomplete delineation that again is meant to help decrease another speck of both the knockdown force of grief and increase the overall acceptance of death. Grief, although brought on by death, once that death is accepted can then become less hindered in its painful exploration of loss, emptiness, loneliness, and longing for a loved one. Grief directly correlates to our level of love, respect, and appreciation for that person, pet, or relationship that has died. A harsh example would be the death of the Cambodian leader Pol Pot in 1998. How many family members of the estimated 1.5 to 2 million Cambodians he either had killed or allowed to die from malnutrition actually experienced grief for his death?

Fearing death and grief is a major problem in our culture. The same sunset analogy still fits; fearing death is like fearing the sun will set. I cannot say the same about fearing dying or the pain, for I have fears of dying. My three biggest fears: I don't want to be caught and eaten by a predator, I do not want to linger in an ICU on a ventilator, nor do I want to experience long, chronic pain or undiagnosed withdrawal while semi-conscious. But I do not fear the moment of my death, for I have never witnessed that actual moment appear to hurt anyone. Quite the opposite, at that last moment I have only witnessed peace and calm. The moments leading up to death, yes, I have witnessed pain and discomfort, but never at the transitioning moment of the last breath or last heartbeat.

Try not to lose a moment of this short, hard, amazing, painful, beautiful, challenging, joyful, failure- and accomplishment-filled gift of exploration and experiences known as your life being wasted in fear of your inevitable, peaceful moment of death. You are worth more than that. So please, attempt to accept death, and hold your voice up and pronounce the words "dying," "death," and "died" with the honor the process deserves. Live your life strong and long, trust that your moment of death will not be painful, and embrace the courage to play with the monster of Grief when you are lucky enough to have it rough you up, because you have experienced the joy of love.